P9-CFU-253

BRINGING GOD

Confessions of a Christian Publisher   **John Hunt**

BACK TO EARTH

BRINGING GOD

Confessions of a Christian Publisher   **John Hunt**

BACK TO EARTH

BOOKS

Winchester, UK
Washington, USA

"Buy the truth, and sell it not."

Proverbs 23:23

ACKNOWLEDGEMENTS

With love to Ros, and thanks for putting up with the hours spent at home on the computer, and with me for the last twenty four years.

NOTE TO READER:

B eing a conservative, traditional kind of a guy, who still thinks in Fahrenheit rather than Celsius, in feet and inches rather than meters, I've stuck to a number of old fashioned routines.

Quotations from the Bible are from the Authorized (King James) Version except where mentioned, because I find it hard to read modern translations and paraphrases, except the GOOD AS NEW New Testament (published July 2004).

I've used BC and AD rather than BCE or CE, though I know it's increasingly seen as incorrect. But it's not as if we're changing the date, making it less Christo-centric. If we dated from the time of recorded history, or from the beginning of Homo sapiens, we would gain a different perspective.

I've tried alternating God as She rather than He, but it doesn't work for me. It's equally anthropomorphic, bears equally little relation to how I imagine God, so apologies to all who think She (or It, or Them, or I, or lower case, or whatever) should have had more space.

American or English spelling is a more serious issue, but I tend to the former, on the grounds that if you can't beat them, you'd better join them (but this doesn't extend to agreeing with their theology or politics).

The book covers a fair bit of ground, and mistakes of facts and judgment are inevitable (hopefully not too many of the former). I welcome comments and correction.

Copyright © 2004 O Books
46A West Street, Alresford, Hants SO24 9AU, U.K.
Tel: +44 (0) 1962 736880 Fax: +44 (0) 1962 736881
E-mail: office@johnhunt-publishing.com
www.johnhunt-publishing.com
www.0-books.net

U.S. distribution:
NBN
Tel: 1 800 462 6420
Fax: 1 800 338 4550
E-mail: custserve@nbnbooks.com

Text: © 2004 John Hunt
Design: Nautilus Design UK
Cover design: Krave Ltd, London

ISBN 1 903816 81 5

All rights reserved. Except for brief quotations in critical articles or reviews, no
part of this book may be reproduced in any manner without prior written
permission from the publishers.

The rights of John Hunt as author have been asserted in accordance with the
Copyright, Designs and Patents Act 1988.

A CIP catalogue record for this book is available from the British Library.

Printed in Singapore by Tien Wah Press (Pte) Ltd.

CONTENTS

I

WHY WE BELIEVE

"Truth is open to everyone, and the
claims aren't all staked yet."

Seneca

I was very naïve when I started work in a Christian publishing house in my early twenties. After a few years studying English at university I had this feeling that words were sacred and authors would be, well, "spiritual," especially if they were the kind who went to church. Obviously, the pursuit of money was gross, and here was a job where I'd never have to do maths in my head or worry about which way round creditors and debtors were, something I still struggle with. People in publishing were bound to be nice to each other and have long, intelligent conversations about the meaning of life over a bottle or two of wine after work in the evenings.

Within a few years I was running a division of a company with headquarters somewhere in the USA, itself soon to become a division of a company which was a division of another publishing company. That was a division of a media company, in itself a division of something whose remote boss was so distant as to make God seem like a friendly neighbor. I was spending most of my time on spreadsheets, making people redundant in the week before Christmas, and publishing books I'm too embarrassed to mention.

One of many low points I remember: we used to sell huge numbers of books to the Protestant community in Northern Ireland. I was listening to a recording of the Revd Ian Paisley's sermons (he's the leader of the Democratic Unionist Party in Northern Ireland, which in the last election got more votes than any other) with a view to making them into a book. Maybe he's a few centuries out of his time, but we'd sell lorry loads, a guaranteed market. I was ready to do it. His voice thundered out, organ music swelling in the background, denouncing the whore of Babylon, the Antichrist in the Vatican. No wonder Christians in Northern Ireland can't manage to live together. This vitriol surely couldn't have anything to do with the teaching of Jesus. And it didn't represent the kind of God I wanted to have anything to do with. If there really was good and evil in the world, this kind of language was evil, and I was on the wrong side of the fence.

There were a number of issues for me that episodes like this brought into focus. Why don't Christians appear to be more loving than other people? Why is the historical record so indifferent? How far can you take the details of scriptures from two to three thousand years ago and apply them today, in the light of different understandings of the world we've gained through the sciences? How sure can you be of what you believe, and is certainty such a good thing if it leads to such division? Why are there so many different beliefs? Might not God be bigger than the various limited ways we describe Him? Or are we better off without God? How do these issues connect? What did I actually believe myself? Was this a good way to spend a working life? And so on.

So as time went on I began publishing more widely, meeting authors from an increasing variety of spiritual disciplines; high church Anglicans as well as evangelical Protestants, liberal theologians, Catholics, Muslims, Buddhists, Sufis, moving on to a wide spectrum of New Age teachers, from acupuncturists to witches. My original co-workers might see this as the slow slide to hell. I'm more inclined to see myself as something of an instinctive conservative and a slow starter, just beginning to learn. And I've learnt something from all of them.

A few decades later and I feel like I've read several libraries' worth of books, and published quite a few of them. I still think of myself as Christian. I don't know Jesus personally any more in the way I once thought I did, I can't quote chapters from the Bible from memory like I used to. I respect the beliefs of those who do, and can, I just wish they would afford the same respect to others of equal conviction who worship differently. I also wish some of them would make more of an effort to follow his teaching. And it is the teaching of Jesus on the kingdom of God that's important for me today, rather than the teaching about him. He seems to me to offer an alternative vision of the world, one that has as little to do with the Bible-thumping mentality as it has to do with the materialist, secular mindset. A vision of giving rather than getting; one which celebrates the weak rather than the strong; one which sees God in hands and hearts rather than temples and doctrine; a God who can be found anywhere, at any time, who is bigger than we can possibly imagine. I believe (I try and preserve my naivety) it would really make a difference if we could follow it.

My desire for God hasn't changed. I just think of Him as more of a way and less of a person. I believe that a view of life based around God rather than self or science is not only credible and possible, it's the best way of living; one that even defines us as human, and is essential to our future well being and our survival. The teaching of Jesus expresses this as well as any other, perhaps better.

But its essential themes are common to all good religion. This takes me to what I see as the real religious question today. It's not so much whether religious beliefs are "true" or "false" (and if you've read this far you're probably not 100% certain either way yourself). That's important, but nothing like as much as the question of which are "good" or "bad." In unravelling the good and the bad we need to go behind the claims and counter claims; the ins and outs of this doctrine or that; the "did it happen this way or not?" events of the last couple of thousand years. To understand good religion and why it's still relevant we need to get back to basics, to answering some fundamental questions. For example: Why do we believe in the first place?

It usually helps to start with definitions. We've got so wrapped up in our little religious and cultural boxes (Christian, Muslim, atheist, or whatever) that we've forgotten what "religion" means. There are two meanings of the Latin *religio*, the root of "religion." The first most people hold in common, the second is where we differ.

The first meaning of *religio* is "relationship." There's a common, universal and ancient thread in religious tradition that takes us back to when "relationship" began. It says that once we were content. We didn't worry. We lived in the Age of Perfection, the Krita Yuga, the Garden of Eden, in innocence. We were at one with nature, because we *were* nature. We didn't know good and evil. We couldn't mess up. We couldn't even think.

So far, so good; most people would agree with this. At some point in our history, whether 70,000 or 7 million years ago (lowest and highest estimates), we became "self-aware." Armadillos specialise in body armor, cheetahs in speed, this is our own speciality, it's what we "do." We began to watch ourselves "living." We divided the world into "me" and "it."

We began naming things, and talking to each other. We began to enjoy the fruits of self-awareness, of communication, and love, and the ashes of separation and uncertainty. Ever since then, since the "fall," we've been trying to put the two together again, the "me" and the "it," turning "it" into "you," figuring out how one should relate to the other, groping around the edges of our lives, wondering what's over the horizon.

We started asking the questions we still ask today: Why can't we just be happy with what we've got? What is love really about? Can it survive death? Why is there anything at all? Is there a Big Truth? A God? Maybe we should shut up and relax. Accept things as they are. But if we could, and did, we'd still be up in the trees, chucking sticks at leopards.

Religion began as a response to the dilemmas that self-awareness created. For instance, rather than act in the interests of the species, individuals could override their biological programing and act in the interests of the self. But to act solely in the interests of the self is self-destructive for everyone in the longer term. Religions grew to connect us again with the larger whole, replacing our lost instinct. It's our "big idea" that ties us together; the one that stops the self getting drunk on its new sense of power. A solid religion creates structures that control the appetites of the self and encourage service and inspiration. The wisdom tradition of Homo sapiens sapiens ("sapiens" means "wise") – of relating to our selves and the world around us wisely, of defining what is true, of practising the good life, of transcending our biology – is what separates us from nature.

So in the first meaning of the word religion helps provide the framework for relating to each other, rituals for the key moments in life, for building societies. It's our means of defining and confronting what is good and bad, honed through millions of years of co-operation and stored in our genes. It gives us benchmarks to guide us, targets to aim for, visions to get us there, standards to judge ourselves and our societies by. If we didn't have religion, we'd need something close to it. And in the hole left in the twentieth century by the ebbing belief in God we've tried a number of different ideas, organizing ourselves around race (fascism), country (nationalism), production (communism), consumption (capitalism). Maybe the jury is still out, but these ideas don't seem to have worked.

Maybe the reason they don't work is because they lack respect for a sense of the "sacred" (for the moment, let's call it God for short), which is the second meaning of *religio*. We may describe this God as an idea of perfection, or a spirit, or in human form, or, as Christian tradition says from the fourth century AD onwards, as all three at once, or in any of thousands of other ways. Each suggests that values are more than our invention. They're rooted in something that's bigger and more important than ourselves, a next level up, something that's beyond our control, that we can't twist to our advantage. To put it in terms of practical relationships, there are things we can't compromise on, where the ends don't justify the means. There are values for which we're prepared to sacrifice more than seems rational.

This is more controversial. What we can't see or measure we suspect might not exist. But we can't ignore it. There's no point in trying to brush God under the carpet and hope that He and the more extreme of his followers will go away. In the US well over 90% say they believe in God, 85% describe themselves as

Christian, 50% go to church. Even in the secular UK over 70% still say they believe in God, 50% call themselves Christian, though only around 7% regularly go to church/synagogue/mosque/temple. The idea first mooted a couple of centuries ago, and common 50 years ago, that religion would die off in the West has proved an illusion. Around the world it flourishes as much as ever.

And it always will. The "sacred" has been with us so long it may even be something hard-wired into the brain, that makes us human. It's what "human" means. The word probably originates from the Arabic *hu*, meaning spirit, or God; and the Sanskrit *manah*, or mind. We think that we are what we have become because we are essentially spiritual beings, minds seeking God, whatever those terms might signify. For tens of thousands of years we've described this search in religion and more recently in philosophy. Religion is usually preferred to philosophy because it engages the heart, even the body, as well as the mind. It offers the medicine as well as the diagnosis. It describes what we have in here as well as how we relate to what's out there.

Religion is primary. So much so that most deeply religious societies don't even have a word for it. Reading, writing, arithmetic, science, these are secondary. They're what we have to go to school for. We have a hunger for the meaning that we describe in religion like we have a hunger for food and relationship. Indeed in most religions these are linked in sacrifice and ritual meals. Communion, eating the flesh of another to partake of its spirit, is the most ancient and widespread of all religious practices. And theology is to religion like cookery is to eating, like love is to sex. We've been doing it ever since our ancestors came down from the trees and started burying their dead.

But do we really need God today to hold our relationships together, when we have marriage and music, laws and police, democracies and global institutions? Why do we still return to this ancient idea? Sometimes it's the young who turn to God through idealism; they feel there's more to life than their parents let on. Or the middle-aged through frustration at not reaching their dreams; they begin to see themselves as they used to see their parents. Or the old because they need new ones; the end is coming like a train and they wonder if there isn't something beyond extinction. Dissatisfaction, the thought that we're being pushed around the edges of life rather than enjoying its center, is a powerful force that leads to belief. Fear can do it still faster. Nothing prompts agonized questioning as much as imminent death, whether of a partner or our own.

But it's also the positive wells we draw on that keep us coming back to it. There's occasional sheer delight at being alive, at the amazingly intricate beauty of nature. There's gratitude at being loved, and at the power of love to change ourselves and others.

A new-born baby, a dying friend, a walk in the woods, maybe even in a church – those usually empty shells of the faith we used to have – at times most of us feel the pull of something else, of being connected to a whole that embraces our little selves. We might describe it as God, variously emphasizing the loving aspect, the beautiful, the true, or the good, or simply as a mystery that we can touch the edges of but can't know. Sometimes, maybe just once or twice in a lifetime, we might experience a moment so strange and wonderful that nothing is ever quite the same again. We might even redefine the priorities in our lives. After all, the world is over there, and it's astonishing. We're here, and we're the only starting point we have. Surely we're related. If there's a meaning behind it we want to know, to be part of it. And in so far as we're rational creatures we need a reason for living and a framework to live by. Rules are useful for that. And life is more than rules and logic. Hope would be a nice thing too.

What most religions agree on, if you look at it broadly, is that when you strip away everything that we tend to think of as constituting our lives – our possessions, home, health, friends, family, even our sense of self – we get down to who we really are, and find there's something there. We're more than a bundle of molecules, more than science has yet described. If you dig deep enough there's a spark, a spirit, rather than empty space. Some describe this as the soul. Connecting with it brings us back to Eden, to the time before we realized we were naked, and invented clothes and fashion, work and worry, religion and psychology. We find we're back in touch with the world. The problems fall away, and nothing could be other or better than it is. We see the true nature of consciousness as eternal rather than transient. That love is real. That life is more energy than matter, force fields rather than flesh. That underneath the appearance all is essentially one.

Many say they encounter a force, which most characterize as loving and healing; many personalize it as a deity, which sustains and informs this world, nudging it every moment toward life rather than chaos.

There is no more powerful feeling on earth. Millions of talented, wealthy, beautiful people have given up ambition, money, and sex for religion. They still do. It can be the assurance of being saved and loved, reconciled with yourself and the world. The moments when you know prayers have been answered, even of foreknowledge. Maybe it's the times when you are caught up in worship, when the veil between this world and the next, between your self and God, splits. It can bring healing, opening up innermost thoughts, bringing to light childhood problems and clearing them. The experience of time, space and nature can be changed by it. The presence of God can be the defining point around which the world turns. We can actually love ourselves because we are part of a greater love. This then spills over into a love for others. It makes sense of everything. It's better than drugs, and without the downside. It can bring us peace: even happiness.

Depending on the channel they've found, some phrase it as reaching for God up there, others as God reaching down to us, others as finding God in here, others as going beyond the idea of God. The voice of God speaking out of the hurricane, the roaring fire, or the still quiet, the voice of reason or conscience, or no voice at all. But all describe the experience as a feeling of coming home, of being welcomed to our true state; a moment that wraps up past, present, and future, self and other, in an explosion of understanding and happiness.

Why we believe in God is easy to see. We always have done. It's a bridge over the abyss, the light at the end of the tunnel. It takes our uncertainties and fears and turns them around, enabling us to believe that what happens was meant to happen, and will turn out for the good. It's what drives us, makes us believe that love is more than sex, relationship more than advantage. That there's a "whole" we can be part of, where life makes sense. That even death is not the end. We're even prepared to die ourselves for a cause as causes can make life worth living. If we can't, if life has no cause, we think of it as having no meaning, no "worth." We all have some form of belief, however mild. It turns self-awareness into a blessing rather than a curse, enables us to love life rather than fear it.

Whether this is true or not, it "works," or we would have given up on it thousands, hundreds of thousands of years ago. Alcoholics are more likely to be persuaded to give up drinking by acknowledging the "Higher Power" of the AA 12 Steps Programme than by being lectured at by doctors. Parents do not lessen their grief by thinking of their dead child as rotting flesh, but by believing their spirits will touch again. We're more likely to act in the interests of others if we can believe in love as a universal principle in life than if we see it as a self-gratifying fiction. We're more likely to be happy if we believe creation is good, and joyful, and continuous than if we think of it as random, painful, and meaningless.

Atheists won't win the argument on the ground in another thousand years because what they offer is not enough. Religion can support you when you have nothing, can give you something to reach for when you have everything. Indeed sometimes the more we have the more we realize there's never enough, and it's not what we really want. It exerts the same kind of power over a millionaire in her New England Hampton's mansion as over a dying Neolithic clan leader clothed in wolf

skins and huddled by a cave fire. In between it covers the lot –
from birth to death, fear to hope, guilt to joy, from poor people
to rich, happy to sad. In a vast and complicated world, religion
gives us reference points, telling us who and where we are.

And there's a point that every religion agrees on – that the key
to understanding is in surrender, acceptance. Most of us have
learned to let go with a partner in the interests of a deeper
relationship: religion is about letting go the world. The trick of
doing it, of having faith (believing beyond the evidence) that the
world makes a deeper kind of sense, comes with knowing for
yourself where that point is, where faith is credible. Where you
can make the jump. Where you can let go, and believe the
unknown will take care of you. The point is different for
everyone, and the average position changes through the
centuries in different cultures. It changes through your own life.

Finding that point is what this book is about. Mindfulness is
staying focused on where the point makes sense. Wisdom is
thinking and acting out of that awareness. Salvation, or
enlightenment, or repentance, or reconciliation, or awakening
(there are hundreds of ways of describing it), happens in the
realization that the point is everything, the doorway through
which you leave behind your self and reconnect with life as it is
rather than the little bit of it we can see.

2

HOW WE BELIEVE

"Faith is to believe what you do not see, and the reward of this faith is to see what you believe."

Augustine

Letting go and living in the love of God, or however you describe it – that sounds great, but it's easier said than done. For the average individual in the West, each of us consuming on average a hundred times more than our grandparents eight times removed did at the turn of the nineteenth century, it's probably harder than at any other time in history. We've got so much more to let go of. As this is a book for novices in matters of religion, written by one, let me come right out and say I've never really managed it; which is why I'll either spend a long time in purgatory (if I'm lucky) or come back as a bug.

The harder I try to believe in a God "out there" the more He seems a function of my own efforts. The more believers shout that He exists the more ephemeral He seems to be – why should any self-respecting God need that kind of help? On the other hand, however much I try to practice Eastern traditions, or the Christian *via negativa*, and lose the "self," there's always that niggling voice: "I'm still here, silly," which I can't quite lose. I've never been completely bowled over and turned into a different kind of person (not that's lasted, anyway). Equally, I've never quite lost the feeling that life without any sense of the sacred is a gray and shabby affair. Revelation keeps popping its head around the corner, but reason always pokes its eye out.

The main problem is *how* we can know we see or hear God. That we're not just talking with ourselves. I get manuscripts every week from people who think they are God, or the sons of God, or to whom God (or angels, or Devas, or whoever) has spoken. Most of our authors believe they have had direct experiences of God. Some would dispute that most others really have had a genuine experience (I try and avoid those). They can't have done, because it's not the same as theirs. But what criteria do we use for accepting some as "real" (if we do) and others not? Aren't all these authors either encountering something "real" or all mad?

Religion relies on personal experience for its validity: "I know it's true, because this happened to me . . . ." But why should our experience be equally valid for others who experience differently? What if they lead to contradictory beliefs? There are at least 100,000 distinct pictures of the divine world that we've developed in our history. And the pattern is really far more diverse, by many factors of 10. There are for instance over 30,000 denominations in Christianity alone, about one for each verse in the Bible, and that's in a fairly centralized and creedal religion.

Each tradition might appeal to sacred scriptures as the source of its authority, as divinely given, but that only shifts the problem along. Why follow one rather than another when they all claim to be true? In the library of sacred scripture for instance the Bible is one book amongst several thousand. It's not the oldest, or the newest. It's not the best written, or the most coherent. It's not the most inspired, or original, or moral. Its authorship is less certain than most (covered variously in chapters 9-14). Only those whose knowledge of the rest of the library is limited or non-existent claim otherwise.

Their arguments are tedious. For instance, Jesus must be the Son of God because he told me so, or because he fulfills the prophecies of the Old Testament, because it's the only explanation of the commitment of the followers, the power of the Gospels, the rapid spread of the faith, the coherence of the text, etc. Muslims use exactly the same arguments for Muhammad. They're of equal merit. Or perhaps Muslims have the better of it. Take the last point for instance. The Qur'an is much more coherent than the Bible, written as it is by one individual in the most extraordinarily beautiful Arabic, in a white-hot heat over 20 years, rather than by dozens of authors from different cultures, in different languages, spread over a thousand miles and a thousand years.

But even if everyone in the world believed in the same God and saw Him in the same way, even if we only had one sacred book, one temple, one church, and had done for the last 10,000 years; even if there were no atheists, no heretics, no believers in other religions, that wouldn't prove anything about whether God is really "there" or not. Any doctor will tell you that the brain can believe anything, even when the evidence of the senses contradicts it. None of us sees "straight." We deceive ourselves. We all feel we have right and logic on our side. It's our make up. We all fantasize, hope, fear. We fall into love, believe it's for ever, and then do it again.

Our minds are "recursive systems," in the language of cognitive psychology. We not only watch ourselves "doing." We think about what we're doing, and then we think about what we're thinking about. We shape our thoughts into ideas and images and ideologies. Then we think about them again. Anyone on the spiritual journey has had the experience of peeling back layers of the mind, like an onion, and wondered; "what could I be thinking about if I could stop thinking? If I could get myself out of the way and just approach God? Or if I could somehow peel back all the layers, might there be nothing in the middle?" And the fear is that if we peel back too many layers we lose all sense of who we might be.

Some psychiatrists even suggest that schizophrenia (and there are more schizophrenics in Western Europe than regular churchgoers) is not due to a lack of rationality, but too much of it. We can't bear too much reality, even if we could see what it was.

All we think of as valuable and real is like a dream dimly-remembered in the morning. We can't even be certain of what we see with our eyes, let alone what god we pray to in our heads. Bees, dogs, us, we all see the world differently; our limited and very different senses can take in only a small spectrum. Interpreting what we see is something different again. People who have been blind from birth and recover their sight don't see cars, trees, houses, but a confusing jumble. Making sense of this is a process we learn. As we age we begin to exercise control over what we see by interpreting it. We build up layers of meaning, making symbols and images, imagining one thing in terms of another.

We create identities at many levels. We read patterns into events to make them better or worse than they are. We lie for our own benefit, or even for that of others. We find reasons to be nice to people we don't like. Experience is as much our perception of reality, interpreted in our heads, as the thing itself. The Vedantic philosophers figured this out five millennia ago (and influenced key European philosophers of the modern age like Schopenhauer when their works were made available in translation in the nineteenth century), calling the illusion of reality that we see *maya*.

This ability to project our imaginations on to the world around us and shape it to our desires has turned into our cumulative wisdom, instinctive and cultural, taking a myriad different shapes along the chain. Out of it in the last 70,000 years or so we've produced art, music, religion, politics, everything that makes us what we are. The "self" doesn't figure all this out on its own. It's created out of our collective definitions of what matters.

At an individual level the relation of the "me" in here and the "world" out there forms an image in our brains. Some neurologists believe they've identified the part of it, nicknamed the "God-spot," that sifts incoming data to enable us to distinguish between the two. But at times circumstances lead to moments of transcendence when the sense of "me" disappears. These can be occasioned by our own efforts, as in worship, meditation, fasting, through drugs, entheogenic plants, in dance, self-mutilation, sex – if you're lucky. Music can also help achieve this, as can nature, love, art . . . religion simply makes a habit of it. Believing in God is a way of relating, a disciplined way of defining the space (or lack of it) between ourselves and the world. If you live in Washington or Teheran you probably see God as "out there," a reality outside our heads, with a gulf in between, which we can only cross with His help. If you live in Paris or Peking you probably see this God as an illusion, and focus on the reality we think we can see, or that we can find within ourselves.

There's no universal spiritual logic to all this. We don't even have this "God-spot" equally. In some individuals the capacity is strong, in others weak. Some are driven to understand, others uninterested. Maybe they're better off. It's a mixed blessing. Saints and prophets, like great musicians and artists, are often on the borderline of breakdown, or over it. More have lost their sanity than held on to it. It's inherited, and not completely under our conscious control; epileptics for instance can suffer from it severely; or it can be triggered by electrical impulses.

The changes in brain patterns are the same across all cultures and faiths. In other words, experiencing Krishna or God amounts to the same thing as far as the brain is concerned. No religious experience is more "real" than another, any more than it's more real to love one person rather than another. Otherwise we would all love the same person, believe the same way. The questions are more whether we've found the right person to love, and the one who loves us. Whether we have a religion that feels true for us, and whether it's a good one. Whether we can move forward in relationship, or whether we're still stuck on the fence.

Religion is nothing special. It's not something you do on Sundays, or in quiet times. It's not something you can separate from loving, or living. It's not different from washing the dishes, or dreaming at night. It's not either "real" or "imaginary." Both God as reality and imagination are just different ways of coming to terms with the polarization of the world into "me" and "it" that came with self-awareness. Maybe there's just matter, and religion is a way of seeing it as miracle. Maybe it is a miracle. Some see it that way, others don't. Maybe it's like whether you see the glass as half empty or half full. It's our response to life that determines what it means for us, rather than some uncertain idea of life itself. And for some, defining their lives as in the hands of God enables them to live better ones. We turn what we see into stories, and imagine better endings. We then act them out; we become what we create. That's what our lives are. The self is not a "thing," but a process, a creation, trailing clouds of memory and potential. Religion is like art, with our own lives as the medium. It's why most of the world's great art has a religious dimension. It inspires us in a way that atheism, nihilism, existentialism, consumerism, have never managed, other than the odd sparkle.

We shape the world we see; the world shapes us. Religion describes the relationship. Believers see God as the measure of it. But we're on uncertain ground here, to be entered with trepidation, shoes and hats off. No one can really describe it for anyone else. Beliefs can lead you to the river, but they can't make you drink. And at the riverbank they look the same. They can all be equally persuasive, equally fragile. Christians in Montana might believe in Jesus materializing through walls (Luke 24:36) and see him appear to them. Animists in Burma see ghosts doing the same. The Uduk in Sudan experience ghosts reading their minds. All these figures are "real" for those concerned. Saying one is real and the others imaginary is chickening out. Saying they're all imaginary doesn't help us understand why we see them. If we want to hold on to our own dreams with integrity we should tread lightly on those of others.

The images we see, the voices we hear, are "real" in the way art and music, beauty and love are real. Also ugliness and evil – the brain takes no prisoners. Religion specializes in the mind's borders, drawing on our strongest emotions, our wildest fears and hopes. Making sense of them with the discipline of words channels nonsense and fantasy into inspiration and guidance. It allows others to evaluate their worth, and maybe share the experience. But the worst thing we can do is take ourselves too seriously, the voices in our heads or the words on the page too literally. Did God for instance really tell Abraham to cut his son's throat on a windy hilltop (Genesis 22:2)? If He spoke like that to us wouldn't we sooner think we'd gone nuts than do what He said? If Abraham tried it today wouldn't we try him for a particularly brutal and appalling attempt at child-murder; view his religion as a sick and dangerous cult; lock him up and throw away the key?

All religions look equally bizarre from the outside. It's not difficult to see how we came to believe differently, how we even came to believe the impossible and imagine it rational, the immoral and imagine it good. If you repeat new understanding often enough it is laid down as a pattern in the brain to be found more readily again. Over time new insight becomes tradition, part of the way the community thinks. Tradition then becomes expectation. Tell yourself over and over again for instance that you're a sinner and you begin to believe it. Practice ritual confession and it becomes necessary for your mental health. Whatever it is that you believe or hope you see you can only interpret it in the expected way.

Over time we encounter the deity we've been taught to expect. In every spiritual experience, vision, dream, near-death-experience, the God we see takes the forms we're familiar with. All beliefs are learned. They're not written in our DNA. If a good Christian had been born in Saudi Arabia he or she would be a good Muslim today. Personal judgement plays a small role. Individual conversions from one religion to another are comparatively rare, and, short of economic or military persuasion, usually cancel each other out numerically.

Sure, traditions are important. Without them we're lost. After all, an individual who thinks he alone has the truth is defined as mad. If he gets a few friends together who think the same, they have a cult. Add in a few states and a few generations, and when it gets up to around a million followers we call it a religion. Incidentally, in the history of religion Christianity is a slow starter. It took several centuries to get to a million followers, around a millennium to reach 10 million, and there are over 150 religions today with a million or more followers.

But there is nothing "definitive" about tradition. Even within religions you can trace the changing patterns of understanding. A few centuries ago for instance virtually all Christians believed that witches rode through the sky on broomsticks; that prophets could do the same in chariots (2 Kings 2:11); that Jesus rose through it to heaven. It's taken the successive centuries for each of these beliefs to turn from accepted fact to metaphor or fiction.

Different traditions within a particular religion also think in different ways. So Catholics for instance might see a miracle in a statue weeping blood. Eastern Orthodox, with their tradition of disallowing statues, see it in stigmata, the imprint of Christ's suffering on the flesh. More commercially-minded Protestants see it in the opportune arrival of cash. There's never real, objective evidence. Where one sees miracle the other sees fakery or coincidence. The intensity of the expectation creates at least the belief of change if not the reality.

Believers overestimate the evident truth of their particular religion. There's no difference in *kind* between the virgin birth of Jesus or Krishna; the levitation of Jesus (for example, Matthew 14:25) or the Buddha; the empty stone tomb of Jesus or Mithras; the ascended Jesus or Ascended Master (see chapter 12). If you want to believe in one, fair enough. But the difference in terms of "evidence" between them is less than you think. And insisting on the absolute truth of one and dismissing the others is plain mean-spirited.

But equally non-believers, and in particular most journalists and politicians, even historians, tend to underestimate the impact of religion as a whole. As organized religion is marginal to the lives of most in the West they read this indifference back into the past, and into cultures different from theirs. But it will still be flourishing when all of our recorded history so far just amounts to the first chapter of our adventures. It's extraordinarily powerful.

Religion pictures the biggest life we can imagine, covering our beginnings and endings, our most beautiful dreams, and our worst nightmares. We've pictured a multitude of heavens and hells, angels and monsters. Gods that are the embodiment of love and goodness, and gods that eat our hearts and livers. It can comfort or terrify like nothing else on earth. It can transform your life or blow your mind away; start wars and sustain them for centuries; depopulate continents (see chapter 15 if that seems like exaggeration).

We end up with a mixed bag, just like we have wonderful meals and junk food; art and rubbish. Most religion has roughly equal proportions of both. A good part of the history of humankind has been the struggle of the good to rise above the bad. Good religion strengthens the bonds that tie us with each other and the world we live in, to make it a better and holier place. It's difficult because relationship is. Having a close relationship with anybody or anything means giving up something of your self. Seeing something as sacred involves putting it at a higher level than yourself. So it stresses service rather than mastery, self-control rather than gratification, humility rather than pride.

Then there's bad religion, which divides: "My leader or view or bit of the world is sacred, yours isn't. The Holy Spirit is a Christian spirit; other spirits are evil. The words I hear in the night, the comfort in the day, the healing, these are the voices and actions of God; yours are of the devil." That's the easy kind. It bottles up the grace of God and puts the stopper on, rather than spreading it around. It can lead us to lay waste to the good around us. It's often justified by appeal to a particular revelation, scripture or tradition. But then there are so many of them. It's not difficult to believe in this god, or that god, out of the 100,000 or so to choose from, or to think that you have the answer and everyone else is wrong. It's a form of religious racism, though there isn't really a word for it. It's the worst kind of "ism" there is. To tyrants and schizophrenics it comes naturally. Trying to understand where we really are in the web of relationships, but holding that in tension with an awareness of the limitations of our own perspective, that's surely the better path.

It's down to us. We, with the help of our parents, peers,

communities, choose how we see God. And of course we don't have to see Him at all. Believing in God is not compulsory. There was no one at your birth saying, "We'll only let you live if you believe in God." There's no one when you die saying, "Because you haven't believed we'll now torture you in hell for ever." That's just sick: a religion for playground bullies to preach and the fearful to practice.

All organized religions have a tendency to turn options into absolutes. They can make it difficult to believe what should come naturally. They can deny knowledge, or even love. At their worst they can promote the opposite, where lies plus hatred equals evil, or illusion. And we're suckers for that because, given half a chance, we'll believe anything. And if it works to our personal advantage so much the better. And it's in the nature of religion and churches to keep inventing more obscure and exotic beliefs, more selfish beliefs, until there's a collective cry of "We can't believe this any more."

Let's ignore bad religion for the moment. Believing in God is not difficult in itself. The basics are simpler than riding a bike. You realize you're an insignificant speck of life with a confused medley of loves and hates and noise in your head. That there's a wonderful world out there, which is informed by a purpose greater than you can imagine. Step one.

You put the two together. Step two.

You let yourself go. Step three.

You then live your life in this light rather than for the interests of your self. Step four.

It may take you 5 minutes, 5 years or 50 to get there, or 5,000 more lives in other traditions, but that doesn't matter, as long as you make a start.

Believing this has been as much a part of our humanity as being born and dying. Religions describe this process differently. Some emphasize the "world out there," that of truth; others how we relate to it, the world "in here," that of love. Ultimately, as all good religion recognizes, they come to the same thing, because each is shaped by the other.

To put it another way, we have minds that want to know, and hearts that want to love. The mind and heart together make up what we think of as the soul. Truth plus love equals happiness. Truth without love is arid. Love without truth, fantasy. Certainty in truth or love makes one the enemy of the other. Everyone draws their own line, leaning this way or that. In what is now a global village we need to draw a wide circle, one that includes everyone. If our vision excludes most people, putting them outside the circle of salvation, it's probably not true, and certainly not loving. It then doesn't deserve to last, and it won't.

And if pushed to describe God, about half of all believers will shape the answer in general terms around truth, and half around love. They're surely both right. Truth is the aim of our journey. Our beliefs, our lives, should incorporate what we know to be true. It's the principle we follow. Love is the measure of how far we've travelled. It's the basis of our practice. For Christians God is our best understanding of both. Jesus is our best example. The supreme one we have in life and words of finding truth through love. He shows the way. And we try to follow.

Some will say that this is all fancy. Others that our failure to see the spiritual more clearly simply reflects our primitive stage of evolution. We're still more apes than angels. Maybe we'll never know. Maybe it doesn't really matter one way or the other. Because the practice of religion is mostly about living life on earth in the light of this bigger vision. It's about translating imagination into fact, about making us better people, and the world a better place. And in what became known as Christianity the supposed founder, Jesus, seems to say as clearly as anyone that it's not the kind of spiritual experience you have that matters but what you do with it. All the good visitations or prayers in the world don't add up to the effect of good action, and we're all capable of that, however rarely we manage it. Which will bring us back later to the lost opportunity that Christianity represents.

3

The Stories
we Tell

"And who is so stupid as to imagine that God
planted a garden in Eden eastward, and put in it a
tree of life, which could be seen and felt?"

Origen

We believe because we always have done. Because it works. It's the way we relate. "How" we believe is more difficult. We can't measure what goes on in our heads like we can measure the outside world. So many of us tend to assume that people who see God are either fantasizing (if we're atheists or agnostics) or that their thoughts are true and good and those of everyone else wrong or evil (if we're believers).

But credible, good religious belief acknowledges that it's not trying to describe the world in the same way as science does. It tells a story. In living a good life we interpret the world we see by the better one we imagine. In doing so we can make the real world better, we can make a difference. Better to have faith and suspend the rational mind than to think straight, see nothing, and have no faith, hope, or love.

Jesus started a religion by telling stories. For his followers that wasn't enough. And over the centuries we've lost the plot, we've forgotten their point. Christianity has stopped making public sense.

For instance the community where I've lived for twenty years is not particularly academic, and certainly not radical. It's literate and conservative, inclined to treat a thousand-year-old institution like the local Parish Church as sympathetically as possible. Regular churchgoers might number 3% or so, but I doubt that more than one in a hundred can wholly identify with orthodox Christian teaching.

I realise this is not true of North America and other parts of the world, but Christianity is now essentially a private concern, and its serious practice in Western Europe involves only a few.

Today we look to anthropologists to tell us how we got here. Biologists tell us what we're made of. Historians and psychiatrists explain why we think as we do. Scientists explore the edges of time, space, and matter. They all have something real to say. Novelists and playwrights take care of the imagination, and give us our stories of today, the ones that explore where and who we are, how we relate. Theology, the "science of God," has diminished as they've grown. It's now a small subsection lost somewhere between history and philosophy. It inspires little else, where it used to inspire everything.

How did it get to this point of irrelevance?

The stories we tell change over time. Religion ceases to be credible when the institutions that have grown up around it hang on to a story for too long. It's happened tens of thousands of times through history. It's seen most clearly in lesser-known religions. They have narrow beginnings and stay narrow. They fade as the world moves on, the followers die off. Their gods of wood rot, stone sinks back into the earth. World religions (though any "religion" is a tentative notion, "world religions" even more so), like Christianity, for instance, followed by more people than any other to date, reflect the collision of cultures, of one way of thinking being illuminated and enlarged by another, in this case the Hebrew and the Greek. They evolve more than others. Their definitions of the eternal, the universal, change with our definitions of what time and space are.

Hebrew religion and Greek culture, the church and a classical education: these formed the Western world. Halfway through the first millennium BC both Hebrews and Greeks believed in a sky god holding court, the Hebrews calling Him Yahweh, and the Greeks Zeus. In Job for instance God chats with his various sons and courtiers, asking one of them, Satan, about what he's found out during his hikes on the earth (Job 1:6-12). The unknown Hebrew writer turned this Babylonian story (and the first verse tells us that Job is not even a Hebrew, but a foreigner from the land of Uz) into one of the world's great meditations on suffering and purpose.

The Greek sages turned outward to exploring the world around us, and created "science." Thales in the sixth century BC has been described as the world's first scientist, and his successors laid the foundations for 2,500 years of discovery. Euclid's *Elements* remained the mathematician's Bible up till the twentieth century, when deep space conditions and added dimensions came into the frame.

If God had asked questions of the Greeks rather than the Hebrews he would have got answers. "Who hath laid the measures thereof [of the earth], if thou knowest?" Eratosthenes calculated its diameter to within 75 miles of the true figure (7,923 miles) by measuring the angle of sunlight down a well.

"Whereupon are the foundations thereof fastened? or who laid the corner stone thereof; when the morning stars sang together, and all the sons of God shouted for joy?" (Job 38:5-7). Aristarchus could have told the writer of Job that the earth didn't have cornerstones, that it wasn't even flat, but a sphere that circled the sun. Today we think like Greeks, pray like Hebrews (at least most readers of this book are likely to: Gallup polls suggest that two thirds of Americans still believe the sun circles the earth, compared to half in, say, the UK, or China).

But how did these different frames of reference merge, especially when in the first few centuries BC the two cultures were antagonistic? The attempted imposition of Greek culture on to the Jewish by the successors of the Greek Alexandrian Empire led to the lengthy and bitter Maccabean wars. They (or at least the hardliners) despised each other.

Both peoples were absorbed into the Roman Empire. The Romans were more interested in getting from A to B than in where Z was. Like most successful empires they assimilated beliefs rather than imposed them. They inherited much of Greek culture and philosophy. Christianity, as an offshoot of Jewish religion, began to spread through the Empire in the first century AD. By the end of the second century leading Christians, known today as the church fathers, were investing huge amounts of time and energy in constructing a belief system that reconciled Jewish and Greek thought, enabling the emerging religion to make sense to the wider Mediterranean world.

The Western half of the Empire then collapsed into the Dark Ages, and the light of civilization in this part of the world was restored during the Golden Age of Islam (ninth to twelfth centuries) by the Umayyad in Spain, the Fatimids in Egypt, the Abbasids in Mesopotamia. In the twelfth century, by pillaging some of these more advanced societies (in a series of jihad-like invasions known as the Crusades), the Christian barbarians of the north began to recover the knowledge of the ancient world. This led to a further synthesis of Greek and Christian thinking, particularly in the theology of Albertus Magnus and Aquinas in the thirteenth century, who developed the classical idea of God by which we know Him today. The Renaissance followed, then the Enlightenment, and by the sixteenth century we were catching up with a picture of the universe that had started to take shape a couple of millennia earlier.

This is overly simplistic; most of the church fathers interpreted scripture allegorically rather than literally. Many in the Middle Ages had a more sophisticated idea of God than many Christians today. By the fourteenth century Gregory Palamas was talking about God as "in His essence absolutely unknowable." Even a virulent Protestant reformer like John Calvin in the sixteenth century considered some Old Testament ideas about the world "baby talk." And during the Enlightenment scientists saw themselves as exploring the majesty of God's creation rather than taking him out of the picture. The greatest scientist who ever lived, Isaac Newton, spent far more time trying to unravel the secrets of Revelation, and alchemy, rather than gravity.

But there's a core of truth in it. In the sixth century BC the Greeks and others were considering the possibility of a world without gods, predicting eclipses of the sun accurately, and speculating on the earth as a round ball whizzing through space. There were half a million volumes in the Great Library of Alexandria alone. Run forward a couple of millennia till the time the Europeans caught up with China and were about to enter the age of print, and there were only 30,000 volumes in the whole of Christendom. Not one of them saw the earth as other than the center of the universe.

In recent centuries science has advanced too fast for the church to keep pace, and our views have polarised. The picture of the world it gives us is centuries, millennia, out of date. It fought against astronomy in the seventeenth century, geology in the eighteenth, biology in the nineteenth, psychology in the twentieth, even, bizarrely, against a better understanding of its own sacred texts. The Vatican took 400 years to admit, in 1992, twenty years after men walked on the moon and after a commission managed to spend ten years looking at the evidence, that it might have "misunderstood" Galileo, and hasn't offered an apology yet. And that's progressive compared with large sections of today's Evangelical community.

So we have two contradictory stories today. To describe what I mean, have a look at the greatest story of all, the story of our beginnings.

To understand ourselves we want to know who our parents were, the family history; we're interested in what makes us the nation and race we are. We want to work out what made us human, and we trace our origins back through history, biology, chemistry, all the way to physics. And the question at the beginning is the same for all of us. Were we planned, and loved, or an accident, the result of meaningless encounters?

We want to believe the first. God created the universe: if not, we're orphans. At the beginning of the twentieth century Oxford and Cambridge University Presses were still printing the accepted dates in their Bibles. There are variations of year, day and month, but 4004 BC comes close, if you work out the biblical chronology.

In perhaps the most conspicuous example of mass willful ignorance since civilization began, over half the people in the world (most Christians, Muslims, Jews) still broadly accept this date, because the books of Moses (sacred to all three religions) can't be wrong.

The drive to a literal reading of the scriptures is strongest in the Muslim world. At first sight that's odd, as a millennium ago Muslims were far ahead of Christendom in science and learning (which is why for instance we count in Arabic numerals rather than Roman). But their fundamentalism has a harder edge. Muslims place scripture on a higher plane than Christians do, so it hurts them more when it's undermined. For them the very shape of the words is sacred. They were literally dictated by God (through an angel, according to the tradition). If you want to worship Allah properly you should do so in Arabic, whereas Christians positively encourage new translations in both English and other languages.

It all depends on where you're starting from. Everyone is to the left of someone else in how literally they interpret scripture, all suspicious about the rigidity of those on one side and the heresy of those on the other. Most Christians/Muslims for example no longer accept the Hebrew view that the earth is flat (14 references in the Old Testament), about the size of Brazil, with Sheol underneath and heaven a few hundred feet up in the air, its light shining through holes in the sky (stars). But a surprising number do. The scriptures after all are "infallible," or "inerrant" (which mean pretty much the same: the Bible doesn't say everything that is right, but it doesn't say anything wrong either). In 1993 Sheik Abd al-Aziz ibn Baaz, the supreme religious authority in Saudi Arabia, declared in one of their many medieval fatwas (something like a papal encyclical) that anyone who believes the world is round is an atheist and should be punished (the penalty for atheism in many parts of the

Muslim world is death, as it used to be in Christendom).

It seems daft to most of us to think of the earth as a flat disc, in a universe of three levels. If you drill for oil you don't disturb the underground spirits (1 Samuel 28:14). If you set off in an aeroplane you end up where you started, a couple of days later, with jet lag. Very few Christians take the Biblical world view literally in every respect.

But thinking of the earth as flat as no more daft in terms of modern knowledge than thinking of it as a few thousand years old. Today no reputable geologist would accept a biblical account of how the earth was formed (or, to be more precise, Gallup polls suggest that even in the USA the number of earth and life scientists who accept creationism is under 0.1%). No biologist would dispute the broad processes or the approximate timeframe of evolution; the questions are on whether it's gradual or punctuated, how it started and what drives it. No anthropologist would agree that people emerged "ready made."

But even in the expensively-educated USA, Gallup polls over the last 20 years consistently show that around 50% of the population believe that God created man in his present form in the last 10,000 years; 40% believe that man has evolved, but God guided the process; under 10% believe that God has had no direct involvement. Two-thirds think "creationism" more likely than "evolution." Creationist Christians (including its updated title, "Intelligent Design") are in the majority, if you count them worldwide.

More "mainstream" (minority) Christians shake their heads sadly at this kind of knowledge-denial. But most of them still accept the events framed by this world-view, where God opens trapdoors in heaven to throw thunder and lightning, shout down to earth, send doves or messengers. Jesus for instance came from heaven to earth, went down into the underworld (as Acts 2:31 implies and the later creeds affirm) and rose through the sky to heaven. They would even say it's necessary to believe this to be a Christian. Some only accept part of the journey as real, other parts as metaphorical. For instance, he didn't really rise through the sky to heaven but he certainly rose from the dead. That miracle happened even if the others didn't. But they're all batting off the same base. The creationists are just being more consistent.

It's a credit to the power of religion that educated people today still feel impelled to take these stories literally. The Hebrews were an undistinguished nomadic tribe (if they existed at all, some scholars doubt it) of the Middle Bronze Age, scratching a living on the margins of the great Persian and Egyptian civilizations. They couldn't write, let alone do science. So when counting the years backwards they confined themselves to a genealogy you could keep in your head if you multiply the average lifespan by a factor of ten or so. The average lifespan of the ten generations from Adam to Noah in the Jewish Bible is 857 years. The nine generations from Noah's son Shem to Abraham reaches a more modest 333. We know from tombs of the period in Jericho (which was a walled town from at least 8000 BC onwards) that most people died before the age of 35, few lived beyond 50.

To step back a moment, of all our ancient scriptures the Bible is one of the hardest to reconcile with a scientific account of how the world came to be. The "Hymn of Creation" in the *Rig Veda* for instance adopts a much subtler, questioning approach, and doesn't assume that humankind is the center of the universal purpose. It's ironic that of all the calendars available, the modern scientific Christian West has based its chronology on one of the world's least accurate. In contrast, the Persians for instance believed the world was created 500,000 years ago. Farther east, in India, each Day of Brahma, each breath of the Creator, is reckoned at 4.32 million years, which improves on the Judaic/Christian traditional view by three factors of ten. Sometimes it's a case of the older the religion the wiser, which is what every religion declares to its rebellious cults.

And it's not just that these stories are harmless, sometimes they get nasty. In the Old Testament for instance God enables Joshua to stop the sun and moon and put the universe on hold so that the Hebrews had enough daylight to finish slaughtering the Amorites, whose lands they were invading and daughters raping (Joshua 10.13).

It surely must stagger even the most conservative Christian mind to take this seriously for more than a few minutes' reflection. We know now that the universe is so big as to be beyond our comprehension. If you think of the space covered by the earth circling the sun as the dot at the end of this sentence you would have to drop it into the Atlantic Ocean to get an idea of the size of our galaxy. You would have to reduce the galaxy to a similar dot and drop it into the ocean again to get an idea of the size of the universe. It's 50 billion trillion miles across, expanding at a billion miles an hour. There are a million stars with their circling planets for every grain of sand on earth. The idea that there is a God who would bring this to a juddering halt to aid mass-rape and murder is completely insane. Today we would be petitioning the UN to impose sanctions on the Hebrews, send in peacemakers. We would put the leaders on trial for war crimes. We would wonder at their delusions of grandeur.

And the consensus of scientific thought is moving toward the inflation theory, which holds that the "multiverse" could be bigger than our universe by millions of powers of 10, and in 11 or more dimensions. It's hard to believe that all this was created for us, for life on earth, present or future, let alone for one small group of aggressive nomads on this planet a few thousand years ago.

We can't square the God of the Hebrews with what we know today, however much refined by tradition. Something has to give. Good religion looks forward, shaping our future to better ends, not backwards, glorifying past evil. In holding on to the Hebrew God of scripture we've diminished Him. The church has driven God to the margins, while our world-view has moved on. And even the Hebrew God was bigger in some respects than our God today. "God" after all is just a relatively recent three-letter word with Germanic roots meaning "good" as opposed to "evil." The Semitic words for God in the first millennium BC, *Elat* (Old Canaanite), *Elohim* (Hebrew), *Alaha* (Aramaic), *Allah* (Arabic), come from roots better translated as "One" or "All." They were at least heading in the right direction, whereas we've reduced Him to half the God He used to be.

The Old Testament authors looked up at the stars and saw the greatness of God in the heavens. They imagined the greatest God they could. We still can, because we still feel the same way. Of course we can live as if our concerns and couplings are all that matters. What religion suggests is that that is not just a life unexamined, but a life unrealized. But times change. The Hebrews had some deep insights into our behavior and how we relate to God. But they imagined Him in their own terms. None of us can do otherwise, which is why we all describe Him so differently.

The God we can believe in today is, again, the biggest we can imagine. Not just twice but millions of times bigger, on the kind of scale that the universe we know today is bigger than the one the Hebrews knew. He includes the gods of the Hebrews and Amorites, the Greeks and Romans, the Inuit and the Aztecs, the snows and the sun. Those that have disappeared, and those that are to come. He's a God for all of us, at every moment, a heartbeat away.

4

THE WORLD THAT'S THERE

"God is the expression of the intelligent universe."

Kahlil Gibran

Can any religious stories be credible in a world of science? It's been the privilege of my job, publishing some 50 or so religious books a year, and looking at 100 times that many that we can't publish, to come across more inspiring accounts of the individual experience of God than most people. I wish we could publish more of them. They all fall on the desk, as far as I'm concerned, with equal weight. So I don't mean to insult anyone's beliefs. But let's try to call the shots straight. There are no laws or truths of religion that can be measured with a ruler, or seen under a microscope. We're talking in different categories.

As far as evidence in the strict sense of the word goes – something that would stand up in a modern court – religious experience amounts to zero. Legally, it's hearsay. Evidence needs corroboration by independent witnesses, forensic examination if it's material, the possibility of repeat performance. Miracles are ruled out, by definition.

As far as "proof" goes there have been a number of experiments under rigorous conditions into questions such as whether prayer helps people get better (though none as yet on the equally widely-held corollary, from a historical point of view at least, that praying against or cursing them can make them ill), but the results are inconclusive. Some say that they prove it, others that they don't, but the $1 million prize on offer for proving any aspect of the paranormal, on any scale, goes uncollected every year.

You can make a good argument that most religion is a comfort blanket for adults who can't grow up, who don't want to take on responsibility for the world as it is, for themselves as they are.

You can argue that the world really *is* one of magic and miracle, but you have to shift the perspectives of the argument. I've felt enough, seen enough, heard enough, to believe that it's possible. Mind does affect matter, even if it's just our own bodies. The heat somehow generated by a faith-healer's hands really can have an effect, sometimes; synchronicity (coincidences beyond what we would accept as coincidence) does seem to happen, sometimes. But you can't legislate for it, repeat it, or describe it in terms that make sense in medicine or science.

How far the mind can affect things at a distance, change the course of events, or how far that's just reading meanings into what happens, I don't know. If everyone prayed intensely at the same time for a meteor to be moved off a collision course with the earth would it have any effect? Could a pebble be moved an inch? I suspect not. It's never been done, anyway, not in a way that can be "proved," photographed. Which is not to say it's not worth praying. In that kind of concentrated agreement we could maybe achieve a few other things, like getting rid of world hunger, or terrorism, or nuclear weapons, any one of which would be a good start.

When religion ignores science it's on the way to irrelevance. When it contradicts it, it's superstition. But then it doesn't have to do either. It plays a different kind of role. It refreshes the parts science doesn't reach. They both come from the same kinds of promptings, the same questionings. Science tells us how to get to the moon, but doesn't tell us why we want to go there. Even the battiest religion can help us get through the day better than knowing everything there is to know about evolutionary theory. And good religion is informed by science, much as science has been informed by religion. Science without religion or morality is the fast road to hell. Religion without reason, likewise.

Literal truth is not the primary question. It may not even be a useful one to bother much about, if you're short on time. Good and evil may be fictions we create, whilst nature is indifferent. But at the very least they're *our* fictions, and we live in the world we create. And maybe fictions have a way of turning into fact if you trust them.

And of course you can have religion without miracle and magic. There are traditions within all religions, like the Quakers in Christianity, that see miracles as unnecessary, or unhelpful. Some believers say that you can leave the supernatural out of it, even that there is no supernature, no God. Buddhism for instance is increasingly the religion of choice for many in the West, focusing as it does on the processes of the mind rather than what it thinks it sees. Jainism, the most demanding religion on earth, the Mount Everest of them all in terms of lifestyle and discipline, has still less room for any idea of God.

Maybe these positions are mutually exclusive, but I don't see it that way. Some want to take their scriptures literally, and believe there is a God "up there" in heaven, sending messengers or family to earth. Others take this (or some of it) as metaphor, and believe in God "out there," outside physical space/time, or off the edge of the universe (not that it has one, which can make the whole idea of God "out there" difficult to get your head around today). Others see Him more as "in here," in the ultimate relationship between self and non-self; the beginning of the road rather than the end of it. That's how it seems to me that Jesus describes the kingdom of God. We find our images to latch on to, but in themselves they're not important.

But here's a diversion for a chapter. Is the idea of a "God" or some absolute truth or reality out there or in here somewhere utterly implausible? Does the world feel sacred because it *is* sacred? Perhaps it's a meaningless question. Meanings are just what we make them, what we read in the stars, write in books. There's no evidence for anything else. But then there's no evidence for something as fundamental to our experience as consciousness either, apart from the fact that we believe we know we have it and see the results. Scientifically, consciousness and God are as slippery as each other.

You can turn over every molecule in the universe and not find God. You can turn over every molecule in the brain and not find consciousness. We have no real idea what it is, or how it works. We don't need it-we've known for a century that enormously complex psychological processes can be wholly unconscious. As far as anybody knows, anything that our minds do they could do just as well as if they weren't conscious.

We don't need consciousness. We don't need God either. Stars explode, galaxies form, life develops, termites build their cathedrals, all without knowledge of God.

But we know we're here. We can enjoy it. We can revel in the existence of our self, and of others. Maybe there's an equivalent perception one level up, of a universal self, of God, which we can equally enjoy, if we can get there.

Millions of words are written every year on whether there's some kind of Platonic reality, maybe a God; whether mathematical truths would exist even if there were no universe for them to be applied in; whether the mind is identical with the brain or whether it extends into a "field" of consciousness. And you just end up with a headache. After a few thousand years we're not much closer to agreement.

Neither side is as conclusive as either thinks. The argument that religion is fantasy is impossible to refute. But equally the materialistic, reductionist one, that we're nothing more than the molecules and neurons that make us up, is impossible to prove. After all each level of description is more than the sum of its parts. Matter is more than molecules. Life is more than matter. Brain is more than life. Mind seems to be more than brain (disputed). More keeps coming from less. The seemingly impossible keeps happening. Life *did* emerge from molten rock, humans from monkeys, cathedrals from quarries. Why shouldn't there be a spirit that is more than mind? Perhaps we're just on the borderline between the two, like a nematode worm between plant and animal, or a chimp on the shimmering edge of self-consciousness. Perhaps when there is sufficient mind it "emerges" into another level of complexity like all the other levels do.

I believe it's possible to reconcile science and religion if you're open- minded in both. By all means, lean one way or the other. If you take a rationalist point of view you may be more attracted to a religion that doesn't depend on miracle. You don't have to hurt your brain and deny everything you learnt at school.

To take an example, let's go back to the creation stories of the last chapter, seemingly impossible to believe today. Good theologians, rather than propagandists in the Vatican, or Teheran, or the Bible belt, say we should read them because they express brilliantly in story form the belief that the world was created for a purpose. That we are here for a reason. If we can't see that, then life is meaningless and let's party or murder as we please, let's do what we can get away with. There's no one to tell us off.

It's not just the Genesis stories. They echo the oral myths of indigenous societies around the world, still handed down today from the Inuit in Alaska to the Aborigines in Australia, about how we came to be self-aware through language. About how the universe is there in so far as we see it, and see it looking back at us. Consciousness brings life to the void, gives it meaning. The world, the landscape, people, are all sung or spoken into existence. The origin of existence is the Word, the creative act, the ultimate definition. God speaks out of His eternal silence and the Word takes on the flesh of creation. It's words that make us, and everything we see. In the greatest and oldest religious texts we know of, the *Vedas*, which may have been started in the fourth millennium BC with the canon being fixed after 1000 BC, the words are part of the fabric of the universe, existing before time itself. In the *Prashna Upanishad* they create the universe at the beginning of each cycle of existence. There's a pale reflection of this in the first chapter of the Gospel of John. Religion is not just art, it's literature.

Religion is not about taking these texts literally, it's about understanding why they're written as they are. We come back to our two meanings of the word. At one level *religio* is our gift to ourselves, the framework we create to live as if our lives mattered, to function without despairing, to give a name to our journeys. And at the level of "sacred" we put God in charge because every bus needs a driver. Most religious believers in the world aren't bothered whether it's literally "true" or not, in the sense that that's not a particularly meaningful question. "Life" is "true," and that's what we make it. That's the human path. If facts were what counted we'd have concentrated on claws and teeth rather than brains and imagination. We know what we are, the question is what we are going to do about it, what we are going to be.

This may sound stupid to atheists, and to any scientist who sees life in terms of its constituent, measurable parts. But it's the way we all *feel*. It's why adults hang on to the idea of God even when churches describe Him in ways children find stupid. In every moment of life we're conscious of affecting things, albeit in tiny ways: no one lives as if life is random. We believe that we can find love, meaning, and indeed in doing so change ourselves, other people, and the world for the better. Our world seems small and friendly (some of the time anyway), not vast, alien, and incomprehensible. What counts is the purpose and effort we bring to things. The relationships we develop, the good we do, the art we create, the choices we make, the footprints we leave behind. If this is illusion, we all vote for it.

And as far as I can work out, the fact that we can do this doesn't fit into physical laws. Free will is not accounted for by cause and effect. However far down you analyze the emotional and chemical and genetic activity behind every thought and action, there comes a point where we turn probability into fact, where we change what might happen. This is what our "self" is, our will, our conscience, our "soul," that indeterminate and troubled space between our genes and God. If mind is equal to brain activity and can be measured, explained, accounted for in terms of our genetic make-up and environmental influences, then we're not responsible for what we do. Religion is not for children, or grown-ups who want to believe like children, it's for people who want to be responsible, and are prepared to be responsible for others.

So how improbable is the idea of a pre-existing purpose present in creation, rather than one we read into it? More cosmologists today believe in God than biologists, though not necessarily in the form of a personal deity. It's a question of perspective. Biologists deal with life on earth, and we know in principle pretty much all that has happened on the way, apart from the question of how it started in the first place and what drives it. On the cosmological scale it's different. Our feeling of control vanishes. Though we can "see" from one end of the universe to the other and back to a few milli-seconds from the beginning, we can't even account for 90% of what should be there. What we know is still very little. Cosmologists are prepared to accept that the universe is more open-ended and mysterious than we can possibly imagine. That there is a further, final "truth out there" to be discovered, and always may be.

It's true we have this impossibly vast universe, in which our planet and solar system are the tiniest of invisible specks. We know today it's taken 3.5 billion years for life on earth to slowly develop, through several mass extinctions, to produce human beings as one of the trillions of possible outcomes. We live in the wafer-thin atmosphere of the planet, crawling about on its surface like bacteria in cling-film around an apple. But, the religion of "the sacred" says, the fact that we're here is a miracle. It could only have happened because it was meant to be.

How it happened is generally agreed. Around 12 to 15 billion years ago the vastness of the universe existed as an unimaginably small point, one of an infinity of virtual particles, smaller than anything physics can measure, with zeroes to 34 decimal places. Maybe it was a "naked singularity," a mathematical point with no dimensions at all. It exploded in a "Big Bang" to create the physical universe of matter that we know (though the Big Bang has its problems and is not definitive, but then nothing ever is in science).

That's so strange that anything else is possible. Nothing else can be as surprising. The question many wrestle with is how we get from this unimaginably colossal "explosion," in the sense of compacted space expanding at huge speeds, to our fragile life on earth. The second law of thermodynamics (the rule that order decays into disorder) would suggest that the Bang should have resulted in almost anything other than an ordered universe. It's been calculated that if the Big Bang had differed in strength by only 1 part in 10 to the power of 60 the universe as we know it could not have existed. That's the rough equivalent of firing a bullet from one end of the universe to the other and hitting a dime. This is called the "flatness" problem. There are others that make it hard to understand how the universe can be as it is, like the horizon and the singularity problems.

There's a raft of similar remote coincidences where, if variables had been fractionally different, the universe as we know it would not have been possible. Similar astronomical odds accumulate with the emergence of our planet and its life forms. We live on a knife edge of probability, poised between huge uncertainties and impossible odds. For some scientists the inescapable conclusion is that there is an element of cosmic design. Sure, it's just the old teleological argument dressed up for today, but it's still forceful. And you can put forward similar arguments for the relevance of the ontological and the epistemological (arguments from being and knowing). Maybe the universe is designed for life, or is self-designing, in the same kind of way that the earth might be. This theory says that the earth evolves in the direction of life. Perhaps the universe does too. With hindsight James Lovelock, who proposed the Gaia theory, may be seen as significant to our way of thinking today as Aquinas was eight centuries ago.

I don't know which is right, and I guess you can think either way, the universe as purposeful down to the tiniest molecular event, or utterly random. Or somewhere in between. No one knows. And it doesn't really matter. Most atheists and believers are not really that far apart. Atheists might say that everything is meaningless and random, but we can carve out of this our tiny portion of awareness where we can live and create and love. Believers might say that the universe is one of consciousness and purpose and love, and we can join in this awareness and find a reason to live. Both can be equally creative and loving. In the statistics of depression and suicide there's no difference between them.

At the largest scale of the universe the idea of a purpose, of a "God" in some form, is a possibility, however remote. Most scientists assume the universe is random rather than purposeful in the sense of being directed. Organizing principles don't amount to purpose, still less to a personal deity. And purpose is hard enough to define, impossible to measure or prove. Because out of the trillion trillion possible outcomes of the Big Bang we could just happen to be in the one that "worked." One sperm in a few million makes it, the others don't. The fact that we're here to see what has happened is just that, a fact. It's absurd to suggest that there's anything more to it than that.

But it can seem equally absurd that the awesome odds against there being anything at all aren't countered by a force of some kind that turns the potential of becoming into being. And if it's there, if it exists at all, it must work through the universe at all levels.

So let's jump for a minute from the biggest to the smallest. Here we go to things as small in relation to us as the universe is large. Atoms themselves, like the universe, are mostly empty space – so much space that if you took it all out of everyone the world's population could fit into a matchbox. If you think of the nucleus of the atom as a marble in the middle of a stadium, the protons that form its shape are the size of gnats whizzing around the perimeter. The particles that make up atoms are also little worlds of their own, and here we get down into a world that's even more difficult to get your head around, that of quantum physics.

There's a further twist here, as far as science goes. It's not only that we can't see the world straight and true, it's apparent that the world isn't "straight and true" either. It may not be measurable. It may not even be there without an observer to see it. Just as it takes two to love, it takes two to exist. A subject and an object to make a "fact."

At this level of smallness there's a widespread acceptance amongst scientists of certain principles that relate to the problem of measurement. This was first expressed in Heisenberg's Uncertainty Principle, which says that a particle can be in different places at the same time. When you see it it's a point, when you don't it's a wave of probability.

There are many attempts at explaining this. One that some quantum physicists stump for is the "many worlds" interpretation. Every time a particle seems to be in two places at once it is indeed just that, but in a separate universe, so you end up with an infinity of different universes that have split off from every particle event. Another, more popular suggestion is the "super string" theory. This suggests that the universe is made of wave patterns of near infinite length, though these waves are mathematical constructions in many dimensions rather than "things." The nature of the waves is such that they cancel out everywhere except in one tiny region, and it's there that the quantum "thing" materializes. So everything is in a sense everywhere but manifests itself at one particular point, which is where you (or the experiment) look for it. There are half a dozen of these string theories, for example, M theory, which says they're all true.

Then there's the Holograph Principle, which suggests that physics is not after all a description of the world as it is, a description of matter, because there is no matter. The matter is really energy. The energy is really information. Maybe the universe is trying to tell us something. Maybe it's God who is real, the point where the deluded known and the illusory unknown meet, and we just struggle to see Her straight.

Related to this is the Exclusion Principle, which suggests that all particles are still in some way connected. Affect one, and you affect another simultaneously at the other end of the universe. How this can happen when nothing can apparently travel faster than the speed of light, is not known. But in some ways the universe still behaves as if it is an indivisible speck. The quantum state stands outside the "now" as well as the "here." Quantum units have no mass, know no distance or time. They somehow encode the probabilities of all possible events. Everything that has ever happened and will be already exists in these patterns. We're a cog in a machine, but standing at the crossroads of multiple paths, every one of which we could take, every possibility of which has been foreseen. Everything follows from everything else.

Some scientists are suggesting that there may be a form of "proto-consciousness" or "intelligent information" that's inherent in everything, as much a fundamental property of matter as is mass. Bell's theorem suggests that there's no such thing as objective reality, and that consciousness is in some way co-equal with matter in its formation. What we see becomes "real." Reality lies in the relation between the two. Complexity and chaos theory add weight to this, suggesting that beyond matter and energy there are patterns of information that we don't yet know about.

Some writers (not always scientists) have picked up on these new insights in science, and ancient ones in religion, to suggest that the world we live in might be no less interconnected than the quantum world. After all, it's hard to have a principle true at one scale and not another. So synchronicity might be "real." Some claim that this "zero point field" explains everything from cell communication to homeopathy and extra-sensory-perception, from flocking schools of fish to miraculous healing. There's an energy flowing through everything that we can't define but grasp at in terms varying from ley lines to chakras, and can touch through ESP or prayer.

This takes us into more speculative, seemingly absurd areas. But there are some in every generation who think they've discovered everything there is to be found, that history has finished, science has ended, and they're always wrong, just like believers who think they have the complete answer to everything. The only thing we can reasonably be sure of is that what we now think of as the weird edge of science is maybe just the beginning of our next steps in understanding.

Most scientists accept that the laws of physics that we have now will be superseded in years to come, much as relativity superseded gravity. Gravitons and sparticles might replace leptons and quarks as the interesting units. To speculate further, perhaps we'll come to see the speed of light as a threshold rather than a limit. The world of matter that we experience might be one small part of our new equation. Perhaps the world of consciousness, of choice and purpose will come to be seen as vastly larger, 99% of what there is rather than 1% or zero. And if anything can travel faster than the speed of light it's likely to be thought. Religion describes it as the Word, the Logos, the principle of reason. God, the final answer, beyond which nothing can be known, nothing exists, talking to Himself, the ultimate conversational loop.

On a daily basis we think of our existence as the reality, and everything else, whether dreams or God or waves of probability, as increasingly unreal shadows. The old stories suggest that it might be the other way round. And today science suggests that our world could be a peephole of fragile consciousness through which we can see an infinitely richer, multi-dimensional one. Time running backwards, different versions of ourselves existing simultaneously, aliens and galaxies made of invisible matter, trillions of universes at the end of our fingertips – these are all theoretical possibilities in the world of modern cosmology and quantum physics.

You can believe you're in the only real universe for you and that everyone else is in a different one, that you live for ever and it's only other people who die. It's perfectly respectable amongst top astrophysicists today to speculate that we're all virtual reality simulations of an infinitely powerful computer, that there could be billions of these simulations and we'll never know whether we're real or not. It's not that dissimilar in some respects from the Grand Omnipotent Deity of the Salafis or Calvinists. Or the idea of some Buddhists that the universe is a projection of the mind. So it's not difficult to believe in God in the twenty-first century as a possibility; in some ways it's easier than at any other time in history. It's just the idea of believing in one version of Him as the absolute and only Truth that's hard.

This is all irrelevant to the practice of religion. That's a question of how you want to live, not what you know. But if you worry about what God is and where He might be it suggests the beginnings of an answer. Medieval theologians turned mental somersaults trying to make sense of how the supernatural worked in nature, down to how many angels could fit on the head of a pin. They'd love to be around today. You can speculate for ever, almost anything could be "right." A central Hindu insight for instance is that when consciousness is focused it contracts, and the ultimate alpha and omega point is one of pure consciousness. Maybe we'll come to see God as the original "point," the singularity, splitting Himself into relationships. Too small to measure, too big to understand. A vast, many-layered tapestry in which all of life is but a single bright thread. To make a huge jump, maybe we'll see the collective choices of all the bits in the universe as His scattered consciousness, making up His "mind," *Brahman,* to which all our actions and thoughts, our share of this consciousness, *atman,* contribute in tiny measure.

We don't know how we link up with this God. But then we have little idea how consciousness works in our brains, or even how life started in the first place. We know little more about the mind of God than the bacteria that make up the bulk of our bodies know about us. There is some evidence though that at the micro-level of about a millionth of a centimeter, where connections between the 100 billion or so neurons in the brain happen, electron-tunneling can take place, much as it does in the quantum world.

To "will" would then be to select from the quantum states that appear, the different possibilities that run through the brain. We "choose" our reality. Somewhere, down in the depths of the mind, remote from us as God is, the real action of the universe is taking place. In every nano-second billions of connections are being made that have never been made before, that are different from anything that has ever happened in the universe. Each of us is a miracle on legs, changing every moment. Somehow out of all this we can think, create, and love. Or hate and destroy. Religion is the thread of sanity we weave into our tapestry of probabilities to create peace and happiness rather than mayhem and murder.

It's not so very inconceivable that we are ourselves part of the process of creation, one membrane out of millions. Or that perhaps, at some level, we can "link up" with a universal mind. Maybe we live within it, our thoughts dreamed into form by mind, a ripple on the ocean of consciousness. When we die our borrowed bodily forms return to the recycling machine of nature, the atoms of which we're made refashioning themselves again into earth, minerals, plants, and people. Our fragments of consciousness return to the background energy-state of the universe, which we variously describe as Dharmakaya, God, Tao, Brahman, the fundamental equation, Noumenon, Reality, the Absolute, Primary Energy, or simply a sea of "things that might be." This is the only thing that is "One," that doesn't change because it includes all possible changes: "I am that I am" (Exodus 3:14), or "The one 'I am' at the heart of creation" (*Shivatashvatara Upanishad*).

It's hard to go to the funeral of someone you've loved and not feel that this must be in some way true, that something of what we are exists outside time and space. Maybe it's wishful thinking. Maybe if you're a left-brained, rational kind of person you're inclined to dismiss it. Maybe if you're a right-brained, living in the moment kind of person you're inclined to believe it. It doesn't matter. It's a possibility, if you want to act on it. The experience of God can be described as the form we give to our relationship with the "other," the definition we give the point where our deepest desires are returned with interest. And in so far as we need a model it's a better one for today than a king in the sky. He is the line we draw at the limits of our capacity for understanding, for emotion, and wonder. We carve out our meanings from the apparently indifferent rock face of existence, and assume there is a rock there that we call God.

And since creation is continuous, since the universe never "stops," maybe God is still developing. He is the original point of energy from which matter is formed, which in turn gives rise to life, to consciousness, which in turn creates energy, completing the circle. Not a being, but Being itself, the "ground of everything," which some Buddhists and Christian theologians describe in pretty much the same way. Our brains are spiders' webs of molecules with the stability and lifespan of summer mist, fleetingly grasping at fragments of this consciousness, much as our bodies are passing hosts for bacteria and genes.

But if God is a process, how did the universe begin in the first place? If the form that reality takes has to await the participation of a conscious observer, how can anything exist before the observer is there to see it? This where we have to take an imaginative leap out of the four dimensions of space and time that we live in.

Imagine an eye with a long stalk in the form of a loop, with the eyeball looking back at its own beginning. That, in the world of quantum physics, may be the most credible explanation of how the universe came to be. Perhaps consciousness is something created by its own workings that has already happened. Religion is simply our attempt to realize where we are before we get there, and it's by doing so that we arrive. It is the practice and growth of consciousness, the universe's way of thinking about itself. Religion is not anti-evolution – it *is* evolution. Darwin is the St Paul of our time. God was not there at the beginning, but He is there at the end, and in the end is our beginning.

5

THE LIFE
WE HAVE

"I sometimes think that God, in creating man,
overestimated his ability."

Oscar Wilde

How big is God today? How does He work? Religion in a broad sense is credible. It's even nice and simple. Consciousness plays a role in the universe, and always has done. Mind and matter are two sides of a coin, a reflection of each other, an idea for which the church burnt Giordano Bruno at the stake 400 years ago. God creates consciousness, consciousness creates God. God is the universal consciousness working through life, the shorthand we variously use for our experience of the world as meaningful, beautiful, loving, and true. Materialism is for dummies. Reductionist philosophies are for people who want to give themselves a hard time, who look for the lowest possible common denominator. But there's not much point in arguing about it, in the limited sense of whether someone called God exists or not. If He doesn't, you're wasting your breath. If He does, He doesn't need your help.

The key religious question is what you decide to relate to. And here we get back to the difference between good and bad religion. It's pretty much the same as good and bad personal relationships. Much religion is self-obsessed. It was the way I used to figure it. I was driven by particular verses. I was a "watchman unto the house of Israel" (Ezekiel 3:17-18), and if I didn't convert one person a week their destiny in hell was on my shoulders. Scattered around the shores and islands of old empires you have thousands of Christian sects today, from Evangelicals several times removed from everyone else in purity of doctrine to Voodoo worshipers and cargo cults, all convinced that their picture of God is alone true, that if they don't follow it the bottom of their world will fall out.

That's bad, sad religion. But then mainstream Christianity itself looks cultish today. It centers on a belief that the Son of God came to earth 2,000 years ago to save humankind. It's why so many Christians claim that the world is only a few thousand years old. The salvation history that the church teaches is written from that understanding.

But religion is at least as old as language, and probably connected with it. Today we have fossil skull shapes of where our larynx would have been that suggest that we were speaking 200,000 years ago. Anthropologists argue over whether there's evidence for drawing and sculpture that dates to 100,000 or more than 250,000 years ago. Every decade or so it gets pushed back another 10,000 years.

This helps put the claims of particular religions in perspective. Christianity for instance has been practiced for less than 1% of that time, during most of which it's been followed by 1 to 10% of the world population. But surely God is not so forgetful that he waited for 10,000 or so generations before sending His Son to save humankind, threatening to come back any day in judgement. Even if we go back only to our immediate ancestors who developed our "modern" culture, from whom we are indistinguishable in every way, and whose genetic tree we can trace in our bodies back to the mitochondrial "Eve," the entire Christian experience barely registers as a blip.

Our understanding of the love of God today needs to be bigger as much as our picture of the universe is bigger.

For instance, what about the other species of Homo sapiens who have disappeared? Didn't God love them? Anthropologists have recovered 500 skeletons of Neanderthal man (*Homo sapiens neanderthalensis*), the latest dating to 34000 BC (estimates of the ages of fossils are accurate to around 10%). In anthropological terms that's like yesterday. Their brains may have been larger than ours, around 1.8 liters to our 1.4 (disputed). They came out of Africa hundreds of thousands of years earlier than we did, and over that time developed a stronger and tougher body than ours, designed to cope with the cold climate. They probably buried their dead with ritual and ceremony, covering them with flowers, placing stones and antlers around the graves, and may have played music. They produced jewelry and pictures with manganese pigments. Most anthropologists say we probably killed them off, whether through warfare or disease or both.

There's a score or so of other ancestors we've discovered in the last half- century, most of whom trod the earth for longer than we have, many of whom seem to have believed in an afterlife. You can't do that without the capacity for abstract thought, the ability to conceive the idea that reality lies elsewhere, beyond this life, a "religious sense." This is why religion in some form will always be with us. It's part of self-awareness. Religious belief involves defining what the "self" is, and is not. The practice of religion is transcending it.

God must have been in the frame for them too. But they would have described Him differently. For instance, the ultimate religious act in most traditions of Homo sapiens has been to sacrifice an individual for the common good, to drink his/her blood and eat their flesh ("Take, eat; this is my body," Matthew 26.26). But if it had been Homo robustus (vegetarians who dug for roots rather than omnivorous scavengers like ourselves) who had survived rather than Homo sapiens, there would have been a quite different idea of how to please God. We eat and sacrifice flesh and see God's offering of His Son as a lamb. Maybe Homo robustus would have seen Him as a plant. Our religion is shaped by our biology even before culture has its say.

We can keep extending the circle of creation with which God is involved. For instance, we're closer to chimps genetically than gorillas are, than two species of clams are to each other. Chimps recognize themselves in mirrors, can make sentences with sign or computer language, have prodigious memories, feel happy, sad, and may mourn their dead, perform primeval rain dances in response to thunder and lightning. Like them, we still prefer to sleep upstairs for security. Anthropologists generally agree that the key distinguishing feature of Homo sapiens is not our brain, or intelligence, or moral awareness, or soul, or even our sense of humor, but our two legs. They came first, the increase in brain size came later.

Most people who work closely with them say it's hard to see any fundamental difference between the three species of homo around today – ourselves (Homo sapiens), Common chimps (Homo troglodytes) and Bonobos (Homo paniscus). Our development of technology and culture over the last million years disguises our much longer period of similarity. It's a question of degree. And as we're the ones driving the others to extinction, perhaps we don't hold the moral high ground. There are only about 200,000 chimps left now. They're gradually being killed off to satisfy our demands for more exotic restaurant menus, for "bush meat."

Apart from our taking the seemingly suicidal step of walking on two legs, reducing our speed and agility, increasing our visibility to predators, Common chimps and human beings have developed along similar lines in all the important respects of sex and social organization. The Bonobos, who split off later than us, developed differently. You can make a case for their having a potentially superior morality. Their family groups are led by females who maintain their position by sex rather than force. Fighting is rare. Killing animals for food, as both we and chimps do, unknown.

What if we had learned from the Bonobos rather than the Common chimps? Our society could have been more peaceable, more "moral." Sex would be initiated by the female to reconcile and reward rather than by the male to express right and power. Our popes, priests, and presidents would be female. God would be Mother. Joseph would be a eunuch rather than Mary a virgin. The Bonobos would probably have been better at managing one of the main problems confronting the earth today – our over-breeding.

We might be no more the favored species of Homo than the Jews the favored people. The more we dominate nature, and the more powerful an image we have of ourselves, the more powerful our image of God needs to be. The worse we become, the more we destroy, and the more sinful we feel, the holier a God we imagine. Maybe Christianity works best for bad people. In a few hundred years' time perhaps we'll all look back on our habits of owning and eating our animal relations – any creatures with faces – with the same kind of distaste that we now have when we view slavery and cannibalism.

Interestingly, a little diversion here, once upon a time most

Christians thought this way. In the first few centuries missionaries took Christianity into the Western reaches of the Roman Empire where, under the influence of Greek philosophy and state control, and assimilating pagan trappings and ideas, it changed into the religion we know. But missionaries also went East. Here, in India and China, they encountered societies more sophisticated and literate than those to be found in Europe after the fall of Rome. The first recorded use of the Christian calendar is in China in AD 641. One of the earliest printed books in the world, now in the British Museum, is a copy of what is probably a Christian calendar. It's dated AD 877, over half a millennium before printing arrived in Europe. Christians in the East followed a policy of non-violence, not just toward people (like the first Christians in the West) but to all living things. Vegetarianism was obligatory.

In the seventh to ninth centuries followers of the "Religion of the Light," as it came to be called, may have outnumbered Christians in the West two or threefold to one, with churches in most Chinese cities, and cathedrals even in remote Tibet. But they were largely destroyed by first the Muslim and then the Mongol onslaughts, much as the English church nearly disappeared under the Viking invasions of the eighth to tenth centuries. Only traces of them survive. The liturgy of the Eucharist that the Nestorian Church still uses, for example, *The Anaphora of the Apostles Addai and Mari*, is the oldest in use anywhere.

We can keep extending our circle of creation indefinitely. I used to look at Egyptian or Indian images of their gods and think, "Gross! How could anyone be as stupid as to think God looks like that (the monkey god Hanuman for instance)!" But for most of history, before we had the technology to easily kill fierce animals and dominate creation, we had seen gods in their image rather than ours – or a mix of the two – half human, half animal/fish/bird; and of course it's still a dominant form in parts of the world. There are still traces of it in the Old Testament. The divine serpent for instance, the symbol on the pharaoh's forehead, is far older than Yahweh, far more widespread. Moses plants a serpent rod in the wilderness so the Hebrews can look on it and be healed (Numbers 21:4-9). The rod is given a name, Nehushtan, and is worshiped for several hundred years before King Hezekiah breaks it in the eighth century BC (2 Kings 18:4).

Maybe the Eastern Christians got it more right than the Western ones. The kingdom of God is not just for us. God is bigger than we think. Sure, God is easier to understand, easier to talk to, if we think of Him in our image. It's hard to ask for forgiveness from a dolphin, or love an abstraction. We make God personal and as physical as we need Him to be. Statues, creeds, rituals, sacraments, scriptures, sacred places – they all help to focus our thoughts outside our selves. But assuming that God really is anything like us is like thinking parrots are human because they can speak English.

And why shouldn't we widen the circle further? It's not just fossils and chimps we're connected to. For several hundred thousand years our ancestors saw life as the purpose, rather than people. It's all sacred and interconnected. We're part of everything else.

They were right. Biology shows us how interconnected we are. It can follow the evolution of our bodies over several billion years. The first circulatory system of our aquatic ancestors was seawater. Our blood is still salty, combining elements of sodium, potassium, and calcium in the same proportions. Our skeletons are still hardened with lime. We can trace the development of self-awareness in our own brains, from the reptilian at the stem to the mammalian at the top. We're part of a community of life, a twig in a forest. Nature is so connected that, incredible as it may seem, every time we breathe we take in about a thousand million molecules that the Buddha breathed out.

God is not just our God, She reflects the whole kaleidoscope, wearing a myriad forms. From cells making pairs, to green shoots in the desert, through to the sacrament of sex, He is the irrepressible drive to life. In India it's seen as a form of cosmic energy called *prani*, farther east it's *chi*. There's no word to describe this in Christian theology as God is generally seen as separate from creation, though the Cambridge Platonists like Ralph Cudworth in the seventeenth century came close.

Small gods live in trees or temples or on mountain-tops, or in the pages of a book. They concern themselves with the interests of an individual, or tribe, or species. They need priests and bureaucrats to translate their demands, to measure them out and keep a percentage. A universal God is just that. Concerned with all of life, with the universe, working through every molecule, every atom. It makes more sense. There's no "point" in life at which matter becomes conscious, at which animals turn into humans, at which we begin to sin, at which God gets involved with life on earth to remedy a problem of His making. The only clear line in biology is between bacteria and everything else. "Soul" is bigger than we think. Boundaries are as much openings as barriers. From the first division of cells in the primeval sea onwards they exist not to enclose us, but to enable more complex exchanges of information. We find ourselves through sharing connections with everything else.

This is not just a pagan or New-Age idea but is central to Middle-Eastern thought, and provides the context in which Jesus taught. Modern scholarship suggests that Aramaic, the Persian lingua franca across much of the region, doesn't draw clear distinctions between "self," "neighbor," and source of life or "God." Unifying them in a comprehensive pattern of belief and behavior was the wellspring of many religious traditions in the area, and has perhaps continued most clearly in Sufism. Just because for centuries our theology was shaped by an aggressive, warrior-based social order that gloried in pillage and conquest (read Anglo-Saxon literature to get the idea) doesn't mean we have to live with that mindset forever.

So why not believe in God as always active, always present, in every birth and death and every falling leaf, in every chemical reaction since the beginning of time, as the architect of all life, all creation, the whole universe, rather than last week's odd-job decorator? He really does notice the death of a sparrow. Let's think of God as everything outside our sense of self. And that's millions of times more than we can see, but that will do to start with.

It's not so much we living life, controlling and deciding, as life being lived through us. And after a few billion years of trial and error, of building layers of complexity till awareness emerges and sees the light, She is now looking around at what He's created and saying, "Yes, indeed it's good." The world is beautiful and true. It dazzles and astonishes. It's amazing every moment that it's here at all. We're incredibly privileged to be here to share it. If we have a problem with life, we've made it. The world doesn't have them, and we're not as important as we like to think. The butterfly is as significant as we are. The difference is, we have the pleasure of being aware of it.

But why should the world be good? It often doesn't seem that way. It often seems pointless, destructive, mad. Our experience of God is usually phrased as encountering an overwhelming sense of beauty, love, and light. But why should God be anything more than an impersonal force? Or one of darkness, evil, and death? The world of nature seems cruel and wasteful rather than benevolent.

And of course God has often been pictured as both, sometimes simultaneously, though cruelty generally triumphs over mercy. All the pain of all the trillions of creatures eaten alive on the planet since life began will pale into insignificance beside the sufferings of hell. This is reserved, in mainstream Christian tradition, for the huge majority of the world's population (generally recognised as 999 out of 1000), where they can be tortured for all eternity.

Maybe the Semitic view of God as good and evil, of the Eastern one as embracing everything there is, is closer to the truth than the later one of God as "good." But perhaps the purpose working through creation really is a positive, "good" one. This is impossible to say, because we can only speak of what we know. And what we know we've helped determine. But travel back in your mind's path to how you used to be 20, 40 years ago. Your memories of your "self," if you can recover them, are likely to be good ones. We like who we are, at least who we were. Now imagine a journey back to our direct ancestors, rat-like rodents. We can trace our similarities; for instance, both rats and human beings still have a common fear of snakes, dating from when their ancestors pursued ours in tunnels under the feet of the dinosaurs. We still mimic a snake's "Shh . . ." as a warning to children. And young rats that are regularly and gently stroked with a brush function better as adults. Being "loved" makes them more relaxed and comfortable. They can actually work out problems better. Their brains get more wired up. This doesn't work with reptiles. It's taken a lot of scientific experiments to prove what every pet-lover instinctively knows.

We're no different. Good relationships develop communication skills, which in turn lead to greater understanding and more complex responses to situations. Children from loving, secure homes grow up with more confidence in their abilities than children from violent or broken ones. As these children acquire greater sensitivity to shades of meaning they find it easier to develop symbols that summarize and convey attitudes. Over millions of years and dead ends, wrong turnings, communication grows the brain, in a virtuous circle. A more complex brain enables deeper love, which in turn spurs the search for meaning. If life forms more developed than human beings exist they are likely to be more loving forms, or they would have destroyed each other (we hope). So, logically, if there is a highest life form we call God who created the universe He is likely to be creative and loving rather than destructive, or He would consume Himself. "In the Beginning arose love," as the *Rig Veda* claims.

"Love" is not the right word for this process, and altruism is not much better. English is a more limited language than many in dealing with these ideas, with one word for consciousness for instance whereas Hindi has dozens, and all language is inadequate anyway. We don't really know what this process is, when it began, what it might become. This is where science turns into religion, where we live by faith that it's what we think of as love that makes the world go round. Imagine it for the moment as simply the highest form of self-awareness that we know of. It has emerged, over a vast period of time, from co-operative relationships, right back to the first parasites.

Love is the point at which co-operation turns into more than sharing out of self-interest, becomes valuing an other for its own sake. We go beyond need, possession, addiction, desire. We value the bonds that enable us to strengthen and deepen that love – honesty, loyalty, faithfulness, and others. In loving God the understanding that we can love everything breaks through, which is why it can be so overwhelming. We feel loved in return by the whole rather than the particular. We experience a love, or sense of connection, that is complete, unchanging, unconditional.

We make gods in our image, and our images change. One of the great insights of the Protestant Reformers in the sixteenth century was that our salvation was not to be bought by money, or by virtue of the sacraments. Perhaps our equivalent perception today is that God, however we describe Her, is not only interested in us. Perhaps He is too big for us to know. He had His doubts about the Hebrews, maybe She still has doubts about us.

Maybe for believers the interesting question is not so much which God we believe in, or whether we have the right religion, as whether we have the right "soul" in the first place. Great idea, wrong species. Perhaps Neanderthal man was more religious than we are. Perhaps God is not particularly bothered whether he is more properly honored in Texas or Tashkent, by white or black, Christian or Confucian, Homo sapiens or Homo erectus.

Perhaps Genesis is more deeply true than we imagine. Perhaps we are all the race of Cain, and have killed off our gentler brothers, cursed by our genes to fight to the finish. We're only intermittently able to grasp the principle that good religion is based on love and life rather than separation and death, on relationship and respect rather than power and glory. The Jeremiahs and Ezekiels of our time, the prophets of today, are those telling us to repent of what we're doing to the rest of creation and change our ways or we as a species won't make it through.

Many religions picture a situation where we are the center of the universal purpose, because we put ourselves first. But in relation to the time the universe has been in existence the period of humankind's recorded history is equivalent to a layer of paint on top of the Empire State Building. To a mayfly, born in the morning and dying in the evening, life is eternal summer on a riverbank. If one of them could think, it might reckon the world was made this way, for its benefit. We're no wiser. We're not the end-product of evolution, we're about one-third or so from the beginning. The evolution of life on earth has most of its time to run, unless we destroy it all.

But here's a thought that millions are starting to accept and spread. Perhaps we're just on the edge of the next level up. We're a step on the way to the creatures God wants us to be, not the end-product. Multiples of 10 often seem to be harbingers of a new level of complexity. A dog for instance has 10 to the power of 9 neurons in the brain. Self-awareness seems to develop at our level, around 10 to the power of 10, or 100 billion, the number of stars in our galaxy. Maybe there's a next level beyond awareness of the individual self, to the collective self, and on up to an awareness of the world as spirit rather than matter, purpose rather than molecules. Maybe in another million or so years natural or artificial evolution could raise the number of neurons in our brain to 10 to the power of 11. Why not?

Is there any reason in theory why we shouldn't evolve toward a level of consciousness as different from the one we enjoy now as ours is from that of our dog? Maybe it will be a different type of consciousness, and self-awareness is a disease, as Kierkegaard suggested, that will one day destroy its host. Perhaps one day we can recover a more archetypal kind of consciousness, of the kind Jung was searching for.

If not in a million years, then maybe in 10 million? The humble hedgehog has been around far longer than that. 100 million? We've got 5 billion years to go before the sun burns out. How far from dog to God? Everything that exists (in this universe at least) is on a line of relationship. Maybe 10 to the power of 12 neurons? 20? 72 (the number of atoms it contains)?

6

THE TALE
WE CHOOSE

"There is only one religion, though there are a
hundred versions of it."

George Bernard Shaw

God is the biggest we can imagine Him to be, but we've made Him too small. We've cut Him up into thousands of stories, as in the Tower of Babel, talking of different gods. Different religions don't represent different truths, they're just the clothes of our spirit, and beliefs the cut of the cloth. And they change with fashion. Imagining gods is as easy as designing dresses, which is why we have so many.

As we probe our common experience, talk over our fears and hopes, forms take shape and flesh. That figure of Woden will keep the wolves from the door. The prayer flags will flutter our thoughts to heaven. The words of a mantra or the Lord's Prayer will pierce the veil. We carve our creations into wood or words and worship them. Faith says our creations represent something real. It says there are moments of honesty that we can reach about ourselves and our intentions, where we can say, "Yes, that *was* true." We step outside our skins for a moment, and tap into the universal current of intention. With practice we can do it at will.

But we're just gadflies on this universal river. A good faith is aware of its failings, that all our images of God are just that, images. But then image, creation, is at the heart of everything. It's all there is. Without it we wouldn't be here talking about it. A good faith says we're not, as atheists or humanists would say, the highest known form of consciousness so everything beyond that is make-believe. It says we've only just started on the road to a consciousness that cumulatively ends up as the creative force behind the universe. Our finest, most beautiful attempts to describe this are the first fumblings of children realizing that they're alive, that they can talk, interact, create. It's not that there's a void beyond our horizon of self-awareness, but that this is a journey without a horizon. We just happen to be aware of the point we're on – as we're aware of our point in time – and can occasionally see a little way forward. Non-believers and believers can agree on where we are. The question is whether we're going anywhere.

We have these tens of thousands of different beliefs about God, and most of them can be described as secondary, as significant as a hemline, and as susceptible to change. But there are certain core differences between good religious ideas that are less easy to explain. Different religions approach God from opposite ends of the "me" and "it," "in here" and "out there" spectrum. Over thousands of years they've sharpened their definitions. The first leads to monism, the other to theism.

Monism teaches that there are no separate gods out there, that all reality is one, and you find it within yourself. The main example is Buddhism. Theism, on the other hand, externalizes God and then prays and worships Him/Her/Them. The clearest example of this today is Islam, which means "submission to the one God."

The two seem poles apart, like north and south, good and evil. But it's not so difficult to see them as different approaches to the same end if, referring back to chapter 4, reality is found in the relation between the observer and observed rather than the subject and object. There is no "thing" called "good" or "evil." The Hebrews saw both as aspects of the same divine reality, as did Jesus (Matthew 5:43-45). Our experience of God is the same. He can be subjective or objective. It depends on how you're looking.

This is hard to understand, but so is quantum physics, and surely whoever God is He's more mysterious and wonderful than that. We have a membrane of skin that mostly separates our insides from out, but there is no such clear distinction between what we think and what we see. Matter, consciousness, imagination, purpose, God – we slice the pie in different ways. We poke around here and there, looking for an easy answer. But no two people can see God in the same way. We don't even see other people in the same way. Our brains are different. We all generate our own pictures, dream our own dreams, succeed and foul up in our own ways.

The problem with theism is that it tends to push God out to the heavens as a remote, separate figure it can be hard to believe in. The problem with monism is that it makes Her or ourselves indistinguishable from the world around us. The extraordinary appeal of Christianity over two millennia has been to combine the best of both worlds by having a transcendent God who incarnates Himself into matter. Its weakness is that it muddles the two different approaches to God, reducing spirit to flesh. Its major internal disputes have accordingly centered on how far Jesus is one or the other.

In practice all the major religions embrace elements of both theism and monism. A monistic tradition like Buddhism for instance also has its theistic elements, particularly in the Amida and Theravada traditions, with prayer to and worship of the Buddha. Hinduism is something of a mixture in that the *Upanishads*, the sacred scriptures at the heart of the religion, are monistic, with their core teaching of *advaita*, or "there are not two things." In practice, though, most Hindus behave like theists, offering sacrifices and prayers to Shiva, Vishnu, and other gods. Indeed in the tradition of *bhakti* yoga a theistic belief in God is seen as an easier, more enjoyable path for those who need that kind of help in surrendering their ego. It's a devotional step on the way to *jnani*, or final understanding, to accepting that "I" is nothing other than a glimmer in the eye of God.

Similarly in theistic religions you have the mystics for whom everything – the dualities of inner and outer, self and other, good and evil – resolves into God alone. In Judaism the writings of Zohar in the thirteenth century, which see the soul as an expression of God, are a good example. In Islam this tradition is represented most strongly by the Sufis, particularly Ibn al-'Arabi of the same period, who preached powerfully on the oneness of Being. The great Sufi leader Hallaj went further and was crucified for saying that everyone is God.

As with Judaism and Islam Christianity has mystics with a monistic vision like Meister Eckhart, Hildegarde of Bingen, Mechtild of Magdeburg, Julian of Norwich, and others. Contemplative branches of Christianity like the Quakers stress the inner light rather than the external forms. The Dazzling Darkness of Christian mysticism, the *via negativa*, is not far from the Way that is Nameless (Taoism), the experience that is beyond language (Zen), the state Buddha describes as Absolute Emptiness, where the mind is void of everything except pure consciousness. Indeed if God is pure consciousness, and consciousness is all there is, it's hard to see how any degrees of difference between Him and us might be established. God as Everything or Nothing? All religions stitch a framework of thought and ritual that leads to one of these conclusions if pursued rigorously, and one is simply the mirror of the other.

The mystics in each tradition have essentially the same teaching. So do those at the more theistic end. There is little difference between Christian fundamentalists, Islamic Salafis and Jewish conservatives who insist most clearly on a God "out there." The words are changed – the Bible for the Qur'an, or Allah for God – but the literal reading of each is the same, overriding the lessons of history and the teaching of compassion.

Perhaps a general truth is that an intense focus on the religious experience often leads to a situation where the "god without" becomes hard to distinguish from the "god within." It's perhaps the greatest tension of the religious life – do you find yourself, or God? What's the difference? As one of the wonderful Sufi poets, Rumi, said in the thirteenth century:

> "So what do I have to do to get you to admit who is speaking?
> Admit it and change everything!
> This is your own voice echoing off the walls of God."

Both traditions have their dangers. Mystics can suffer depression and madness in confusing themselves with God. Conservative theists are prone to take their God so literally they are prepared to condemn and murder people who disagree with them. Some have had happy experiences of both monistic and theistic traditions, and say they are not dissimilar.

We can reach a stage of desperation about ourselves and the human condition, or an overwhelming sense of its beauty or mystery, which is then crystallized into a Higher Being, or God. Or we can progress through stages of enlightenment where we realize that we are part of Being, which includes all desperation, beauty, and mystery. Ultimately it's meaningless to draw too much of a distinction between them. Our brains can't process these concepts without relevant sensory information, which in this case, by definition, doesn't exist, since God is not a "thing." And at the deepest level of reality we know, that of the quantum world, reality does not exist independently from the act of observing it. If we do not see God, He is not there. If we do, She is.

This is not to say that all pictures of God are of equal value. But they're cultural and personal. To claim them as uniquely true is meaningless. The disputes between different Protestant sects over who is saved and who is not seem mad today, the differences between Protestants and Catholics inconsequential. The fact that they gave rise to so much suffering, including one of the longest and bloodiest wars in Europe, the Thirty Years' War, is a monument to our bigotry. The fact that the differences are still important remains a monument to our arrogance. The differences between Christianity and other religions are matters of interpretation. Perhaps we can simply accept each other, even learn from each other.

For example, to take two seemingly conflicting viewpoints, Christians say that God is personal and that to find salvation we reconcile a personal self with a personal God. Buddhists say that neither we nor God are personal because neither exist. Reconciling nothing with nothing makes for enlightenment. In the Christian experience of salvation you make a huge choice.

You wrestle your soul to the throne of God's judgement and lay it at his feet. You give up your own claims to goodness and happiness in joyful abandon and experience an astonishing peace of mind. In the Buddhist experience of enlightenment you realize there is no choice to be made. You have no soul, there is no God, no claims from Him on you or you on anything else. You go beyond them all in joyful abandon and experience an astonishing peace of mind.

Who's right? It makes no difference. The brain patterns produced by both Christianity and Buddhism are the same. The advice on how to live is similar. Wisdom and compassion are the twin pillars of both. Prayer works as well as meditation. One emphasizes the outer path of forgiveness, the other, the inner. Both exist as working possibilities, as aspects of a larger whole, of something we have little knowledge about. We're playing mind games. We'll never know if they're real or not. Faith is living as if they are. Good religion is holding the two in tension, the outer journey and the inner.

We need to understand our separateness before we can be reconciled. We need to practice love before we can understand what it means to be loved. In giving love we create the potential for love to be returned. To the extent that we know and love ourselves we are known and loved. God is love. By believing in a God of love we bring Him into life.

If you dig deep enough into Buddhism and Christianity you may find they both have their origins in the ideas first formulated, as far as we know, way back in 5000 BC, and earlier, by the Rishis of the great Vedic civilization of the Sarasvati valley in India, that we share the same consciousness, the same

"I." We are joined in one spirit (1 Corinthians 6:17). The material and spiritual are two sides of a coin. If for a moment we forget politics, the play of personality, the noise of the self, the demands of religion, and reach into the quiet space within us, we find God. And then the world is one.

In today's universe, as described by science, we are all part of the continuum of life. What is true of the material is also true of time. Time is not an absolute, but just another dimension through which we move. There's no dividing line between this moment and the last, or the next. All exist in an equally real sense, now. And there's no clear distinction between this world and the next, between us and God. To ask, "Did God create man, or man create God?" is like asking which came first, the grass or the grazing animals, the chicken or the egg. They developed together. Life is a process. The line may curve, swing around corners, it might zigzag. But it has never stopped and started again. Not on our planet anyway. Reality is not sliced like salami. It includes what we create, even what we think, what we dream. In the bigger picture there is no time. There is no space. There is no matter. There is only light. Reality is "one," which is why the experience of "oneness" is at the heart of religion. You are not alone.

"While ye have light, believe in the light, that ye may be the children of light."

John 12:36

7

THE WORDS WE WRITE

"Truth did not come into the world naked, but it came in types and images. We will not receive it any other way."

Gospel of Philip

To sum up where we've got to. Religion matters. It bonds us to each other and the world around us. We're all related, the universe is relationship. Spirit and matter are codes we use to describe relationship at different levels. Our definitions vary through culture and time. Ignorance and arrogance lead us to assume that the tradition we happen to be in at a particular point in time is the universal truth for everyone at all times. Every now and again we need to disentangle the good from the bad, rethink what's worth retaining, and what we should leave behind.

In the rest of the book we look in more detail at how the Christian religion developed, where it went wrong, and why the teaching of Jesus still matters today. Not just for ourselves, but for our collective future. For the next three chapters we focus on how its mother religion, described in what we know as the Old Testament, developed.

By most measurements it's a pretty new religion. Around 60,000 years ago our direct ancestors stood on the edge of Africa, with the world in front of them empty of their kind. They were as rational, intelligent, superstitious as we are, with paint on their faces, spears in their hands, and spirits in their heads. There may only have been a few thousand – DNA samples suggest that all people alive today descend from no more than half a dozen women. As they spread around the globe they built different societies and cultures, and beliefs diverged, naturally. Worshiping a sun god doesn't make the same kind of sense in Alaska as in Mexico. Christianity would look different if the Romans had executed criminals rather than crucifying them. Religions are shaped by culture as well as geography, biology, and history. When our ancestors came into contact again in relatively recent times each assumed they were right, the others wrong.

For tens of thousands of years people probably practiced what we describe today as Shamanism. Shamans lose their sense of self in nature. In their trances they can warn and guide, pronounce oracles. They can call on the wind and rain and fire, bring plenty or famine, work through wild animals. There is little organization or hierarchy, the community recognizes the closeness of the individual shaman to the spirit world, and turns to him or her for advice and help.

It's impossible to put precise timelines on these religious ideas. They overlap, merge, continue longer in some cultural traditions than others. You can still see the Shamanic tradition at work in the Old Testament. Elisha for instance orders two bears to tear up forty-two small boys because they teased him about his baldness (2 Kings 2:23-24), a level of gratuitous violence that our worst serial murderers today don't match.

You can see the same tradition today in monotheistic religions. Sects of Islam like the Dancing Dervishes or Howling Rufais promote a direct experience of the Great Spirit or Holy Spirit that breathes through life, transcending the self through trance and dance, inspiring prophecy, and speaking in tongues, creating a sense of power over the direction of daily events. As Christianity has lost its intellectual edge through the twentieth century it has similarly recovered some of its charismatic power through the Pentecostal movement.

When did a sense of Spirit turn into belief in God? The differences between them are obscure. They can both be seen as either masculine or feminine. If you want to think of God in terms of gender, seeing Her as Mother makes better sense than Father. Biologically speaking, at conception, the female chromosome is produced first, the male chromosome is added later.

So the oldest concept we find of God all around the world is as a prodigiously fertile Mother. Fertility symbols (Venuses) go back at least 30,000 years, one figurine (Berehat Ram) has even been claimed as 250,000 years old. The idea has always survived, even in the most patriarchal religions like Christianity. The first mention of God in the Old Testament is of a female spirit, *ruach*, a Persian word, which sweeps over the waters. The feminine never wholly disappears. For instance, another female Persian goddess or demon called Lilith hovers off-stage. She's mentioned in Isaiah 34:14-15 ('screech owl' in the King James Version is *lilith* in the Hebrew), and survives in a separate Hebrew tradition as Adam's first wife. Her children are referred to as "lilim" (Numbers 6:26). Rather than being created from Adam's rib she emerges from his unconsciousness when he is in a deep sleep and wakes him up. In later Gnostic tradition she is seen as independent and even superior to Adam, with her favored sexual position being on top rather than underneath. How different life might have been for billions of Jewish, Christian, and Muslim women if Lilith rather than Eve had made it into Genesis. Just trying to imagine it shows the power these stories still have in our own culture and psyche, however remote the later church teaching may seem.

Goddess worship amongst the Hebrews diminishes as their religion becomes more patriarchal. The Mother Goddess recovers some prominence amongst the first-century Christians, in non-canonical gospels like the *Gospel of Thomas*, the *Gospel to the Hebrews*, the *Apocryphon of John*, the *Gospel of Philip*. Later in the Christian tradition Mary, the mother of Jesus, becomes a goddess in all but name. In AD 431 at the council of Ephesus, the city of the virgin huntress Diana, she was given the title "God-bearer." By the twelfth century she was seen as miraculously conceived by her mother Anne, who became the center of a further cult. Her semi-divine status strengthens even in the nineteenth and twentieth centuries with the doctrines of the immaculate conception (like Jesus, she never sinned) and the bodily assumption (like Jesus, when she died she was transported direct to heaven) established as articles of faith for Roman Catholics. If it were possible to track the focus of devotion down the centuries she has probably been more significant for the majority of Christians than Jesus.

But despite the resurgence of the goddess in New-Age literature today most of us are more familiar with the idea of God as Father. Historians generally agree, in very broad outline, that this concept developed as societies became more complex and hierarchical, with stronger authority figures ruling them. This process began with hunter-gatherers changing into pastoral nomads, shepherding their food source around with them in the form of livestock, rather than having to search for it afresh every day. Some, perhaps first around the Caucasus, or more widely around the Middle East, figured how to "plant" food in the ground, leading to agriculture, around which grew villages, bringing the gods of the seasons and weather.

Out of the villages, cities developed, a mere 5,000 to 10,000 years ago. They enabled the accumulation of wealth and power, leading to kingship, class, and rule, and to the increasing division of labor, specialized functions, and to male dominance. Kings came to be seen either as gods or as ruling by divine right. Their sons became sons of god. Power, class, and divinity became inextricably linked, to the degree that it's only in the last couple of centuries that we've managed to separate them in our thinking.

The Roman Catholic Church remains something of an exception in this process, as it frequently does. As the divine right to rule of czars, emperors, and kings crumbled in nineteenth- and twentieth-century Europe, that of popes actually increased. The doctrine of papal infallibility was pronounced in 1870, and all bishops in the Roman Catholic Church were appointed by Rome from 1917 onwards. Under the present papacy it is being increasingly molded in an absolutist, superstitious image.

As cities enlarged the extent of land and people under their control, more complex hierarchies of gods emerged to reflect increasing power. With advancing civilization kings turned into emperors, leading to the idea 3,000 to 5,000 years ago of henotheism, one god holding absolute power over the others. Competing gods began to reflect the politics of the new warring empires. So sky gods (the first male sky god that we know of is Dyaus Pitar of the *Vedas,* which through various incarnations ended up as the Greek Zeus Pater and Deus (Jupiter) in Latin and our own "Father in heaven") became more powerful, and as human beings increasingly dominated nature the gods, particularly the supreme sky god, took on human shape.

We began to believe that we could talk to God directly, and He began to talk back. He communicated through words of power and truth rather than visible manifestations on earth – extremes of weather, or graven statues. And around 5,000 years ago, maybe much earlier, words began to be translated into writing. Writing has been described as the second most important thing that's happened on the planet, the first time since the arrival of DNA that information could be stored and retrieved. After tens, hundreds of millennia of expressing religious insight through dreams, trance, divination, signs, singing, people began to shape the words describing our experience of spirit into pictures, then letters. Put religion and writing together and you have an extraordinarily powerful new force in shaping the way we think and live.

This is nowhere expressed better than in Genesis. Like the many other stories of the region which they draw on, the Genesis stories were revolutionary in their time. They reflected this new, widespread understanding around the world that human beings could be more powerful than nature; we could shape it in our image. So God Himself is vaguely human. The Hebrews, Greeks, Hindus had all come to believe that gods and people were related. So naturally they had the same desires and were often visiting the earth from the sky or underworld, particularly for extra sex. They raped, kidnapped or fell in love (or did all three) with the prettiest girls. The children of such crossbreeding were usually male, often larger and stronger than other children. In Genesis 6:2-4, for example, the sons of God copulate with the daughters of earth to produce giants. Blue eyes, representing the sky, were also a common feature of these children. In Hindu stories the children of such partnerships could be blue all over.

The majority of the world's population today believe that God exclusively revealed Himself to humankind in written words of different scriptures. God wrote them Himself, or communicated them to authors so directly that even if the authors wrote in their own styles they couldn't say anything He didn't want them to say. It's similar to people believing today that spirits communicate through channeling, automatic writing, or ouija boards.

"Revelation" has nothing to do with scripture as such. It best describes the moments of collective inspiration, expressed in particular texts, when new insights shift our common perspective. The point of revelations, much like scientific discoveries, is that they are always being improved upon. The most conservative positions on the Bible or the church are simply the most conservative ones in society. There's nothing necessarily "religious" or "Christian" about them. Indeed Christians often take the low moral ground, reading the Bible through the lens of the social prejudices of the time. For instance, the founders of twentieth-century Evangelicalism and the doctrine of biblical inerrancy – Charles Hodge, Robert Dabney, James Thornwell – believed in slavery as "some of the plainest declarations of the Word of God" (Presbyterian General Assembly Report 1845). Catholic conservatives held similar positions – as late as 1866 the Vatican defended slavery as part of natural and divine law. The conservative church is often a generation behind the rest of society in its moral position, a couple of generations behind its humanist opponents.

Or worse. The trouble is, the early Old Testament reflects the social thinking of a tribal nomadic people of 3,000 years ago. Carrying out the 600 plus laws of the books of Moses would involve murdering or casting out most people with a job in a modern society, not just homosexuals and adulterers, or women who have sex before marriage (Deuteronomy 22:13-21), but hairdressers (Leviticus 19:27), farmers (Leviticus 19:19), restaurateurs (Leviticus 11:10), footballers (Leviticus 11:6-8), bankers, and dozens of others – there would be no one left to throw the stones. I'm not suggesting the Laws of Moses are uniquely bad, they're paralleled in the Laws of Mani in Hinduism, and reflect the concerns and attitudes of many of their contemporaries. But they're not for today. If you want to take scripture as infallible rather than think the issues through, then join the Taleban. Even better, the Khymer Rouge. Pol Pot and the horrors of the Cambodian killing fields would be the logical result of taking Leviticus literally.

The Bible is the collection of sacred documents we happen to have ended up with in the West, through a long sequence of accidents, violence, inspiration, and debate. The texts mix contemporary events with dimly-remembered history and law, legend and chronicle, myth and prophecy, as often as not assimilated from other traditions. The first stories of Adam and Eve, the Tree of Knowledge, Garden of Eden, Noah, are all adapted from earlier epics like that of *Gilgamesh*, which had been written down up to a thousand years earlier, and had still older origins. Their sources are as distant from the time of the Hebrews as the Hebrews are from us. Some of the psalms and parts of Proverbs are taken from Egyptian writings, praising very different gods. Ecclesiastes seems more inspired by the skeptical philosophy of the Greeks than the Hebrew idea of God. The Song of Solomon is erotic poetry included because the compiler mistakenly thought it was by Solomon. The authors, like all artists, were taking their material and shaping it into new forms. Far from revealing an unchanging God the Old Testament gives us the clearest example in religious literature of how we change Him according to our needs and desires.

We downgrade the Old Testament by ascribing it to divine dictation, to some form of magic. At the human level it's fascinating enough. It's the most extraordinary record in world literature of a single people's experience and understanding of God as it changes over a millennium. It records the transition from a local god on earth, worshiped by sacrifice of food and life, to a universal God of love, worshiped in the heart and mind. It plumbs the heights and depths of our experience of life, of pleasure and pain, happiness and despair. That's why it's still worth reading. So if you find the Bible inspiring try paying the same kind of attention to other sacred scriptures. If you find it boring or irrelevant, just turn it around in your head. Think of it as "work in progress," maybe 10% revelation, 90% description and error. We can read it to learn how the Hebrews got God wrong, not right, and how they learned along the way from their mistakes.

But it's difficult to read the Old Testament today. The cultural gap between us and the nomadic Hebrews is vast. Most Christians find it hard enough to relate to the faith of Muslims, who worship the same God and live in the same century, often in the same city. Another difficulty is that the events it purports to describe were written down half a millennia or more after they maybe happened.

For instance, we (Jews, Christians, Muslims) date our understanding of the one God back to Abraham, a Hebrew. The Hebrews, *Habiru*, were probably not a defined race. The term has connotations of mercenary, robber. Some Old Testament specialists say Abraham was a Chaldean shepherd who left Ur in Mesopotamia roughly around 1400 BC (there are no dates in the Bible, though plenty of ancestral lists). Others say he could have been a tribal chieftain of the Amorite people, or a Canaanite holy man, or a literary invention of many centuries later. A few biblical scholars say the Hebrews and Israelites were entirely separate peoples.

We'll never know if Abraham was a real person or not, there simply isn't enough information. Dates for his proposed life vary over a 1,000-year period, about the same distance in time as today back to King Arthur, and his historical existence as an individual is about as certain.

What is interesting about Abraham's story is what it tells about the gods of a pre-urban, pre-agricultural society of nomadic people. Their god is not universal or all-powerful. He doesn't even have a clear name of his own. English translations gloss over the different names of God as "God" or "Lord." But Abraham's god is described in the Hebrew of the Old Testament as El, with variations such as El Elyon, El Olam, El Shaddai, El Berit. He's the name of the highest god of the Canaanites, and present in many Middle-Eastern religions. This is why words beginning or ending in "el" in the Bible and the Middle East are so common. The most obvious of course is "Israel" itself, which some scholars think is a compound of the Egyptian gods Isis and Ra with El while others prefer "strength of El."

El is also referred to over 1,500 times in the Old Testament in the plural as elohim. He is to the elohim something like the fairy king is to the fairies, the main god among many. He's not special to Abraham, he's not significantly different from the gods of his neighbors. He speaks in dreams to kings as well as to Abraham and Jacob. He's recognized as a god by the pagan priest Melchizedek (Genesis 14:18-24) whose own god Abraham also recognizes. He's not all-powerful (Genesis 19:22). Like the other gods in a region where elder sons became a threat to the father, he favored younger sons (such as Abel, Isaac, Jacob, Joseph, David, in the various Bible stories).

He's a low-maintenance kind of god, a nomad's god, carried around with the luggage, of the kind Rachel could steal from Laban (Genesis 31:17-35.) He doesn't demand temples or priests. He's for pastoralists, advising on the direction of travel, where to graze the flocks, on domestic issues, family relationships. He needs feeding and honoring like any other guest. He's the kind of god that has been around for tens of millennia, and still is in many parts of the world. He still plays a large part in the lives of Christians, who ask him for advice and confirmation on their decisions in life, such as where to live, who to marry, and to intervene on their behalf or that of others.

He also of course helps with the main issue in the lives of the people of biblical times, that of fertility, promising successful reproduction – an aspect of his powers that we've rather forgotten today. Indeed he's an unusually powerful fertility god: though Abraham is childless from his seed will come a great nation (Genesis 12:2). It's such an ambitious promise (particularly as he and Sarah are over 90) that Abraham wants guarantees. So they bind themselves together in a covenant, in much the same way as people do in a legal document (Genesis 17:1-14). The covenant is confirmed in the act of circumcision. This was a common practice in the Middle East, particularly with the Assyrians, and all over the world, from Pacific islanders to Aztecs. Its origins are uncertain, but probably have to do with the sacrifice of the first piece of flesh after copulation to insure good growth for the next year's crops.

If you want to take Abraham literally he's not an attractive character. He's in the old tradition of the trickster, even twisting fate and his god to his advantage. He prostitutes his wife (who is also his half-sister) "at every place, whither we shall come" (Genesis 12:11-20; 20:1-18), much to the disgust of his hosts when they find out that the two are married. This doesn't seem to worry El, who is not a "moral" god in the sense that we understand God and morality today. He backs Abraham up by sending plagues and threatening death to those he has deceived, whilst rewarding Abraham's pimping with prosperity.

Up to this point Abraham has been making reasonable arrangements with his neighbors, like taking his herds in a different direction from Lot's to avoid conflict over grazing. But now he wants more. El promises Abraham and his descendants the land of Canaan, but doesn't ask the people in Canaan to leave the land first, so setting the scene for thousands of years of trouble, a conflict that still makes the news every week.

Abraham becomes the shepherd's nightmare, the guy who won't co-operate, who wants it all for himself. He worships a god who reflects his own interests rather than the powers of nature, common to the time, that affect everyone alike. El becomes the god of Abraham alone, "mine," a tribal god who even divides families down the middle: "Yet I loved Jacob, and I hated Esau" (Malachi 1:2-3). He represents the worst kind of religion, where personal material or spiritual gain come above common decency, morality, even parental instinct. A god of individual greed rather than collective responsibility. His spiritual followers today are the Muslim terrorists, Jewish Zionists, Christian fundamentalists, who all believe in the same god of Abraham, believe they have his ear, and (like Abraham himself) put a higher value on their creed, or their land, or their money than the lives of children.

Not many people today read the Abraham story in this way, though many of the early Christians did (see chapter 13). Many Jews take it literally: the story is what it says it is. God gave Abraham this land, they are His descendants, so the land is theirs. God says so. Some Christians today agree with this and support the US Government in its $3 billion a year subsidy of the Israeli army. Some Christians look for other meanings, more suitable to their own times and circumstances. The Dutch Boers for instance trekking into the African interior, saw it as a story for them: God was giving them the land they saw before them. From this and other Bible passages the Dutch Reformed Church developed the doctrine of apartheid.

More liberal and mainstream Christians today look for less aggressive interpretations. For instance, Abraham wasn't a bad guy. And El wasn't really going to let him cut his son's throat, whatever Sarah thought about it. The story represents

Abraham's understanding of a new idea of God, one who doesn't demand human sacrifice. God identifies with the victim, not the oppressors. And in the New Testament it's clear that God now cares for all people, not just the Hebrews, even offering His own Son as the scapegoat for the sins of humankind.

We all read the idea of God that we want to believe in back into the text. All we know for sure is that the three great monotheistic religions trace their history (and in the case of Jews and Muslims their race) back to Abraham. If he existed, he was the most influential person in history. No conflict has been so enduring and bitter as the one the Bible credits him with starting. No idea in history has been as powerful as the one that a universal deity will occupy Himself to your personal advantage. Over half the people in the world today (Jews, Christians, Muslims) believe in Abraham's new personal God. They read the promises to Abraham as applicable to them, whether it's of land, wealth, or salvation.

With Abraham's more immediate descendants the scene shifts from Canaan to Egypt for the great story of the Exodus.

8

THE MONSTERS WE TAME

"Man's last and highest parting occurs when, for God's sake, he takes leave of God."

Eckhart

The most interesting question in the Old Testament is how exactly does the minor but ambitious El turn into the ferocious and ruthless battle-leader YHVH or Yahweh, who then becomes the moral and almighty God.

Like the cunning and commanding Aeneas in the *Aeneid*, the equivalent Exodus story for the Romans, Moses dominates the Exodus. Again, whether he actually existed, whether the Hebrews were ever in Egypt, are much disputed, with a vast literature on the subject. The main problem is that, apart from the Old Testament, there is no mention of the Hebrews in the hundreds of thousands of records of the period. Most scholars would say there is some factual basis for the stories, maybe there was a series of such migrations out of Egypt over a period of centuries, which are conflated or most vividly expressed in this particular story. But what we're interested in here is not so much whether or not the stories happened, but what they tell us about the God the Hebrews believed in.

Moses sees God differently from Abraham. He may even be a different God altogether. El has now taken on the majesty of the higher gods – the ones like Zeus who the Greeks believed would burn you into ashes if you saw his true form. Whereas El would pop down for supper with Abraham, and wrestle with Jacob, Moses has to wear a veil so that his compatriots aren't blinded by the glory of God reflected in his face, after he's caught a glimpse of His backside (Exodus 33:18-23).

Where did this new powerful God come from? If the Hebrews were in Egypt it was probably between 1400 and 1200 BC. During this period the Egyptians had developed the idea of one all-powerful Sun God to reflect the glory of the pharoahs. Aton was worshiped as the only God by Amenhotep 1V around the year 1360 BC. One theory is that the Hebrews were a group of Aton worshipers fleeing the persecution that followed Amenhotep's death.

Another theory is that Moses adopted Him in some form from the polar opposite, the moon god worshiped by the Midianites. Moses lived most of his life with them and married the daughter of the high priest (Exodus 2:16-3:1). There are many other theories. Alternatively, more conservative scholars suggest that after a virtual absence from human history for a few million years or so God decided the time was right to enter the human stage again. At least in a small kind of way, setting fire to a bush and speaking to an outcast from a tribe no one else had heard of or bothered to mention.

But whoever She is, it's not yet the Almighty we're familiar with today. Some of the miracles that God does through Moses, the pharoah's magicians can also do. It's a question of degree, not nature. And He doesn't seem all that familiar or friendly to the Hebrews either. Moses' view of God seems to be more one of war and death than fertility and life, a view represented by the bull of their ancestors, which they believed had delivered them from Egypt (Exodus 32:4; translated into English in Genesis 49:24 as "the mighty God of Jacob"). The Hebrews are so uncertain of this new God that Yahweh wants to massacre them all for their lack of commitment, sparing Moses alone (Exodus 32:9-10), but Moses persuades Him to change His mind because it would encourage their joint enemies, the Egyptians. It's hard to see where Moses stops and Yahweh begins. Yahweh repents of His evil thoughts (Exodus 32:14) but Moses then acts on His behalf, calling on his elite guard, the loyal sons of Levi, to "slay every man his brother, and every man his companion, and every man his neighbour" (Exodus 32:27), which they do, killing 3,000.

The Hebrews realize they've saddled themselves with a tyrant-priest, and rebel. Nomadic tribes, after all, tend to govern themselves through consultation and kinship ties. One of the world's first recorded attempts at participatory government ends in mass-murder when the earth opens and swallows the leaders with their women and children, taking them all down into Sheol. The morning after, there's another rebellion, leaving 14,700 dead (Numbers 16). Later, 24,000 are killed later when some of the men start having sex with the local Moabite women (Numbers 25:1-15).

The climax of Numbers comes in chapter 31 with the battle against the Midianites. The Hebrews slay all the males, but Moses is angry with them for sparing the women, so they get the plague again. Moses orders them to murder all the women except the virgins, who they can keep for rape. This may be the first example in writing and practice of the "holy war" ideology, later to become institutionalized in Islam as one aspect of Jihad, and to find expression in Christianity through the Crusades. Some detailed instructions on how to wage such a war are given, including ritual cleansing before battle (Joshua 3:5); abstinence from sex (2 Samuel 11:11); rules of engagement are provided in Deuteronomy 20. There was probably more in *The Book of the Wars of Yahweh*, referred to in Numbers 21:14, but this has been lost.

Time and again Yahweh (or Moses) wants to go over the top

and kill. Even when a man is found gathering sticks on the Sabbath, and the people aren't sure what punishment should fit the crime, Yahweh commands that he be stoned to death (Numbers 15:32-36). The continual complaint from them both is that the people aren't brutal enough in their treatment of their enemies. It's not as if this was inevitably the culture of the period. The drama of poetry like the *Iliad* (written at roughly the same time) lies in the sympathy with which the Greek poet treats the Trojans, particularly the hero Hector whose death is the poem's tragic centerpiece. Similarly, Aeschylus imagines the Greek defeat of the Persians through the eyes of the Persian women left at home. Throughout this period you can find better morality (and much better language) in the writings and gods of "pagan" cultures than in the pages of the Old Testament, as many early Gentile Christians were later ready to point out.

These chapters are so rarely read that we forget what a brutal God this is; mad, bad and dangerous to know. We shake our heads wonderingly that people are prepared to follow leaders like Milosevich and Saddam Hussein, but we only need to read our own sacred texts, or look at our own recent history, to see how easily we can approve of genocide, or turn a blind eye to it. El hadn't thought what to do with the people already in Canaan. He promised without being prepared to follow through. The second time around Yahweh knows. He will "blot them out," and dictates a military strategy for doing so (Exodus 23:29-30).

The difference between El and Yahweh can be summed up in the different treatments of Abraham and Jepthah. El lets Abraham off the sacrifice of Isaac. Yahweh gives Jepthah, the judge of Israel, no such help. He has to burn his daughter alive

(Judges 11). In all of the stories in all the sacred books of the world religions these episodes are among the least enlightening, the most barbaric. Many of the early Christians understood this, and saw that, like Moses, we all make God into who we want, a reflection of ourselves, good and evil. The difference is, He's easier to change. We can turn bad gods into good ones.

After the Hebrews settle in Canaan they appear to give up this God of terror and war and adopt the customs and beliefs of the tribes around them. This is again a disputed subject, but for the Bible reader it is made clear when in 621 BC, several centuries later, King Josiah sends his secretary to the Temple to collect taxes. The high priest Hilkiah gives him an old book he's just found buried in the Temple somewhere among the cast-offs. They believe this to be all or part of the "book of the law" written by Moses (2 Kings 22:8) and Josiah realizes that for centuries they have been worshiping the wrong gods and have forgotten about the God of the Exodus. He tells the people to celebrate a Passover feast and the writer of Kings adds: "Surely there was not holden such a passover from the days of the judges that judged Israel, nor in all the days of the kings of Israel, nor of the kings of Judah" (2 Kings 23:22).

So if Josiah hadn't heard of the one God of Abraham and Moses, when did monotheism (one God) rather than henotheism (one god amongst many, for example, Psalm 82:1-8) really take root among the Hebrews? It's much debated. Most scholars would say that there's no sudden emergence of a single God, that there's a dual narrative running through Judges, Samuel, Kings and Chronicles. On the one hand, the later scribes record the doings of the men of God. On the other, there's the almost buried but frequent acknowledgement that "the high places [the foreign altars] were not taken away" (2 Chronicles 15:17). There's the continuing thread that the Hebrews don't deserve to have this God to themselves, and that He hedges His bets, supporting other peoples as well: "Are ye not as children of the Ethiopians unto me, O children of Israel? saith the LORD. Have not I brought up Israel out of the land of Egypt? And the Philistines from Caphtor, and the Syrians from Kir?" (Amos 9:7).

The generally accepted overall picture amongst the specialist historians rather than Jewish/Christian/Muslim scholars is that Yahweh was originally a child of El, god of the sun, and perhaps had a mother, Asherah, goddess of the moon (in the Hittite tradition Yahweh is briefly married to his mother). He is one of many children. Baal (the god of rain and fertility) is one of his brothers. Another, who he frequently battles with, is Yam, the seven-headed sea dragon, the god of storms and destruction, mentioned in Job 9:8 and Psalm 74:14.

The name Yahweh is first given to El at the beginning of the First Book of Samuel, where it means "Lord of hosts", suggesting that He is now the supreme High God, displacing El, ruler of the elohim. The Hebrews (increasingly called Israelites) begin to adopt him as local to themselves. By the seventh century BC there's no question for them as to who is in power: Yahweh guides and controls the elohim (Deuteronomy 33:2) and uses the stars in battle (Judges 5:20). By the fifth century BC El and the elohim have largely disappeared and only Yahweh is left.

The main motor of this change is the Exile, an event that most

historians regard as historical, in contrast to the Exodus. One of
the first events to be mentioned both in the Bible itself (2 Kings
17:1-6) and elsewhere is in 722 BC when Assyrian records tell of
the conquest of the Northern Kingdom of Israel. Ten of the
twelve tribes were carried into captivity and disappear from
history, leading to later fantasies that they could be found in
Africa, or America, or any other unexplored territory. The
southern tribes of Benjamin and Judah were left to carry on the
nation. During the following century the Babylonian Empire
replaced the Assyrian. In 586 BC Nebuchadnezzar, the
Babylonian monarch, destroyed Jerusalem and carried the
remaining Hebrews of the Southern Kingdom off to captivity, to
the land that Abraham had been called to leave a millennium or
so earlier.

They were now one of many minor races shuttled around
within the Babylonian Empire. They had lost the land and the
Temple. Their religion had to change. The all-conquering war
God is dropped, and the religion is slowly transformed into one
whose purpose is to preserve national identity through ritual
and law. It became important to preserve the stories of the race
before they were forgotten. They had to be collected into a
book, and that's the origin of the Old Testament.

All scholars, conservative and liberal, accept that the process
of revision and re-interpretation of the existing material whilst
pulling it together was continuous and lengthy. The gaps and
joins still show. Different writers describe events in different
ways, reflecting changing beliefs and agendas. For instance, in 2
Samuel 24:1-2, written before the Exile, David's decision to take
a census is said to be due to God's anger with his people. But in

1 Chronicles 21:1, written after the Exile, the inspiration comes from Satan.

The Israelites were in exile for about seven generations. It's a crucial period. They couldn't help but be influenced by the society in which they lived, much as early nineteenth-century immigrants to the USA have, over a similar period, now become part of that culture. While they were there the Babylonian hierarchy of Empire was replaced, in 539 BC, by the Persian, and the exiles adopted the Persian Aramaic as their first language (the one Jesus and his disciples later spoke). Thereafter Hebrew was confined to temple ritual and law, much as had by then occurred with Sanskrit in India and would later happen with Latin in Europe.

The Persians created a vast Empire stretching from Libya to the border of India. They followed the ancient religion of Zoroastrianism, inherited from the Medes, several empires earlier, and already had their own sacred books, the *Zend Avesta*, now mostly lost. Their priests were called Magi, and the later wise men who came from the East to the birthplace of Jesus were probably seen as such – Zoroastrianism was still flourishing then. The Magi had been studying the stars for thousands of years – the world's first observatory, the Temple of Belus, is believed to have been established in 2350 BC. They introduced the zodiac, dividing it into 360 degrees, and the Sabbath, the full moon day, the *shabbatum*.

Persian religion was more sophisticated than the carrot and stick religion of the Hebrews, where being faithful to the right tribal God was rewarded with wealth. They asked the kinds of questions we ask today: Why should good people suffer and innocent children die? Zoroaster answered that wrongs and rights will be sorted. Justice will be given to all. The world was created by a wholly good God of truth and light, Ahura Mazda, who defined himself as "I who am" (*Ahura* means "lord", as does the Hebrew *Adonai*). Later comes his evil brother Ahriman, god of lies and darkness, who fights against him, and rules for 7,000 years. All men and women must choose between good and evil. All have immortal souls. It is the duty of all people to love and worship God, show compassion to all living things, and do as you would be done by.

The facts of this aren't in dispute, just the interpretation. Some Christian scholars say: Okay, there are similarities between Persian beliefs and the later Israelite religion. The Israelite religion is inspired, with the Holy Spirit revealing the truth to humankind, whilst the Persian religion is not.

But most scholars would say that this is putting the cart before the horse. The Persian religion came first and was overwhelmingly more important in the first two millennia BC, influencing all others over an area of several thousand square miles. The Holy Spirit itself comes from the Persian Spenta Mainyu, through whom Ahura Mazda fights the cosmic battle. The equally widespread, common Hebrew idea of a God particular to a single tribe (or family, village, or city) who could do both good and evil, change his mind twice a day, and give help in battle slowly changed under Persian influence into a holy, just God. Evil came to be embodied separately in Satan, and by the time the New Testament was written had begun to take on flesh. Along with God and Satan came other Persian ideas like life after death, heaven and hell, resurrection, the judgment of the dead.

To take an example of the change in beliefs: there is for instance little sense of heaven and hell in Hebrew tradition prior to the Exile. There was no judgment of the dead. There was nothing basically wrong with this life. Blessings for the Hebrew patriarchs are counted by the number of years you've lived, the number of goats and children and servants you've collected or stolen. It's why the two major themes of the psalms are unfairness and desertion by God. The psalmist demands and pleads for justice now. There's no sense of justice to come, now is all there is (for example, Psalm 6:5). They have a sense of heaven a few hundred feet up in the air, but it's not a place where people go as a reward for a good life, but where the gods live. People go down as shadows to the underworld, Sheol. This is another universal belief, a similar place to the Greek Hades or the Norse underworld ruled by the goddess Hel, from which we get our "hell" (the word that's used in some modern translations for several different ideas in the Old Testament, blurring their meaning (Ezekiel 31:14; Isaiah 22:13; 1 Kings 2:1-2). A few outstanding individuals are treated specially and rise up through the sky like Elijah to join the gods in heaven. But even key biblical figures like Samuel are in Sheol, as grisly underground ghosts (1 Samuel 28).

After the Exile it's different. Zoroastrian teaching said that the dead will be brought back to life with newly-resurrected bodies. A great judgment will follow, with metals turning into rivers of molten liquid, valleys and hills being leveled, and the coming of the kingdom.

The seven archangels of Zoroastrianism turned into the seven of Jewish tradition, resurfacing in the Dead Sea Scrolls and still seen in the seven-branched menorah (candlestick). The final prophet (to be born around AD 2341), the world savior, born of the seed of a prophet and a virgin mother, will overcome disease and death in a final cataclysmic battle. These ideas fed into Islam as well as Christianity, and influenced Hinduism and Buddhism.

Most scholars date the return of a party of Israelites to Jerusalem, as described in Nehemiah, as the moment when the Jewish religion really came into being, and it's from now that most historians talk of the "Jews" as an identifiable body of people. By the fourth century BC many of the Old Testament stories went through their final compilation and editing. The writers retrospectively ascribed the grand deeds of their semi-legendary ancestors to their worship of the one God, Yahweh. The God we know and love today has arrived.

9

THE GODS WE SHAPE

"We pick out a text here and there to make it serve
our turn, whereas if we took it all together, and
considered what followed before and what followed
after we should find it meant no such thing."

John Selden

My apologies for going on for so long about the Old Testament, but this is our heritage. These old stories from a small Middle Eastern tribe have helped make us who we are. But we can step back for a moment. The enforced "time out" in Babylon that eventually led to the creation of Judaism, Christianity, and Islam is worth putting into a wider perspective. Then, as now, beliefs (however strongly held at the time) were tenuous, provisional ideas that washed across cultures, geography, time. That's one reason why the Old Testament is so interesting. It was compiled at a time that may have been uniquely creative in the cultural history of humankind.

By the fifth century BC we're about halfway through the story of civilization. There was a new literate class across the Old World. People had begun to look skeptically at the older religions that celebrated survival and promoted fertility. Power was in the hands of kings and emperors rather than spread around small tribal units. These rulers had taken on the qualities of gods, and the gods themselves had correspondingly been pushed from earth up to the heavens. The idea of absolute power, represented in the heavens by monotheism, was widely current.

But there were also contrary trends. For seekers who were uncomfortable with the idea of bowing the knee to absolute power on earth religion became more a matter of inner development. The idea of "universal spirituality" and rules of personal conduct applicable to everyone became significant. Some, particularly in Greece and China, even began to see gods as the products of human imagination rather than real beings, with man as the measure of all things. The question of what is "real" became central to reflective thought, leading to philosophy. With an absence of gods on earth pessimism about the body, the world, this life increased and the idea that there is a better world out there, of which this is just a shadow, began to take shape. By a few centuries later, in the time of Jesus, the question of personal "salvation," of how to be redeemed from a fallen world and enjoy the real one, was the concern of dozens if not hundreds of schools and cults: Greek, Egyptian, Jewish, Persian, and many others.

It's hard to underestimate the extent to which the way we think today was shaped around this time. A long-lived Marco Polo in the fifth century BC on a pilgrimage across the Old World could have started in Italy with Pythagoras, the West's first great mystic, who realizes that the nature of the universe can be expressed in maths, who teaches reincarnation (or the Eternal Return) and the sanctity of all life. Then across the water in Greece he could have sat at the feet of Socrates and Heraclitus as they teach their vision of the Supreme Good, before moving on to the Middle East where the Old Testament is taking its final shape, and Jeremiah (in Palestine) and Ezekiel (in Babylon) are talking of a holy, just God to whom we are individually responsible. Over in India there's Buddha's experience of Nirvana and the first readings of the *Upanishads*, as well as Mahavira's religion of non-violence to all living things. A thousand miles away to the east, in China, Confucius and Lao Tsu are teaching the philosophy of the good and virtuous life, with human principles at the center. We would struggle to find a comparable group from the last two millennia. In that respect it's been downhill ever since.

All these traditions are "major" today. We're most likely to find what is good and valuable in them by focusing on what they have in common. At the heart of each is the question of knowing and being yourself, the moment of understanding when our inner beings touch the universal law, described as Dharma, God, Torah, Tao, or whatever. This loving relationship came to be phrased and felt differently over the generations in different parts of the world; they emphasized different aspects of how to live truthful and holy lives, and where salvation lies.

For example, the Eastern religions of Confucianism and Taoism tend to look to the past. To find our right place in life we align ourselves with the spirit and wisdom of our ancestors. Two key religions originating in the Indian sub-continent, Hinduism and Buddhism, look for it outside the present moment. We free ourselves from the cycle of time and the world's illusions. The Middle- Eastern, monotheistic religions of Judaism, Christianity, and Islam place it in the future. Our past and present may be hopeless but God's plan is for all creation to be redeemed. The Eastern and Indian religions led to the wisdom tradition, emphasizing the interior search. The monotheistic religions developed the prophetic tradition, emphasizing relationships with others and changing society. The particular genius of Jesus was to combine the two.

But they all overlap. All say that understanding our past is crucial to understanding our present. All have traditions that place some form of salvation in the future, whether that of Jesus, Buddha Maitreya, Krishna, or the Zoroastrian Saoshyans, with the literal-minded in each tradition and generation fixing one date or another to frighten or thrill us. But all say there are values outside of ourselves, outside society, embedded in creation itself. To find happiness we realize them in our lives. The deepest happiness we can find is in the present moment, living fully right now, with the past forgiven and the future secured.

Each religion is colored by the culture it arises from and the circumstances of the founder – Christianity for instance began among a poor group within a marginal people who had been mostly under foreign rule for centuries and looked for future salvation. In the case of Buddhism, its founder was an aristocrat from an ascetic tradition dissatisfied with the sensual life of court, seeking true happiness and enlightenment. Each has millions, even billions of followers who find salvation, enlightenment, peace, fulfillment in their own traditions. They all feel their identity dissolved in creation, hear the voice of creation itself speaking to them, redefine the focus of their lives from the "self" to "God" or "other." There are thousands of accounts in print of lives being transformed, and with the alteration of a few words it's often hard to tell in which religious tradition the experience took place.

The simplest summary of their teaching on how to live the good life is the Golden Rule: "Do to others as you would want to be done to." We tend to identify this with Jesus, but it was a frequent theme in Judaism. Rabbi Hillel, a near contemporary of Jesus, used much the same language, and managed it without reference to God. Confucius based his philosophy on it 500 years earlier. His key concept is *ren*, "the love of man" (*Analects XII, 22*). The basic Buddhist precept is that you should consider all beings as like yourself. The same ideas are central to Jainism and Islam. It's simple, direct, and if you follow it you can't go too wrong.

The winnowing process of the last few thousand years has developed this as the central commandment, with an associated range of virtues like self-control, moderation, service, generosity, faithfulness, and so on. It acts as a counter to the increasing division in society over the millennia caused by the accumulation of wealth in the hands of a few. It's a radical alternative to greed. But all the great spiritual leaders say that relationship is more than a social benefit, it's at the core of life, the reason we came to be here.

It's probably no accident that it was around the fifth century BC that "science" also made huge strides. In the last few centuries science has stormed ahead again, but religious ideas and language haven't essentially altered since then. We're still reading the same books. That's why the twenty-first century may be one to match the fifth century BC – religions have a lot of catching up to do.

This change in God from a local tribal deity to an omnipotent sky God, who then becomes increasingly abstract and withdrawn from the affairs of humankind, can be traced in broad outline in the Old Testament. The stories you might remember from childhood are mostly in the first part. Of the 41 kings of Israel Yahweh speaks only to the second and third. From events we guess at being dated at around 1000 BC and earlier there's 1,000 years of the Old Testament story still to be told, and He doesn't appear so directly again, becoming a God more of vision than event. He "hides his face," a phrase used increasingly in the major and minor prophets. It's the best-recorded, most drawn-out disappearance of a God in history. Much of the power of the psalms is in their reflection on why He does this, and on how we can survive without Him. In Esther, where the Jews are saved from being massacred by a woman who is the wife of the Persian King Ahasuerus, God is not mentioned at all. The story is about the power of the Persian rulers over the Jews, not the power of God over the enemies of the Jews. (Ahasuerus, incidentally, is better known in history as Xerxes, whose defeat by the Greeks was one of the great turning-points in European history.)

So revelation slows, and ends. By the time we get to Jesus the Jews had no doubt that there were inspired scriptures, but they had fuzzy edges. Some Jews thought the writings of Moses were the only authoritative scriptures; others, all the books in the Greek Septuagint translation; yet others only the books originally written in Hebrew. So when Jesus refers to scripture it's not necessarily scripture that is now in the Old Testament (for example, John 7:38).

The Old Testament itself wasn't given its current form in Judaism until a couple of generations after the death of Jesus, when the destruction of Jerusalem in AD 70 scattered the Jews (and the Jewish Christians). The response of the Jews was similar to that during the Exile. Having again lost their Temple and their homeland they turned to the holy writings to keep their faith and identity. The surviving scholars came together at the Academy of Jamnia, near Jaffa in modern Israel, under Rabbi Jochanan ben Zakkai, and in AD 90-100 at the synod of Jamnia, decided which books would go into the Hebrew Bible.

The text itself was not finally agreed till the seventh and eighth centuries AD. But they perhaps sensibly always regarded Rabbinic commentary (the *Talmud*) as having nearly equal status. Most religions have a similar approach. The Hindu have their sacred texts, *shruti*, and the commentaries, *smriti*. The title of the greatest work in the East, the *I Ching*, means "classic" and "warp;" it's the warp upon which the weft of the commentaries is written. Christians, on the other hand, with their lack of established commentaries, have to reinvent the wheel of interpretation in each generation.

So, getting back to the Old Testament, what's its relevance for non-Jews? These chapters have probably given a very lopsided view of the Old Testament. Undeniably there's a strong thread that describes God as an average physical deity, built like us, with a preference for particular perfumes (Exodus 30:34-37), frequently perverse, deceiving his own prophets (Ezekiel 14:9-10). He's also represented in the usual terms of a weather god, thundering through the devouring fire of Zoroastrian tradition, hail and earthquake (for example, Psalm 68:7-8). He's also at times a jealous God, a bigoted, racist, murdering, evil kind of a God that you wouldn't wish on your enemy. We no longer want a God that encourages us to hate our enemies and God's "with perfect hatred" (Psalm 139:22), or that threatens us with cannibalizing our children if we don't follow all the tribal laws of Leviticus (26:29), and condones human sacrifice (Leviticus 27:28-29).

But as the Old Testament moves on more sympathetic ideas of God come to predominate. It is in many ways more interesting than the first half. The idea of God changes. He broadens and deepens. Many of the themes and narratives of the first part are common to many cultures, but there's little to compare in world literature with the suffering expressed in Lamentations, the cries of the prophets. The awareness develops that there's no short, quick answer to injustice and agony. God comes to be an expression of our hope rather than our might. He's found in our despair and weakness. He identifies with our suffering rather than our victories. God becomes a loving Father rather than a war-lord, as first seen in the Song of Hannah (1 Samuel 2). There's the compassionate God of the prophets, the idea of God as the embodiment of moral holiness. This is stronger in the latter part of the Old Testament (and in the Gospels) than in any other religious literature.

The question throughout the Old Testament is not so much whether God exists or not, that's taken for granted. It's more what kind of God was necessary for the times. He can be seen as developing from a "primitive" God of dance and music, war and slaughter, through the period of highly organized sacrifice in the Temple, to the focus of the prophets on an interior God, one seeking a repentant heart rather than the sacrifice of pigeons and goats. Various traditions of Hinduism go through the same process in the same period.

Some Christian writers explain this by saying that God only reveals Himself to people in so far as they can understand Him. The understanding develops through the Old Testament and into the New, and we move from a God of anger and violence to a God of love and justice. This rather misses the point that the God of the Revelation to John at the end of the New Testament regresses to Old Testament behavior, slaughtering humankind wholesale like the God of Moses and of Noah. But in any case why not take this thought further? We can continue to change our idea of Him. We can build on the growing perception through the Old Testament that God is not a mighty warrior who defeats our enemies, but a universal God of unconditional love.

Most Christians still retain the Jewish idea of God as a Spirit separate from us who (in the Christian view) incarnated Himself into an individual on earth. Though slowly edging out of sight in the Old Testament He explodes back into the world in the New, appearing as a baby rather than locking Himself in an ark or temple. But maybe if there is this God of all relationships in the universe who acts out of purpose and love, who is the God of all consciousness, He does indeed disappear as we realize Him into being, because God is not an idol, but consciousness itself. The disappearing God of the Old Testament suggests that as we grow up we find that God's choice is our choice, His love is our love. In the Old Testament God gradually becomes not so much a deity telling us how to behave but the embodiment of the way we should behave. By the time of Amos (eighth century BC) some Jews evidently see Him as rejecting the earlier picture of Himself as an almighty ego in the sky demanding worship and sacrifice like the neighboring idols. He becomes a principle of justice:

> "I hate, I despise your feast days,
> and I will not smell in your solemn assemblies . . .
> Take thou away from me the noise of thy songs;
> for I will not hear the melody of thy viols.
> But let judgment run down as waters,

and righteousness as a mighty stream."

Amos (5:21-24)

It's summed up in Jeremiah 31:31, 33 (see also Jeremiah 31:34; Joel 2:28).

In some ways the Judaism that had developed by the first century AD was more attractive than the Christianity that later grew out of it. It was concerned with how we lead our lives, how we treat each other, with social fairness, with the heritage we leave our children. It had become in parts at least a religion of community and forgiveness. Following many centuries of oppression the prophets tried to imagine a better kind of life, a kingdom of God where oppression did not rule. The time was ripe for a prophet who would spell out the implications of this new thinking, who would see God in people, in the way we live, revealed in action from the heart rather than in laws issued from a God up there.

One of the forerunners was John the Baptist, who saw that the collective rites of the Jewish people were no longer sufficient for purification, that the work had to be done individually. It was taken further by Jesus, who didn't seem too bothered about rituals like baptism but asked individuals to commit themselves to a new kind of life. But he did not drop out of the sky with a new message, he was a product of the times like we all are, a credit to Judaism, challenging his contemporaries to continue changing their idea of God.

The new covenant Jesus taught, the fulfillment of the law, replaces for Christians the one made with Abraham and his descendants that kicks off the Hebrew story. The promise of land to Abraham is not relevant to us today, any more than Solomon's Temple. In the new covenant God is no longer an objective deity but is shared, entering our inner life. We move from the gods of stone and wood, through the written descriptions and images of God, to God-consciousness. The people of the land, who became the people of the Book, are to become the people of Spirit. Jesus fulfills the Old Testament in the sense that he symbolizes God becoming embodied as humankind, as truly self-aware, to the point where the distinction between self and God disappear.

This is what the Old Testament has been leading up to, and Jesus was the greatest of the prophets, too radical for most, including the Jews themselves and the future Christian church. Maybe we can take it further and say with Nietzsche in the nineteenth century that the search for truth has killed God. We can take the words of Jesus on the cross: "My God, my God, why hast thou forsaken me?" (Matthew 27:46) as a metaphor for own experience of God. In so far as we kill others, we kill Her. If we don't realize Her in our lives, She's not there. It's only through redeeming our image of Her that we can redeem ourselves.

THE LOVE
WE LOST

"Happiness is the only good; the time to be happy is now, the place to be happy is here, the way to be happy is to make others so."

Robert Ingersoll

W e're about halfway through the story of written religion, halfway through the book (thank God). We come to the life of one of thousands of religious reformers, one who has perhaps had more impact than any other on the way we think today. Though we know less about him than most. He's one of the few for instance for whom we don't have a record of his words in the language he spoke. The bulk of Christian scholarship, in trying to work out the exact meaning of the Greek text in the Gospels, is chasing the wrong camel, as he spoke in Aramaic. It's a language that depends on inflection rather than a root grammatical system like Greek. "Body" and "spirit" can be the same thing, depending on emphasis. "Father" is not about gender, need not even be parenthood, but could imply universal creation.

It's not just the language we're uncertain of. We have no record of his early life. He suddenly appears, preaching and healing. And there are no contemporary accounts at all. He doesn't seem to have been noticed. A biographer in the modern sense of the word wouldn't have a single "fact" to go on. The first references to him, in Paul's letters, speak of him more as a spiritual channel to God than a real person of recent memory. There's no mention of Galilee, Nazareth, Jerusalem, or virtually anything he said or did. The Gospels come after Paul's letters – all scholars, conservative or not, are agreed on this. They are interpretations of his life, made by faith communities in the light of what they had come to believe about him (this is where scholars begin to differ). Their provenance is unknown. No records of their authorship are attached to them till the late second century AD.

This isn't the place to get into all the detail, read the theologians for yourself. The output is enormous, millions of words a year. It's all speculative. Much of it revolves not so much around whether Jesus actually said these words or those, out of the 60,000 or so recorded (half in the canonical Gospels, the others in the non-canonical), but whether he lived at all, and if he did whether we can really know anything about him for sure. The vast area of doubt allows every kind of theory to flourish, from the serious (for example, that he's a fictional version of his brother James) to the bizarre (arrived from space). Conservative arguments that the weight of later Christian documentation and Gospel manuscripts suggests that his historical existence is more certain than that of, say, Julius Caesar or Alexander the Great, are simple nonsense. The historical evidence for the existence of both is overwhelming. But in any case that doesn't mean we accept them to be divine simply because their followers believed them to be so.

None of it really matters. Tell Confucians or Taoists that Confucius or Lao-tzu may not have existed and it probably won't make a scrap of difference to the way they think and live. We overestimate the contribution of individuals to events, or traditions, or beliefs. It makes us feel better, to have someone to emulate, to look up to. It makes it easier to remember the words if we can visualize a person speaking them. We need a picture. But it's the words that count.

The majority of scholars accept that there is a historical Jesus behind the stories. But we don't really know whether he was more of a prophet or a healer, a rebel or a priest, an Essene or Messiah. What we do know is that he was a great story-teller.

And those who doubt the source of much of what he said all agree that we come closest to his words when we read the parables. They're a world away from Greek philosophy or Rabbinic theology. Galilee in those days was a fertile place of fields and scattered villages, and the parables draw on the imagery of the countryside around. Like Zen or Sufi tales they're mostly in the form of paradox and riddles. They ask questions rather than give answers. They turn the contemporary understanding of life upside down, as much now as then.

And what scholars also agree on is that at the heart of the parables is the kingdom of God. At the age of 30, the ritual age of spiritual maturity in Zoroastrianism and many other religions, Jesus set out to preach it. "Repent: for the kingdom of heaven/God is at hand" (Matthew 4:17; Mark 1:14). It's not in the distant future, it's here now.

That still doesn't make it easy to be sure of what the parables are, let alone what they mean. The same parables are treated differently in different Gospels, with different emphases, different styles, and the later writer of the Gospel of John scarcely includes any. But in looking at the whole rather than focusing on particular verses it's possible to get an idea of what Jesus was on about.

The subject of almost all the 65 or so parables is what the kingdom of God is, and how you have to be ready for it. It's the "economy" of true Christianity, the forgotten heart of the message. It has little to do with what we think of as Christian today. There's no theology. It's not "consider the creeds," but "consider the lilies."

The most common theme is that the kingdom is worth

everything (Matthew 13:44-46), but it's free. It's always open for you (Matthew 20:1-16). Indeed it seeks you out. It will grow and take over (like the mustard seed, Mark 4:30-32). It's not incremental, a question of doing a little bit better, it's a different way of living (Luke 5:36-39). It's turning to a new reality (Mark 1:14-15; Matthew 4:17). Jesus is not here to restore a lost state of union with God but to show the one you already have. It's more a question of recognition than of choice.

Life is not a burden, a shadow from which we need to escape, from which God will redeem us. It's a gift, a grace. It's a feast, a wedding (Matthew 22:1-14), a celebration. Your true nature is not a material one, subject to time and decay, or a sinful one, but an ever-present innocent spirit. Love, joy, and peace: these are your virtues, this is how you are, if you can realize it. So live openly and freely. Live like the flowers do, without a care. Live in the present moment. Enjoy it. Now is all that counts (Matthew 6:25-34; 10:29-31; Luke 12:22-34). Now is all there is. If you acknowledge this gift, saying thank you for what you want, you'll find you have it. If you believe you have it, you will. Belief is creative. It can move mountains (Matthew 17:20-21). Anything you ask for you'll get (Mark 11:24). There's no mystery, no hidden truth. You are free to ask for and imagine anything. If two or more believe the same thing, and ask for it, the power is multiplied exponentially (Matthew 18:19). The universal Father wants you to have everything.

The kingdom is not for the few, it's for everyone. It ignores the distinctions that scarred Jewish society, indeed defined it. Jesus reaches out to those who God has cursed, like the disabled and blind (Leviticus 21:18-20). He mixes happily with prostitutes, tax-collectors, even lepers, who everyone believed must have committed the most terrible sins and were strictly segregated. He goes further: every individual is of supreme worth (Matthew 20:30-34; Luke 15:4-7). It's what you are in yourself that matters, made in the image of God, not how you look, what your family is, what your race is, what you believe, what you think of yourself. It doesn't matter if you're ill, poor, or criminal (Luke 14:16-24; 19:1-10).

But that doesn't make it easy to get into the kingdom. The Jews (along with virtually everyone in the first-century world) saw tolerance as weakness, open-mindedness as sin. God blessed distinctions, and rewarded those who practiced them. The more you gained and the more powerful you were, the closer you were to God. He gave you a hard time if He was displeased with you. But the kingdom of God Jesus described is the reverse of theirs and ours. Those who are ahead in the social exchange have more they need to lose. They're still trapped in the race for gain, for self-esteem. The more you have, the farther from God you are (Luke 14:16-24). The first will be last, the last first (Luke 14:7-11; 18:10-14). It's those who suffer now who will be blessed (Matthew 5:3-12). God is embodied in the powerless, not the powerful. It's not the fittest, or cleverest, or wealthiest who get to the kingdom, but the sick, the children, and the poor.

The kingdom demands a different attitude. You must treat others as God has treated you. It's reciprocal. Forgive people what they owe you (Matthew 18:23-35). The more forgiveness, the more love in return (Luke 7:41-43). It seems not too far from the law of returns, called karma in the East. If we can forgive unconditionally we receive unconditional forgiveness. You have to forget calculation, the measurement of benefit to yourself. It's in giving that we are blessed, through giving love that we receive it. Loving your neighbor is a given (Luke 10:25-27), but this is not enough. You must love your enemy too (Matthew 5:38-48; Luke 6:27-34; 10:28-37). If someone hits you, let them hit you again. Offer no resistance. Don't harbor injustice, hatred, bad feelings. In the eyes of God you are them. If you see yourself in a leper or your worst enemy you've understood.

The key to the new attitude is giving up the "self." Free yourself even from all ties of obligation and family (Matthew 8:21-22). Forsake all that you have (Luke 14:33). Overcoming the world is not conquering it, but realizing that it doesn't matter. Lose yourself, become like a child, love for its own sake, and you can enter the kingdom (Mark 10:13-15; Matthew 16:24-25; Mark 8:34-36; Luke 9:23). Accept life as it is. Let the self die (John 12:24). When we lose it we dissolve into divinity. It's only when you can really give up everything you want, everything you think you are, that you understand who God is. Then there's no separation. We go beyond forms, beyond choice, and God takes over. We share His peace. Our true self, or divine self, the "I" that experiences, is inwards: "The kingdom of God is within you" (Luke 17:20-21). Understand this, and you will live in the love of God, as Jesus does (John 14:21).

Freud called loving your enemy the most impossible commandment ever written. It outrages our sense of boundaries. But Jesus says there are no boundaries. God even loves the good and the evil in creation without distinction (Matthew 5:43-45). It's only when we realize this that we see the kingdom. It's only when we forget ourselves that we find God. Because God is to be found in everyone else. We can be happy in so far as everyone is happy. The kingdom is in the midst of us (Luke 17:21). We are in him, and he in us (John 17:21). Everything created is a manifestation of God. There is not so much difference here from the central Hindu perception that "there are no others."

The Jews regarded God with such reverence that they did not address Him by name. Jesus calls Him "Dad," Abba. We are all sons of God (John 20:17). We are all one (Matthew 25:40). We can never be separated (Matthew 28:20). Jesus models the way to live in conscious union with God (John 14:6). There really is no divide between Him and us, us and the world. Jesus is simply the mirror in which we can see ourselves. Is this the best you can do? Can you go further?

In going further toward God we see Him coming toward us. When we realize this we no longer need divine beings "up above." Contrary to the experience of Moses, Micah, and dozens of others in the Old Testament God is no longer "visible" (John 1:18; 5:37). The kingdom of God is "spread out on earth," and made real in ourselves, by forgetting our selves (Mark 1:15; Luke 4:43; 17:21-23; Matthew 4:17). God is as much like our twin brother as He is like an almighty deity up in the sky. It doesn't matter which mountain you go to to worship God (John 4:20-23), He's not "up there" any more. He's "down here," "in here."

The kingdom is not a place, but a relationship. And it escapes more exact definition because it comes across in the life and words of Jesus as not so much a "state" as an "attempt." The more closely we try defining it the more we end up with another set of boundaries that will need jumping. He's unstoppable in his pursuit of it. Family, disciples, Pharisees, Romans, none of them could persuade him out of it. It's not a search that can easily be mapped out in steps because it's internal. It's what you make of it. It's a process, not a formula. It challenges you in so far as you're open to being challenged. He never tried setting it down in writing. He never turned it into laws; laws are there to be broken. He didn't set up a community or suggest working arrangements for living together; he seems to have overturned whatever living arrangements he could find. There's no practical advice. There's no mission statement, no soundbite. It's just "go further." If you've given some of your money away, give it all away. If you've forgiven your enemy seven times, forgive him seventy-seven times. If he hits you, let him hit you again. There's no hedging of bets, no qualifications.

It's as demanding a teaching as any on earth. All our instincts say that living in an orderly society is a question of compromise. You give a bit, take a bit. The kingdom even offends the evolutionary logic of altruism – that co-operation works in the long run because if we help others they might one day help us, because cheats will be found out and punished. It asks us to shed all our instincts for self-preservation, developed over millions of years. Living in the present, not worrying about the future. Untying the laws that keep society sane and ordered. It asks us to abandon the rational mind, the main asset that distinguishes us from the animals, and instead just trust. Have faith. No matter how tough it gets. It's faith that makes us what we are. Faith and love. They can achieve the impossible. Don't worry about the evidence all around you that they don't exist. Live like a child of God with the stars in your head and the flowers at your feet. Give like a child of God who has everything and needs nothing. Believe like a child of God with complete faith in your fellow-children. And it will be true.

Is this daft? We go back to the beginning of this book. We need a big idea to make sense of the world we live in, to make it a better one, to provide a large enough incentive to act in the interest of everyone rather than ourselves. It's our recognition of the never-ending difference between what is and what could be that enables us to make things happen, and turn from indifference to love, apathy to action, animal to spirit. This is what the evolution of life and consciousness is about. There are no brick walls, glass ceilings, other than those we create for ourselves. There's no one stopping it, other than ourselves.

We start as insignificant. As individuals we all are. Jesus is no different from us. But we could have a great future together. The kingdom places the highest possible value on every individual life. Bringing them together in love creates the kingdom of God on earth. But we can't do it on our own. Just loving our neighbor isn't enough to get us going. We need to recognize that the demands of love and goodness are more than we can manage, and we have to imagine further. We need this bigger idea to aim for, the sacred ideal, this idea of truth and love that we call the kingdom of God, the idea of a larger, universal purpose that we call God, or we'll find ourselves in an evolutionary dead end. We'll die the death of a thousand wars and pollutants, till the crust of the planet we live on runs out of patience.

Jesus doesn't stand outside the tradition of great spiritual teaching down the ages, as some kind of divine interloper a

THE LOVE WE LOST

couple of thousand years ago, but bang in the middle. At the heart of the experience of all religions is the feeling of reclaimed oneness with creation, both what we see and what we can't, of belonging to a whole that is both divine and beautiful, true and loving. And at the heart of his teaching is the ancient idea that God is in him, he is in God, we are all in God, God is in all of us; and the proof of the inner realization is measured by action in the world, giving ourselves unstintingly, singing our hearts out, patiently building the kingdom of God on earth brick by brick.

To sum it up, life is just what it is, and being a Christian is just a particular way of living it rather than looking for a different one. We're in the kingdom of God if only we could see it. It's not the next world that's important, but this one. Not the future, but now. Not the kind of beliefs we have about God, but the kind of people they help us to be.

It's not history that's important, it's the myth. History is just what has happened, where we've gone wrong. Crucifixion is what we do to others and may suffer ourselves – the loss of loved ones before their time, cancer, madness. It's the myth that matters, the expression of what we hope to be, resurrected in a brighter world. If we could really follow it, we would change our selves, and bring a better world about. But we can't seem to do it. We can manage it in pieces. Individuals can create it between themselves to some extent. Many of the best relationships are based on the idea of sacrificing your own interest for the benefit of your partner. And we can extend that to the family. Some saintly individuals manage to extend it further, to communities of the disabled, or the poor. But for most of us it's an ideal that rarely happens. But it's there though, as an idea.

And that's the potential power of Christianity, the power of Jesus, today, that he taught again this wonderful idea that would make us all happy if only we could all take it on board at once. And it would have to embrace everyone, because humankind is one. But none of us can be the first to let go of what we have. We don't believe we have the courage, or the love. We're content, more or less, with the image we have, with the religion that tells us we're okay if we confess. The one we've inherited, absorbed from our peers, developed for our protection. We would feel stupid if we abandoned it. The kingdom is for the fools of this world.

11

THE KINGDOM ON EARTH

"And if we reach, or when we reach, heaven's scenes, we truly will find it guarded by United States marines."

Ronald Reagan

The kingdom is what life should be like, what it could be like. It's what it is, if we could realize it. But we change the teaching. We corrupt the insight. We create new creeds and laws. Control turns into oppression. Inspiration turns into deceit. We threaten to drown in our own creations. Every now and again a teacher picks up the original manual and says: "This is how we're meant to do it. We're all on the same side. Love each other." Then we sink again.

So what does the kingdom mean in practice? Can it still fire the imagination?

There are many aspects we could cover – repentance, freedom from the self, from time, equality, closeness to God, inner peace, nature, love, forgiveness. We could talk about health, stress, healing, the environment, community, justice, gender, war and peace, and much else. But this is a book of snapshots. Let's just look at one, which might seem a bit prosaic at first, what Jesus says about money.

There are two main ways of thinking about money in the Old Testament. One is that God gives wealth to those He favors. It's the measure of His approval. The other, which comes later with the prophets, is that the wealth is not ours, it belongs to God and is for sharing. Every jubilee year we should redistribute it. Where does Jesus fit in? Let's take the Gospels literally for a moment.

In the first three Gospels, the earliest in the New Testament, there are about ten times as many verses on money as there are about going to the cross. Around half the parables are on money and possessions. Which makes it surprising that the cross seems so significant in Christian teaching and money rarely covered.

We've built up a lot of teaching *about* Jesus without paying the same kind of attention to what he *says*. Perhaps we just don't like it.

We might take the view that these verses on money aren't so relevant now. Society is fairer, most of us are middle class rather than poor, we don't have huge numbers dying of starvation in our streets. But it's not just our neighbors down the road we should be thinking of. The world today is more of a global economic unit. Most of what we buy comes from abroad, as food and manufactured goods, or more often as raw materials to have value added, often by a multiple of several hundred times from cost to retail. We've exported our cheap labor and the associated hardships. Economically as well as spiritually, everyone is linked to everyone else.

In the time of Jesus Palestine, and every small region of the world, was self-sufficient. The relative discrepancies in wealth between different regions and nations were close to zero. It remained this way for about 1,500 years until the Christian nations (successively the Portuguese, Spanish, Dutch, Russians, French, English, Germans, Italians) began their empire-building, plundering the resources of other countries (at the end of the eighteenth century the largest GDP in the world was that of India). Two hundred years ago the ratio of wealth between rich and poor countries had reached 4 to 1. Over the next century it rose to about 10 to 1. Today it's 60 to 1, and still increasing. Today it's we in the developed world who have the money, who are rich.

Of course capitalism is a hugely successful economic system that has brought great benefit to the countries practicing it. But the overall percentages of rich to poor in the global economy are just as bad today as they were in Palestine in the first century AD. Then the top sixth of the population (governors and priests) owned around 60% of the wealth. Today, globally, the top sixth (that includes you, or you couldn't have paid for this book) control 80% and have an average income of $70 a day; 60% of the world's population live on less than $2 a day; 25% on less than $1 a day, the United Nations' official minimum survival level. The daily income of most people in the world wouldn't buy a cup of coffee in the West.

The theory of capitalism suggests that everyone benefits from increasing wealth. The reality is that a minority do, but at the expense of the majority. It's just that our definition of the majority changes. Today they're in the Third World rather than down the street. This translates into harsh realities as grim as anything you could find in the first century AD. Four out of five people in the world live in substandard housing with no decent sanitation. Over one-third are malnourished, with no clean water. Access to telephones, computers, forget it. Less than 1% of the population. These are the toys of the rich. Every year around 10 million children die of starvation, many times more than from preventable diseases, while 100 billion dollars of food gets thrown away in North America alone. Whereas the Third World can't find enough to eat, the main health problem in the First World is eating too much. For most people, life is not much different from 2,000 years ago.

The higher up the scale you go the worse it gets. The richest 200 people in the world *increased* their income last year by $100 billion. That increase alone is roughly equivalent to the amount the poorest 500 *million* earned. It's hard to see the disparity in wealth in the world today as other than obscene, as evil.

So if Jesus were around today he would probably have had as much to say on money as he had then. What are his words to the rich? Rich people cannot enter the kingdom of God, period. Christian commentators consistently water down the message by saying that it's the love of money he condemns, not money itself. But that's not there in the Gospels. It is by the time Paul writes to Timothy (1 Timothy 6:10), but Jesus doesn't sugar the pill like that. He never says: "Money's okay if you use it for good, if you give a portion to charity, if you don't let it rule you." He says if you have it, give it away (Luke 6:30). If you hang on to money you'll be corrupted; you don't understand how dangerous it is. There's no ambiguity here. You simply can't be rich and follow him in a world of poor people. If you really treated the poor as you would like to be treated, if you saw God in them as well as yourself, you couldn't be rich. You couldn't live with yourself.

The most vivid teaching is given in the parable of Lazarus (Luke 16:19-31), who is the only parable character to get a name. He lives on the crumbs from the rich man's table. The rich man doesn't do anything wrong in the parable: he comes across as a decent enough guy, concerned about his family. He's just rich. He probably thought he was doing Lazarus a favor by leaving him the crumbs. After all, he'd earned his wealth, and it trickles down from the top to benefit everybody. No doubt Jesus' listeners thought, as we might, that Lazarus' poverty wasn't the fault of the rich man. Maybe the fault was even with Lazarus. Perhaps he should have found himself a job. If the rich man had given him more he would probably have gambled or drunk it away. But the condemnation of the rich man is absolute. He doesn't get a chance to repent. He doesn't even get a chance to warn his wealthy brothers of the burning fires of hell that are waiting for them.

In case we haven't got the message, it's repeated many times. On judgement day the people God rejects are not the ones who aren't saved or born again, but those who haven't helped their neighbors (Matthew 25:42-43, 45). The rich young man who does everything right is told to do just one more thing: to give away all he has (Matthew 19:16-22). There isn't a clearer message in the Gospels.

There's a sad irony here. The wealthy top sixth today largely live in North America and Europe. As 75% of Americans say they have made a personal commitment to Jesus Christ, the rich are mostly Christians. The majority in the world are like Lazarus, outside the gates.

If you're in the top sixth today, earning $25,000 or so a year (the average income of the West), there's little doubt about it: if you take the Gospels literally, you're damned. The confessions you've made, the numbers you've converted, the time you've had with Jesus himself, are all irrelevant. The Western Christian church is going wholesale to hell.

Of course it's hard, if not impossible, to live on a Third-World income in the West. But that in itself is a judgment on the kind of global society that we've largely shaped. Because individual responses are not enough. A kingdom of God with a few individuals present is as meaningless as a heaven with a few saved souls. It's a contradiction in terms, because we're all in

God, all one. A true kingdom response to the inequalities in the world would mean redefining what we mean by society. Rethinking the definition of money. We should think about abolishing altogether the idea of an economy based on debt and individual success. Get rid of "interest," which was morally condemned by most religions, including Islam, Christianity, and Judaism (with 14 condemnations in the Old Testament), up until around the sixteenth century.

We should think about creating a society where the income all around the world is nearer the average of $7,000 a year. Extend basic human rights to cover education, clean water, decent housing, and keep any surplus for the benefit of the environment. Recover the Old Testament idea that decisions should be made for the benefit of the "seventh generation." We should be as wary of people who want excessive wealth as we are of those who want excessive power or sex at the expense of others.

Would this simply involve redistributing wealth to people who haven't earned it? The parable of the vineyard (Matthew 20:1-16) says we shouldn't worry about that. But is the wealth of the West all down to honest hard labor anyway? To take an example from chapter 15, perhaps we should repay the 20 million or so kilos of gold and silver looted from Central America in the sixteenth and seventeenth centuries. At a rate of interest about half that we charge Third World countries today for debts incurred largely for the benefit of Western businesses (particularly arms manufacturers) the accumulated debt would run to several hundred digits and bankrupt every Western government many times over.

Sure, there are plenty of arguments to say that life is getting better, capitalism is working, we're turning the corner, the wealth will eventually trickle down. This has been said for centuries. But the rich keep getting richer, the poor poorer. The more we have, the less we want to share. The richer people are, the meaner they are. The richer the nation, the less generous it is in giving aid (the USA is the meanest of all the developed nations). Where your treasure is, there will your heart be also.

Of course this teaching is fantasy. To change like this is impossible. It goes against human nature. Difficult enough to make life work as it is without giving your hard-earned income to people you don't know, and who probably won't thank you for it. But the message of Jesus cuts through it. It *is* a simple one. It's radical. All religious founders are more radical than their later followers imagine possible. That surely is the point of the Gospels. Jesus went the whole way. He said better to live the impossible than the immoral. The degree to which Christians think this is absurd is the measure of the distance the church has traveled from his teaching.

Maybe even if we're not going to sort out the present, we should try to sort out the future. Because after all, there is enough food and fresh water to go around. If we acted in love and treated everyone equally, we could all live without worry. We don't actually need all the bits of plastic and possessions that we have. They don't actually make us happier. They don't give us more time. The kingdom of God on earth is not that far away.

But we all want that bit extra for ourselves, to put more into our cupboard than into our neighbor's, to protect our own interests. We need more and more possessions, bigger houses to put them in. We need more space, more privacy, more technology, more money to pay for it all, and the merry-go-round spins faster and faster, while many starve to death, and most suffer for want of a few dollars. It's insane. "The world has enough for everyone's need, but not enough for everyone's greed," as Gandhi said. Maybe we'll give up a bit, but only if everyone else does too. Few are prepared to go out on a limb. And if we do it gets chopped off. Going to church is so much easier. We get saved, without really having to lose anything. Perhaps that's what Jesus meant by taking up your cross and following him. We really do have to be prepared to lose it all.

This is not to suggest that Jesus was some kind of radical socialist or anarchist. He was driven by a vision of the whole person, of the whole world, how we relate to each other and to God, not by economics or politics. It's only when we have no vision for something better that we want to accumulate. If we knew we were going to die next month we'd look back and wish we'd given more of ourselves to others and invested in relationships rather than furniture. We'd spend the next weeks working out how best to give things away rather than getting more. And the vision Jesus had was to live as if now is all that matters, where the world and God are indivisible, where sickness, evil, space, and time itself are overcome by love.

The teaching is not unique to Jesus. Great teaching never is unique to one person. The Buddha underwent a greater degree of personal deprivation. Mohammed too lived an ascetic life. Giving up everything to go on the road with just a begging bowl is more a characteristic of Hindu teachers than Christian. But going further than you might think reasonable or possible in the cause of other people seems central to what Jesus was about. And again, we can only speculate on what he really said. But even scholars who doubt the existence of a real Jesus would put the teaching against the evils of wealth at the center of the "teaching of righteousness" out of which the first stories about him grew.

This teaching on money is not the radical edge of Christianity but part of the bottom line. It's the modern emphasis on salvation without lifestyle sacrifice that's heretical.

Others select different texts and come to different conclusions. Most Jewish scholars see Jesus as an erratic but essentially orthodox Pharisaic leader, maybe teaching much the same as Hillel with a sprinkling of Essene thought. Some Christians see him as a teacher of inner wisdom and enlightenment, with the kingdom being entirely spiritual. Most see him as a kind of apocalyptic, universal super-hero, who has risen from the dead and will return one day to rule the earth. Maybe unconditional love was at the core of everything he said and did, with the second coming and judgement being written in later. This tradition may have come from John the Baptist (whose followers some of the disciples probably were) rather than Jesus. But everyone finds something different. It's like trying to get a message out of Shakespeare.

Maybe there is no "message." He was just living and speaking without the kinds of boundaries we hem ourselves in with. He really was completely open to God, to goodness, and life. And when you are, there's not really much more to say other than remain completely open. Treat others as you would want to be treated. Take it where it leads you.

It's fair to say that if this kind of kingdom really was at the heart of Jesus' teaching it was short-lived. The first disciples "had all things common; and sold their possessions and goods, and parted them to all men, as every man had need" (Acts 2.4-45). But their successors grabbed the devil's temptations that Jesus had rejected, turning the kingdom of God into the kingdom of gold leaf, with the church being the richest organization in the world over most of the last millennia rather than one of the poorest. It soon lost sight of the "world" as the "kingdom," full of the presence of God, with every person, every relationship sacred, there to be realized and enjoyed. In the process of building a church and conquering the world Christians forgot about saving it. They turned it into a collection of individuals who could be converted one by one and pay their dues, with the church as the turnstile clocking them in. It's been heading off in the wrong direction ever since. Jesus would have disowned the religion the church created, and would have been appalled at the idea that even one heretic had been tortured in his name.

There's a choice we all have. It's not so much a question of what Jesus taught as what you're prepared to believe. We make him into what we want him to be. We create the kingdom we want. We get the world we deserve. It's not difficult to believe in gods coming to earth, in being born again, in our selves living on after death, most people have believed one form or another of this for the last 10,000 years and more. Believing that God can be what we make Him, that we can create the kingdom of God on earth, that what we create is worthwhile whether we live on to enjoy it or not, that's the hard part.

12

THE IMAGES
WE CREATE

"John, there must be one man to hear these things from me; for I need one who is ready to hear. This Cross of Light is sometimes called Logos by me for your sakes, sometimes mind, sometimes Jesus, sometimes Christ, sometimes a door, sometimes a way, sometimes bread, sometimes seed, sometimes resurrection, sometimes Son, sometimes Father, sometimes Spirit, sometimes life, sometimes truth, sometimes faith, sometimes grace; and so it is called for men's sake."

The Acts of John

The choice is a stark one. God on earth, amongst us all, created by us all, differences abolished, all working for the good of all. Or God in the heavens, sending a Son to earth, his successors ruling on his behalf, mediating God to humankind.

For me the idea that Jesus came from the heavens in 2000 AD is a hard one; an example of the way we change good religion back into superstition. To look at this more closely for a chapter, if he really did, couldn't he have tried a little harder? He doesn't write anything down, he appears when most of history is already over, in a remote province of a particular empire, after dozens have already come and gone. He doesn't even travel farther than you could drive in a car today in a couple of hours, depending on the traffic. He could more logically have arrived tens of thousands of years earlier. He could have waited another 2,000 years till we had television or radio. He could have written his message in lights around the planet. Just think how many more people would have been saved.

Christians might say that that's too obvious, that we need to have room for faith. But this is exactly how God does seem to behave in the Old Testament. He appears in pillars of fire, sends earthquakes and lightning strikes on demand. He has no difficulty in providing the equivalent of detailed architect's drawings for the Tabernacle, the Ark, the Temple. He issues laws that cover every aspect of behavior, for every moment of the day.

Verses in the Gospels are quoted to show that this Jesus himself believed in his divine mission, verses like John 14:6, "I am the way, the truth, and the life." Maybe he did, but then tens of thousands of people have. Maybe he was mad – his own family thought he was, at least at one point (Mark 3:21-35). In any case, the Gospel of John, though incorporating earlier oral tradition, is written in a very different idiom from the other Gospels, and is a generation or two later (with the first three dating from a generation or two after Jesus lived). Most scholars would say it's the least likely Gospel to reflect what Jesus actually said.

Read as a whole, the Gospels show a Jesus who doesn't seem as interested in this kind of role as later teaching makes him out to be. He never tries to "prove" a particular definition of God, he offers no arguments. It doesn't even seem to bother him whether people believe in his God or not. Living in Nazareth (if it existed, there are no records of it at the time), a morning's walk from Herod's cosmopolitan and Greek-speaking summer capital of Tiberias, Jesus must have rubbed shoulders with worshipers of Zeus, Osiris, Mithras, Ra, Mercury, Diana, Isis, Adonis, and a host of others. He doesn't mention any of them. The fact that the Roman centurion and the Syro-Phoenician woman whose daughter he heals believe differently is not an issue for him. It's how you act that counts, where your heart is, not whether you believe in one God or another. He talks about loving God and loving your neighbor, and that one doesn't count without the other. They amount to the same.

Maybe if Jesus had lived longer he would have passed on his ideas in more detail. By comparison Mohammed had over 20 years between his revelation and his death. The Buddha had 45 years, Confucius maybe 50. They had more time to develop their teaching, pass it on coherently to their disciples, write it down, organize the succession. Jesus was a relative youngster. He taught for only one year (if you follow Matthew, Mark, and Luke), or maybe three (if you follow John). He was gone before most of his contemporaries knew he was there.

He's as good an example as we have of the dynamic master teacher, storming in from the desert, blowing away the cobwebs and structures that self-interest has created, bringing people back to universal themes of truth, justice, freedom, equality, spirit; of "oneness." After his death there's a vacuum. The awed disciples, without the same intensity of vision but with an average mortal's share of self-interest, scurry around stitching up the hole and recreating the world as it was before. With time the bureaucrats parcel out the vision into prescribed chunks called doctrine, adding their flourishes; the leadership types organize groups into communities, sometimes called churches; the salesmen go out with the one and only true original product and knock everyone else's; the accountants start to look for profit. It's true of business and governments as well: the path from vision to hierarchy, co-operation to tax. Much the same happened in Islam, where Mohammed's followers proclaimed him the last prophet soon after his death. Though unlike followers of Jesus they didn't go as far as proclaiming him divine.

We have too many gods, and the Christian church underestimated Jesus by turning him into another one. He was a Jew, in the tradition of the prophets. He wasn't the son of a sky god. The Jews were the least likely people in the Empire to believe that, one of the few peoples who saw an impassable gulf between God and humankind. They were so upset about identifying anything human with God they were prepared to die in their thousands in protest against Roman soldiers carrying standards bearing human images into Jerusalem.

Conservative Christian scholars argue differently, with some reason. Jesus is frequently referred to in the New Testament as "Lord" (though this can mean anything from "sir" upwards) and "Christ," maybe not identifiable with God but indicating divinity in some form. In one of the earliest documents, in 1 Corinthians 16:22 ("Our Lord, come!" NRSV), the suggestion is that Jesus is prayed to, and Jews prayed only to God. There may have been many Jews whose perception of God as holy and separate was not as clear as others. Who believed that the coming Messiah would be divine. At no point in the first millennium can you say there was a monolithic certainty amongst Hebrews or Jews as to what they believed.

Jesus is also referred to frequently in the Gospels as Son of Man and occasionally as Son of God. "Son of Man" means pretty much "mankind" (Psalm 8:4). Adam, Israel, and kings of Israel are all referred to in the Old Testament as son of man. The meaning overlaps with Son of God. "Son of God" is another vague phrase with multiple meanings (capitalization is a late seventeenth-century addition to the Bible text). Adam, David, Jacob, Ephraim, angels are all called sons of God, as were other prophets around the time of Jesus. Jesus calls peacemakers sons of God (in the Greek text of Matthew 5:9).

Moreover, many verses in the Gospels suggest that Jesus defined himself as "man" in the ordinary sense of people as sons of God. He frequently distinguishes between God and himself (Luke 18:19; 22:42; Mark 13:32). This is particularly so in the first of the Gospels to be written, Mark, where there's only one reference to Jesus as Son of God, and that of doubtful authenticity. The references increase through Matthew and Luke, a generation later.

Outside church-related institutions the overwhelming scholarly view is that the idea of Jesus' divinity developed because non-Jews who believed in him as the "way" to God (and in the first century AD they were increasingly in the majority) would have assumed he was one himself. They couldn't understand him *not* being one. Even so, it wasn't till the fourth century that the phrase "Son of God" was promoted to mean "God the Son," as co-equal with God. Almost all scholars, even conservative Christian ones, would agree on that.

The Christian church has got this the wrong way round. It wasn't the early Christians who converted the Empire to their way of thinking, but the Empire that converted them. The first "Christians," Jews, did not believe in Jesus as the Son of God. That was blasphemy. The later generation Christians, Greeks and Romans and others, did. It would have been surprising if they hadn't. The predominant Mediterranean world-view of the time, described by Hesiod eight to nine centuries earlier, was that life was a ladder with animals, people, heroes, angels, and gods on different steps. But they all interacted. Gods in heaven were too remote, they were always coming to earth. Their offspring returned as heroes to heaven. They metamorphosed into one another. An emperor could be divine almost by definition, indeed usually was. You were liable to be crucified for disputing it. Even a great athlete must have something of divinity about him. These divine or semi-divine characters were expected to heal and do miracles, that's why they were followed.

We can see examples of this polytheistic way of thinking in the New Testament itself, as soon as we step outside the world of the Jews. There are two curious episodes in Acts. One is at Lystra (Acts 14:8-13), where Paul heals a cripple and as a result he and Barnabas are hard put to prevent the locals from thinking they are the gods Jupiter and Mercury. Another is in Malta (Acts 28:6) where Paul is declared a god because he has survived both drowning and snakebite. I used to put this down to the ignorance and superstition of the locals, amongst whom Paul was moving with the light of knowledge of reason and faith, like a brave nineteenth-century missionary. Far from it. These were prosperous places, much closer to the center of the Empire than Judea. This was normal, it was the way people thought. Almost everybody (apart from Jews and skeptics) believed that gods had sons and they came to earth and had sex with virgins.

To put this in a broader context, sons of god in the first century AD were as common as celebrities today. Every other hilltop had a god, a brooding presence or a hyper-active deity chucking thunderbolts or kidnapping the prettiest girls for sex. Zeus fathered hundreds of children by women, mostly virgins. His son Hercules is the best known today, thanks to Walt Disney. Alexander the Great, Plato, Augustus, were all believed to be born of virgins. In fact they're common all over the world. Greek gods and satyrs, Arabian djinni, Celtic dusii, Hindu bhuts, Samoan hotua poro, various demons good and bad, all had human sons and daughters. The births were usually noteworthy in some way, being in difficult times, in the obscurity of a cave, in hiding from angry tyrants, with innocents being slaughtered, with miraculous signs and stars in the sky, foretold by prophets and wise men, under divine protection. This particularly applies to the more prominent sons, like Buddha, Krishna, Mohammed, Zoroaster, Jesus.

Every town in the Empire had statues and temples to a variety of these god-men, drawing variously on a common stock of imagery, iconography, and tradition. Asclepius for instance was a popular one, born of Apollo and a mortal mother, with hundreds of cult centers in the Empire. He heard prayers and healed people, and even raised a man from the dead, but was killed by Zeus for his impertinence. Later he was restored to life and deity. His symbol, like that of the early Hebrews, was a snake coiled round a pole. In contrast, Jesus could not only raise the dead, but defeat death itself (Hebrews 2:14). In this he out-trumps even Hercules, the deliverer and protector, perhaps the most popular god-man of all.

As Christianity developed, the followers increasingly added these themes and stories to their own tradition. Take any competing god and you can see the parallels. Mithraism was one of the most popular cults, originating from the old Iranian God of light (still followed in Hinduism today with the god Mitra). Most scholars accept his followers had rituals similar to those of Christians, but which predated Christianity: for instance, baptism, anointing with oil, a eucharist, and Sundays. Christian bishops still wear a *mithra* or mitre and carry a shepherd's staff in imitation of the bishops of Mithras, much as they adopted the dog collar from the Roman civil service and the purple of the bishop's robes from the imperial dress. We still call priests the Mithraic "Father."

Like Jesus, Mithras seems to have been worshiped as "the way, the truth, and the life," as redeemer and savior. He was born on the traditional date for gods born of virgins (as also happened with Adonis, Attis, Bacchus, Horus, Krishna), our 25 December, a date which the Christians took over in the fourth century. The shepherds and the Magi visited him as a baby. He performed miracles, healed, was buried in a stone tomb, and rose on the third day, in March, at the time of the spring equinox. The similarities were such that Augustine later said the priests of Mithras worshiped the same God as he did.

Another was Dionysus, born to a virgin goddess in a cave, eaten by the Titans when he was a baby, later resurrected. The symbolic act of eating meat and drinking wine, the flesh and blood of the god (John 6:54-55), at a special meal brought union with him, and he in return granted eternal life. Turning water into wine was his speciality. Maybe the church adopted this tradition into its texts, which is why at a wedding Jesus turns water into a thousand bottles of wine (John 2:3-11), a truly Dionysian quantity for a small village. Maybe it was a useful text of the time which could be turned to illustrate how the "new wine" of the gospel replaced the inferior "water" of Jewish law. The similarities between these incidents in the life of Jesus and those of Attis, Adonis, Osiris, and others are endless.

This is not to say there is no historical basis for these Gospel stories. Take the water into wine for instance. It may be that this scenario appeared first in oral tradition because it was based on Jesus' own wedding. Virtually all Jewish males were married, it would be surprising if Jesus were not. That explains why his mother was the main guest, why the host turned to her for help when the wine ran out, why Jesus felt it his responsibility to supply it. A later writer or compiler may have edited the identity of the bridegroom out of the text to accommodate the increasing sense of Jesus' divinity.

As another possibility, of course, there's the orthodox view that this was a genuine miracle, whatever that means, and the Son of the God of the universe of 100 billion galaxies had nothing better to do with his short time on earth than help a local wedding party get drunk.

Most of the miracle stories can be read today in terms of new knowledge (mental illness rather than demons), misunderstanding (he inspired the 5,000 to feed each other rather than multiplied loaves and fishes), mistranslation (walking "by" the water and "on" the water use the same word), or later elaboration. Read the theologians for the ins and outs of which miracles are more credible than others. The number that are seen as such, even by conservative Christian scholars, diminishes with every decade.

Few for example would accept today that the ascension, more significant than the resurrection in Western art, literally happened as the New Testament describes it. It's clearly meant to be taken literally: the disciples are shown looking intently up into the sky as Jesus disappears from sight. But quite apart from the miraculous aspect there are more mundane problems. For instance in Luke 24 Jesus ascends on Easter day itself, whereas in Acts 1 it's 40 days later. Two of the Gospels don't even mention such an apparently significant event. But the main difficulty today is that the account is so clearly based on the world-view of the time, which situates heaven a few hundred feet up in the air. If it was still there now jumbo jets would be knocking holes in it and people falling out. If it's off the edge of the universe, and Jesus is still ascending, he would barely have started to cross our own galaxy yet, even traveling at the speed of light.

Still, this kind of belief works for many. Billions have believed, and still do, that the soul takes flight to the heavens through the hole at the top of the shaman's lodge, rises in the smoke of the fire, scatters in the sparks, descends to the underworld through a tomb or cave. Most scholars though, even conservative ones, would say that to take the ascension event literally undermines rather than reinforces faith.

So Christians tend to apply a sliding scale of credibility and significance to miracles. Most you can question, or ignore, but the resurrection is different. If this isn't true, then nothing is. Faith is meaningless, Christianity pointless. It's like Custer's last stand.

Which is an odd position, as the story of the resurrection is written and believed in by the same authors who wrote the others. It's not so difficult to believe in it with a small "r." The after-life, the idea of rebirth, renewal, drives religion. God representing creation and the Son renewal is as old as Adam and Eve, it goes right back to the agricultural corn-gods. And by far the best argument for the resurrection, which Christians rarely advance, is that Jesus rose from the dead because people *do* rise from the dead. The world really *is* one of magic and miracle. Millions, perhaps billions of people, have had experiences of accessing patterns of information, of forms, or people, that are incredible in terms of modern science – the effect of healing hands, or of seeing an angel, or a dead relative, or being watched (by some estimates up to 90%), or other forms of the paranormal.

All over the world, from the zombies of Haiti to the Fang people of Gabon and every inhabited place in between many people still do believe in the dead walking, in Elvis Presley still playing, in ghosts, demons, and the supernatural, as a matter of daily experience. There's a vast amount of literature detailing experiences of leaving the body, returning after brain death, communicating with spirits, better documented than the resurrection of Jesus, and more rigorously checked. For New Agers, Christians, Hindus, animists, this is the way the world is; it is interpenetrated with the actions of God/gods/spirits. Many have had experiences of this world shading off into a different one, of encountering a different kind of reality, and they believe it. Others haven't, and they don't. But most people in the world could believe in Jesus appearing in *some* form to his disciples after his death, or at least that the disciples believed they saw him in some form.

The real difficulty is in accepting that the resurrection of Jesus was unique, physical, and the saving act of God, which transformed the fortunes of humankind, the world, the universe. Most religious people in the world might say that it's the Christians who are lacking in faith, skeptical of the world of spirit and potential, believing that just this story is true and similar ones are not.

If you can believe in the resurrection, good for you. May it make you a happier and better person. But believing in the resurrection isn't necessary to belief in God or being a Christian, any more than believing in the ascension. It's like saying you're only allowed to enjoy Christmas if you believe in Santa Claus. Forcing the issue creates a problem for anyone who wants to think rationally about it. The trouble is, we're relying on stories written by people we don't know, from sources we don't know, with no record of transmission. In this respect the evidence for UFOs, for example, is vastly greater than that for the resurrection, in that there are 3.5 million Americans alive today who claim to have seen one, and can be interviewed.

The more incredible a story is, the higher the level of "proof" needed to believe it. Imagine the kind of proof we would want if it were claimed of someone today that they had risen from the dead; the interviews with the risen person, the medical evidence, the video footage, the eyewitness accounts. The amount of evidence needed to convince a reasonable person that someone who had died came back to life after three days would be enormous.

But, if we examine this in terms of evidence, no one even claims 2,000 years ago to have seen Jesus rise from the dead. No one records it at the time. There are various stories that circulated later about followers who saw an empty tomb. But the accounts are all different. Different numbers of women, or men, with different names, in each case. They see different things, angels, or men, or Jesus, or nothing. Compare the accounts for yourself if you want to check it out. Jesus doesn't appear again (in Mark, the last verses of his Gospel are not in the most reliable manuscripts and almost all scholars agree they were added later), or he appears in Galilee but not Jerusalem, or Jerusalem but not Galilee, or both. The appearances are also uncertain in that Jesus is variously seen as physical – ready to be touched, eating fish – at other times not, appearing suddenly in their midst, not wanting to be touched. Sometimes he's recognizable, sometimes not. Indeed the first chronological mention of the resurrection, in 1 Corinthians 15, uses the Greek word *ophthe*, which can mean either physical appearance or vision.

The resurrection of Jesus as a physical, bodily event doesn't seem to feature in the first Christian documents, the letters. There's no mention of the empty tomb, or Mary Magdalene or the other women, or any details. In so far as Paul does talk about the appearance of Jesus to Peter, then James, and all the disciples, then the 500 (who don't appear in the Gospels), and finally himself, he mixes up these supposedly factual sightings with his own visionary experience. To put it perhaps more crudely than Paul would have wanted, any individual's vision of Jesus is as good as anyone else's. So whereas a Christian today might say that the bodily resurrection is essential, the litmus of the claims of Christianity, it didn't necessarily seem to be that way for the first disciples. It began with vision, not event.

Associated with the death and resurrection there are various supernatural events. In Mark (around AD 70) there's darkness over the land. Matthew (around AD 75) has an earthquake and tombs opening, with the dead rising. Luke (around AD 80) adds the curtain of the Temple being torn in two. Astronomers know there was no eclipse at the time, no darkness. With both the appearances and the supernatural effects it does seem that the detail increases as time goes on, though the latest Gospel, John, doesn't mention them at all. As with the virgin birth, John may simply have considered these divine special effects too crude to be taken seriously. They are in any case rather mouse-sized to accompany the death of the Son of the Ruler of a universe of billions of galaxies. You would at least expect them to be felt around the Roman Empire – even around the planet. If no contemporaries on the spot noticed anything out of the ordinary happening, why bother?

The story is expanded further in other gospels not included in the New Testament. In the *Gospel of Peter* (AD 50-100) the soldiers on guard at the tomb see two gigantic angels who come down to bring Jesus out with his cross. Other non-canonical gospels take a more "spiritual" line. In the *Gospel of Mary*, Mary sees Jesus in a vision, not in reality. Peter is suspicious of the vision but Mary is vindicated and joins the apostles as they go out to preach. Later tradition provides a further variety of interpretations. One says that James was the first witness; another says Peter, rather than Mary, giving him more authority. Maybe the New Testament Gospels are more reliable than the non-canonical ones, but there's little clear reason for saying so, apart from tradition having declared them to be such.

Of course it's hard to read Matthew's account of the passion – the most detailed of the four – and not feel moved by it. Look at all the detail. Nobody would have bothered to invent it all, or had the nerve. And we know it happened because we experience the presence of Jesus. When Peter denies Jesus and the rooster crows, it crows for all of us. We all know that we're weak, we all betray the good when we're afraid, and it's Christ alone who can save us. If he wasn't a saviour, who is there to forgive us? How can God forgive if He doesn't understand what it means to be like us?

But things don't just happen in the Gospels because they "happened." They could only happen because God meant them to happen, because He had already foretold it. The writers couldn't conceive of life outside God. Every act, every moment, had spiritual meaning, as it still does for many today. They wrote in the tradition of "midrash" rather than history (more of a Greek tradition), interpreting today in the light of the past. In spiritual autobiographies and missionary stories of today you see the same process at work. The writers lived and breathed scripture every moment. They searched it for a word or a phrase that had similarities to the event they wanted to describe. These words were often taken completely out of context, or mistranslated, or misunderstood, or all three.

Most scholars (taking them across all traditions, Jewish, as well as secular and Christian) see Matthew's story as a later theological construct rather than fact. It's not difficult to see how and why it takes the shape it does. His Gospel is dominated by the debate between the Jewish and early Christian communities as to whether or not Jesus fulfilled the scriptures. Matthew's 60 plus references to the Old Testament are there for that purpose. At the time he wrote the Jews were throwing the Christians out of the synagogues, and the cult was fighting for survival as a strand of Judaism.

Matthew is writing an idealized spiritual picture of his Savior. So the ride on a donkey into Jerusalem is there because it parallels Zechariah 9:9. Indeed because Zechariah confusingly mentions an ass and her foal Matthew seems to say that Jesus rode both at the same time (21:7). Overturning the money-

changers' tables suggests Malachi 3.1, Hosea 9.15, and others.
The Gethsemane experience on the Mount of Olives brings to
mind David in tears. The arrest and trial echo dozens of
references about being surrounded by enemies; making no
answer, Psalm 38:13-14; Pilate washing his hands,
Deuteronomy 21:6; the suffering on the cross, Isaiah 53:3-12;
the two thieves on either side, the evildoers circling the psalmist
in Psalm 22; the wine and the gall, Psalm 69:21; being forsaken
on the cross, Psalm 22:18; dividing the clothes, Psalm 22:18;
thirty pieces of silver, Zechariah 11:12; Judas, Obadiah 7;
hanging himself, 2 Samuel 17:23; Jesus not having his legs
broken, Exodus 12:46; darkness over the land, Amos 8:9;
earthquake, Joel 2:10; rising on the third day, Hosea 6.1-2. And
so on.

This is not to say none of this happened. And of course maybe
Jesus chose to ride a donkey, overturned the tables, because he
saw himself as fulfilling scripture. No one would claim that of
Pilate or Judas though. It's just that it's hagiography, it's "spun,"
it's not history, or documentary. And we know Matthew was
writing his story in the light of scripture because we can see him
doing it. For instance, he claims that Jesus was born of a virgin
to fulfill an Old Testament prophecy (Matthew 1:23) because
he's quoting the Greek Septuagint version which by that time
had gained that meaning. But the original Old Testament
Hebrew simply means "young woman."

The sources for a physical resurrection are tenuous,
unconvincing, contradictory, absent, or even point to the
opposite conclusion, and there's no way of questioning them.
Apologists say this doesn't necessarily mean it didn't happen.

Indeed it may even make it more credible in that if the whole thing was a stitch-up the disciples would have made a better job of it, wouldn't have used women as witnesses, etc. Which is somewhat convoluted reasoning. But the point is that it's easy to see how the story might have arisen.

It's not a question of "hoax" or "true," of believing that the disciples were either liars or honest men. That's too simplistic. The only thing that all four Gospels agree on was that Mary Magdalene (exactly who she was, an individual, a mix of people, fictional or real, is much disputed) went to the tomb. Of all the followers she may have been the most committed, or the bravest. Perhaps it's significant that in John's Gospel the disciples don't see the angels in the tomb but she does, after they've left. Perhaps she hallucinated under the stress of the times – even today 10% to 25% of people say in surveys that at least once in their lives they have experienced a vivid hallucination. Perhaps she was an epileptic, prone to visions and imaginary experiences. After all Jesus had healed her of seven devils.

Perhaps it was less dramatic than that. Experimental psychologists know that it is relatively easy to create false memories that can be stronger than memories of real events. That our real memories are often confused as to their source. That they are influenced by other people's memories of the same event. That we can change our memories in the light of later experience. Perhaps Mary believed she spoke with Jesus but was simply mistaken. Perhaps the gardener was just a gardener. Perhaps she simply went to the wrong tomb. Perhaps she imagined it all much later, having stories drawn out of her by excited grandchildren. Perhaps she lied. In any case, whatever the motive, she started a hare running.

Then as the story gained ground some (but not all) of Jesus' later followers believed it. Other women wanted to be part of it, and added experiences of seeing Jesus, or an angel, or both. Perhaps they couldn't tell the difference. Some of the disciples started to add their bits. A generation, two generations later, after the traumas of the destruction of Jerusalem and the scattering or death of most of the population, second-, third-, or fourth-hand accounts turned into the collection of different stories we have now.

So how should we think of the resurrection today?

In the scales of experience and knowledge we all balance the weights differently. For some the experience of encountering the risen Jesus or the many other figures perceived as divinely present after their death is such that the resurrection must be literally true whatever scientists and scholars might say. The power of love makes anything possible.

For others there are many truths. They recognize the equal power of the experiences of those of different beliefs. The resurrected Jesus might work for me, the re-incarnated Buddha for you.

But for most belief and knowledge need to go hand in hand, enriching each other. Faith is not credulity. It's personal, and starts from where you are. It's not holding an impossible belief, it's having the courage to live in the light of a good one, the best you can manage. For some Christians the resurrection is true in a spiritual sense. We don't need to believe it happened physically to believe that it expresses in the form of a story, in the later reaction of the disciples, the fact that consciousness in some form survives death, that there are larger dimensions to the world than space and time, that everything that has happened still is, that memories of yesterday are as powerful as the events of today, and shape what happens tomorrow. The impact of Jesus on his disciples was such that his continuing felt presence was more vivid than most.

Some can believe in miracles, others can't. Some have experienced them, most not. A faith for everyone doesn't depend on miracles. It says that there's a vast range of possibilities, from molecules to spirit, and we choose our point on the line. For most in the West our hearts want to believe in the resurrection, our minds can't. Not today anyway, or not as a once-only event rather than a matter of common experience.

An argument for the relevance of the resurrection and that of similar stories might go something like this: we shape our experience and our hopes in terms of the story we're given, much as billions of believers in other religious figures do. Humbled, scared, thrilled, reconciled, supported, uplifted – these emotions are the common currency of all religion. We give them labels and denominations that make sense to us, or we can't use them. Underneath the labels the emotions run deep. Break the thin ice and our minds are full of shadows, images, fears, the good and bad. Psychology explains some – life hasn't been the same since Freud described the battle between the id and the ego, the subconscious and reason. Perhaps as Jung said we collectively create archetypes that can be more real to us than our individual selves.

Religion can't be defined as fact, but it's more literal than symbol. Neither of these languages expresses the world in our heads where the important things in life happen. It models a relationship between ourselves and the world. It pictures a reality that answers our needs. The idea of the man who becomes God or the God who becomes man is one of the most widespread ideas we've developed to link our consciousness with a possible universal one.

Some models are better than others. They, with their stories, change as our views of truth and reality change. A "displacement" model of God sacrificing Himself for humankind is better than the "literal" model of people sacrificing each other for God. Better still is a model that recognizes itself as only a model. The value of each lies in the extent to which they develop us as individuals growing in awareness and practicing love. Not in the miracles that grow up around the models, obscuring the meaning.

The miracles surrounding the birth and death of Jesus are no more important to Christianity than those around the Buddha are to Buddhism. And they are few and trivial compared with those in Hinduism. Our power of will is not so developed that we can turn water into wine or putrefying corpses into living flesh, nor that we can alter our eternal destiny in the universe in a moment. Believing otherwise may be nice, but it's religion in a hurry. Maybe miracles happen, and some are more able to produce them or see them than others. But resting your faith on one is not necessarily helpful, or good religion. It doesn't help us practice it here and now. If it's miracles you want, go to India.

We don't know what happened to Jesus. Any of the legendary accounts of what happened to him, such as that he survived the crucifixion and travelled to Kashmir, as many Muslims believe, are much more credible than the resurrection. His bones aren't going to be found. Crucified people weren't given burials, they were left for the dogs and crows. Nor is he going to appear in clouds and lightning tomorrow to judge who believes in him and who doesn't. That's B movie, Hammer horror religion today. But a belief that he expresses more clearly than anyone the divine dimension in human beings, that in some sense he lives on, that maybe we all do, focuses our desires for a life beyond the material, unconstrained by time.

The story expresses our belief that it's the quality of our lives and deaths that's important rather than quantity. It's by believing we can do good that we do it. By doing it that we become good. By believing in God that we live as His image, aware and active players in the slow grinding of the universe towards self-realization over billions of years. In some way it's by saying yes to life that makes life happen.

13

The History We Change

"And the Son of God died, which is immediately credible because it is absurd. And buried he rose again, which is certain because it is impossible."

Tertullian

So how did the kingdom of God on earth for everyone turn into the kingdom of heaven for a few? This is the subject of the next couple of chapters. If you're bored with history, skip to chapter 16.

Tradition and scripture, like history, are written by the victors. Orthodoxy is just what people like us have made it to be. After thousands of years the chances of it being close to the original are vanishingly small. None of us think like the first Christians did. At a distance history smooths over the bumps. Imagine back 300 years from now, to AD 1700. The ship's wheel has just been introduced to replace the tiller. The Swedes are defeating an alliance of the Russians, Danes, and Poles, and capture Warsaw. The French gain control of the English forts around Hudson's Bay and settle in Texas. Virtually everyone in the West still believes in a divinely-ordained class structure that has kings at the top and slaves at the bottom.

The world looked very different, and anyone living then would be astonished to see it today. The difference between first- and fourth-century (when Jesus achieved the status of co-equality with God) Christians is of the same order.

It's hard for us today to understand the degree to which all religions evolve because we're so used to thinking that there's only one God, with one right interpretation, whether or not He exists is a black and white question. We read the Gospels as if everything happened just down the road, yesterday. Jesus either rose from the dead or he didn't, it's all either true or false.

The Roman view of religion was perhaps more sophisticated. They were in some ways more credulous than we are, in others more skeptical. They were aware of many gods, both of their own tradition and of the many peoples they had conquered. They judged them on their merits. They used different gods for different purposes, much as we've farmed out their functions to doctors and dentists, priests and lawyers. They knew that religion was a two-way street, what you got depended on what you put in. Gods were not gods if they weren't worshiped, offered sacrifices. They were there as long as you gave them house room.

There's a simple reason why Christianity succeeded. It didn't emerge clear-cut, as a new, distinct religion with a worked-out creed, to be accepted or rejected. It evolved into a belief that made sense to a lot of people at the time. They turned it into what they wanted. It was as much a reconfiguration of existing religion as a new one. Beliefs evolve out of consensus. Religions all work with the material to hand. They don't appear out of thin air, they are not that different. All the practices, rituals, and symbols that we think of as Christian (sacraments, icons, Christmas, feast days, Sunday, incense, prayer, the Eucharist, speaking in tongues – the list is endless) have been absorbed from other cultures and beliefs. The cross itself, that ancient symbol of the point where God meets us, is a pre-Christian icon, representing the Sun God in Assyria and Central America, Osiris in Egypt. Actually, of all the Christian symbols it's one of the later ones, not really appearing in art till the fifth century AD, when Christianity took on a more violent edge. The rosary managed to travel through several traditions, starting off as an aid to meditation in Buddhism, adopted by Islam, and arriving in Europe through the Crusades. All Christian teachings are ancient, universal beliefs that the church has adapted in a particular way. Salvation, eternal life, the second coming, Son of God, heaven and hell – anything you can think of.

Over a period of centuries Christianity absorbed existing traditions, rolling up the specialist providers into one divine package headed by a single almighty God. The followers of Jesus overlaid Him with aspects of other gods and heroes and the church took over their temples, festivals, symbols, and the Old Testament itself. The more powerful the church became the more it adopted the trappings and beliefs of competing pagan cults, till it was to all intents and purposes indistinguishable from them.

Christianity was successful in the Empire because it was the right religion at the right time. It had the ingredients of a genuinely populist movement. In fact being rich and powerful was a positive liability. The new faith was for the 90% who did not have "rights" in the form of citizenship, or the money to buy God's favors. Christianity gave people a new sense of worth, a new dignity. It inherited the Judaic principles of caring for widows and orphans, the poor and oppressed. Christians looked after each other. In a world ruled by force of arms, where life was generally short and brutal, they offered love and hope rather than stoicism and suffering. This didn't last, of course. In a few centuries the church was the largest slave-owner in the Empire. But in the meantime not being noble, or wealthy, or a famous soldier, was a positive virtue. Through Jesus the poor had the chance to save themselves. They might not have the villas but their souls were secure and they would be rewarded in the next life. For most, it was the best deal on offer.

But what did the first Christians actually believe? Most

scholars agree they were known as "Nazareans," or "Nazarenes" – probably nothing to do with Nazareth but implying strict observance of the Law. They were one of many groups opposed to the Temple establishment and Roman rule, probably a minor one compared with the Essenes (who the contemporary Philo writes a whole book on), and the Mandeans (still surviving today as the Marsh Arabs where they fled after the destruction of Jerusalem, still claiming John the Baptist as the true Mandean), or many others.

There's little doubt they saw themselves as practicing within the Jewish faith, worshiping in the Temple. Virtually all scholars, Christian or not, would agree with this, both from the internal evidence of the New Testament letters and from later writers like Clement of Rome. Indeed they may have followed the Law more zealously than the Pharisees. To get a flavor of what early Christian worship would have been like you would do better to go to a Sufi mosque today than a church, or, if you can, to one of the Christian Churches in West Syria. There, just down the road from Galilee, they still worship in Aramaic, the language Jesus spoke, foreheads touching the ground, bottoms in the air, a practice later largely dropped in Christianity but continued in Islam.

Where scholars begin to differ is in what the Nazarenes believed about Jesus. Christian scholars tend to read back into the first generation the beliefs of the later New Testament writers. But over the last few decades the majority of scholars, including many Christian ones, have come to the conclusion that the Nazarenes considered Jesus to be an ordinary human being, naturally born, but one who managed to follow the Law perfectly. His actual life was probably not very important to them, his death still less so. The Epistle of James scarcely mentions him, nor does that of Jude. They probably believed in the resurrection, but not as a unique saving event for humankind. Jesus was taken up into heaven in the same manner as Elijah, a similarly divinely anointed prophet with a special relationship to God. For them Jesus was in the radical, uncomfortable tradition of the prophets, calling Judaism back to true, unadulterated worship.

There's also some evidence that the Nazarenes saw Jesus as the true Prophet, particularly in the Jewish communities from Syria to Iraq, a tradition that again was later taken up and developed by Mohammed. But first and foremost he was a good Jew. In other words, what virtually every Christian believes today about Jesus developed as later teaching. The first Christians weren't "Christian," as we know the word today.

The majority of scholars, across the board, would agree that the first leader of the Nazarene community was James, the brother of Jesus, for whom there's more evidence outside the New Testament than for Jesus himself. He was probably stoned to death by the Jewish religious establishment around AD 62, and by AD 85 the Nazarenes were excluded from synagogues, with the liturgy condemning them. In exile they prayed facing Jerusalem, as the Muslims today face Mecca.

They became known as the Ebionites, which means "the poor," perhaps staying true to Jesus' teaching on wealth. Eusebius, the major church historian of the early centuries, describes them as still being strong in Palestine and Syria 300 years later, still believing in Jesus as a mortal. But the Nazarenes had by then become an embarrassment to the Gentile church, which had moved away from Judaism. Early on writers begin to edit them out of the story, they came to be persecuted as heretics, and by the end of the fifth century this original Christian church had died out.

But there were many other strands of Christian teaching that developed in the first generation. Maybe they spread out from Galilee and Jerusalem and changed as they did so. That's easy to understand – journeys were carried out largely on foot, in difficult conditions. There was no Bible, no creed, no church. Teachers had to support themselves as they went along, making converts on the way, sometimes being converted in turn. Or, some scholars say, the teaching developed separately in a number of different centers, and elements of it focused on the figure of Jesus as giving it human definition.

In the absence of any documentation of what Jesus said or thought churches and individuals could interpret him pretty much anyway they wanted. Among the earliest, for example, were the Elchasaites in Syria and south-west Turkey. Compared with the foreign offshoots of Christianity springing up in far-away places like Rome, they were just down the road from Jesus' home patch of Galilee. The Elchasaites retained the Jewish law, circumcised their children, rigidly kept the Sabbath, and didn't accept the heretical innovations of Paul. But they believed that two angels had appeared to their founder, Elchasaios, and told him that Jesus was reincarnated anew every century, and born of a virgin on each occasion. Much as Buddha reincarnates for the salvation of humankind. There were many other churches in the area, each with their own angle. Some held that

Jesus was being continually incarnated in many individuals, a belief that eventually fed into the Imam doctrine of Shi'ite Islam, as did the "perfect man" tradition and others.

Another teaching was that of Thomas, which spread to Persia, and became known eventually as the Nestorian Church. In this form it spread to India and China, where it survived for a thousand years. One convert, called Mani, developed it further into an attractive religion embracing Eastern ideas, with priests committed to poverty and celibacy. In its early days it spread West back to the Roman Empire. Augustine, the most important figure in developing Christian teaching after Paul, was a Manichean before his conversion to Christianity.

Being dedicated to non-violence, Manichean teaching got up the noses of the establishment everywhere. Mani was hanged by the Zoroastrian Magi, and his followers were persecuted in the Roman Empire first by pagans and then by Christians when they had the power. Manicheans survived persecution in Europe till the seventh century, when they disappear from the record.

Christianity didn't begin with a common belief, but was more like a wave of ecstatic experience that in a few centuries rippled around the old world from the Atlantic to the Pacific. It was driven by the Jewish belief in a high, single, universal God who actually loved humankind. This love was manifested in a particular man who had died for their sake. They absorbed this new insight into their own traditions, shaping it in a way that made sense to them.

One interpretation of Jesus, which eventually fed through as the dominant one into what we think of as Christianity today, was that of Paul in the first century AD. Most Jewish scholars see him as the real founder. Christianity as we know it today is after all based on the assumption that Jesus didn't really manage to get his message across, and that Paul had to come along to explain it. None of the 27 books in the New Testament are by Jesus, 13 are attributed to Paul, though 4 to 6 of those are probably the work of others.

In contrast to James, Paul saw Jesus as more than a prophet come to renew Israel's faith. As an educated, cosmopolitan Jew (probably, but a few say Gentile) he would have been familiar with the various competing descriptions of the channel between a transcendent God and people on earth – an intermediary Son, the Greek Logos, the Jewish Wisdom. Paul scaled Jesus up, making him the Lord Christ, a cosmic player in the heavenly drama. He may have developed the idea from a "world ruler" prophecy current in Israel at the time, mentioned in the Dead Sea Scrolls. Other widespread contemporary themes were the Man of Righteousness and the Primal Man, and he may have turned this into the beginning of the doctrine of original sin, linking Adam to Jesus. Paul never comes straight out and says Jesus is divine. There are one or two verses that suggest it, like Philippians 2:6 ("being in the form of God"), but the balance is on the other side. Adam was the first man, from the earth. Jesus was the last, the spiritual "man of heaven," who lived such a perfect life of service that God "designates" him to be His Son (Romans 1:4). Jesus is not equal to God, but he shows the way.

This adoption of Jesus as God's Son seems to happen for Paul at the resurrection (for example, Romans 1:3-4). Mark, writing later, seems to move it forward to the baptism, starting his story when the Spirit of God descends on Jesus in the form of a dove.

Matthew and Luke, writing later still, bring it further forward to the birth, with their two very different narratives. John, the last of the New Testament Gospels, skips the birth and says that there was no time in history when Jesus was not God's Son.

Paul's vision of what Jesus was about was one the Gentiles could understand. He could speak their language, literally and figuratively. He introduced pagan sacraments like the taking of bread and wine (1 Corinthians 11: 23-26), the food of Demeter and drink of Dionysus, to flesh out the new faith with appropriate ritual, claiming to have received knowledge of this through dreams and revelation. But he went too far for most Jews. This quickly threw up questions about what the faith actually was, leading to bitter arguments between Paul and the main Nazarene establishment. In Galatians 2 Paul criticizes James for trying to reconvert Paul's converts back to following the Jewish Law. He was mocked by his fellow Jewish Nazarenes as a "man of dreams," or "liar," or the "enemy of God" (Galatians 4.16.) The *Pseudoclementine Recognitions* even records a possible physical assault by Paul on James.

Of course this is all disputed. The balance of scholarly opinion changes with every decade. Scroll forward from now and the outcome by the end of the twenty first century could be that Jesus is seen as a more historical, political, essentially Jewish figure, and the movement he represented maybe emphasizing the Law still more strongly than the Pharisees. The reverse is equally possible, that Jesus could be seen as a more mythical figure whose essential teachings are irrecoverable. All we can be sure of is that our understanding will be different from the one we have now.

That our understanding has changed in crucial respects over the centuries is surely undeniable. For instance, to take one particular doctrine, mainstream Christianity is unique today amongst the major faiths in that it teaches that humankind is basically lost, damned, in Original Sin. We're condemned from the time we're born, unless we accept God through His Son, or the sacraments, or whatever. The logic is inevitable. If there's no original sin then no savior is needed, no sacrifice by God to save humankind, no need for a literal resurrection. Conservatives are right in that once you start to pick the thread it all unravels.

But the doctrine of original sin goes against the grain of the Jewish Bible, where it's not mentioned. The Hebrews saw life as innately good. The Jews, whose story it is, see Genesis as a hymn to the greatness and goodness of God, not as an account of the fall, which leads to redemption. The idea of the individual rather than the family or tribe having clear responsibility for his or her actions doesn't seem to appear until around the sixth century BC with Ezekiel (Ezekiel 18:2-4, 17-21).

Original sin also runs contrary to the teaching of Jesus, who goes out of his way to affirm people as good rather than bad. The people he condemns are the religious leaders who say the opposite. He says you have to be like a child to enter the kingdom of God (Luke 18:17).

It runs contrary to our understanding of human development today. There is grounding for the idea of inherited traits, sure. Many psychologists say that around half the variation in personality and behavior is inherited, the outcome of our genetic make-up. But the idea that we are all condemned before we start, through an action that had nothing to do with us, goes against common sense. Nobody today believes their child is born evil. The idea is obscene.

It's also immoral. No teaching has led to more mental agony, physical suffering, and villainy. If an individual's original sin condemns him or her to eternal hellfire, then torturing their bodies to save their souls makes sense. It would be wrong not to. Most Christians down the ages have agreed with the logic of this, including all mainstream church leaders and saints up till a few centuries ago when humanist values began to spread through society. The hardline church leaders of today are the inquisitors and witch-burners of yesterday, mellowed by secular society.

At a more prosaic level it simply cuts off believers from everyone else. It's not impossible to love people you believe are intrinsically evil, any more than for poor people to be honest in a community of rich people, but it's a lot harder.

The idea of Original Sin runs counter to everything science tells us, from anthropology through to zoology. It is contrary to the teaching of Jesus, the Bible, common sense, experience and morality. So why do Christians give it a moment's consideration?

Most scholars would agree that the first Christians did not have the sense of original sin and consequent salvation that church tradition has today. The idea was first sketched out by Paul, seven centuries or so after the Genesis story of the fruit and the fall was written down. Paul interpreted the death of Jesus as a sacrifice made by God on our behalf. It was extended by Augustine a few centuries later, another individual obsessed by sins of the flesh. For him Adam and Eve were real people, and their sin of disobedience was passed on down the generations through the act of sex.

But many of Augustine's contemporaries disagreed with him. Pelagius, for instance, Britain's first significant theologian, quoted the Gospels to support the idea that people are born innocent (for example, John 1:17; 12:31-32; Mark 3:28; 1 Corinthians 15:21-22; Romans 5:18; 11:32; 1 John 2:1-2).

Augustine vigorously attacked Pelagius, who was tried three times for heresy, and three times acquitted. Augustine eventually persuaded the Emperor Honorius to pressurize Pope Zosimus into excommunicating his opponent. Augustine was made a saint, and the writings of Pelagius were condemned. Some later churches further hardened this teaching on original sin, as in sixteenth-century Calvinism. Not only were you born evil but God had predestined most for damnation, and they had no chance of salvation. Others rejected it, like the eighteenth-century Quakers.

But was Pope Zosimus right? Maybe you prefer Augustine to Pelagius, or Jesus. The idea of original sin has its uses. If your life is desperate and miserable, if you can't control your appetites, can't stop doing wrong, you may feel that you're in a state of "original sin." In that case, you might jump at the chance of entering a state of grace. But it's Christianity that generated that definition of sin and grace in the first place. There is no sin in nature, it just is. The lion doesn't eat lambs because it's sinful, but because it can't chew and digest grass. There is no "perfect" creation to fall from because it's constantly evolving. Sin came with self-awareness, with society, with laws. Before laws there was nothing to sin against. God is not so small that we can offend Her.

More helpfully, perhaps, the idea of original sin reflects a deep understanding that we have the potential to do better, and have screwed up. We keep falling into "evil" rather than rising to our destinies. If we seek perfection we're bound to fail, and that needs an explanation. As a spin on the Genesis story it explains how we're capable of the most horrible acts, much as being made in God's image explains acts of greatness and self-sacrifice. It encourages you to search your heart, see what you're capable of, to understand the evil to which you can sink. And we're all complicit in the world's suffering. Any religious teaching, even the worst, can stimulate the individual to improve, to have courage, to complete the self in God. That's why religions take hold and survive. They all have these steps that force you to see your self anew and transcend it, to find a deeper happiness than momentary pleasure.

Hinduism, for instance, describes our condition as one of impermanence. In reading and meditating on the sacred scriptures we recognize this and come to an understanding of our "real" selves, the state of *thuriya*. We can restore ourselves to harmony with the cosmic order by offering everything up in a spirit of sacrifice, and become one with the inner reality of all things.

> "He who sees Me everywhere,
> and sees everything in Me,
> I am not lost to him,
> nor is he lost to me."
>
> *Bhagavad-Gita*

THE HISTORY WE CHANGE

This experience is similar to the new birth that Jesus describes. But, and here's the main difference from the later approach developed by his followers, the Brahmins teach that basically people are good, a teaching that is not just good for you psychologically, but makes sense metaphysically. If reality is truth and goodness, then lies and evil must be the illusion. Good must triumph. Islam takes a similar approach, believing that humankind was originally sinless and peaceful. If, on the contrary, you believe that people are intrinsically evil, and you expect that of them, you're likely to get what you look for.

Buddhism takes the theme of self as process even further. I identify my "self" with my sensations, feelings, emotions, my character, and beliefs. Behind that we all have "Buddha nature," *anatta*, no-self. We understand who we really are by going beyond these, to the awareness that all living things have in common. We can realize this suddenly, or, more likely, through a long process of deepening awareness.

Every religion has a different technique. In Taoist China if you've been a prodigal son and strayed from the right path, you can return to the fold by reconciliation with your family and ancestors. All these beliefs work for the people who think in those ways.

No one is condemned through Adam's disobedience. No one starts life with a core of evil. That's Satanism, not Christianity, or not what it should be. Of all the teachings in the world this is one of the furthest from good religion. Let's start with the idea that creation is good, that life is an incredible gift. Recognizing it and being thankful for it is the start of the road to happiness and wisdom. We're all in need of forgiveness and grace. But this is a virtuous circle between ourselves, our neighbors, and God. Not a one track line between God and us. We're not so blesssed with goodness that we can afford to dismiss the little we have. The point of believing in God is to expand its area in your life and the world, not diminish it.

Maybe if it hadn't been for the Jewish rebellion of AD 68-70 and the dispersal of the Jews things would have turned out differently. We wouldn't have ended up with this guilt-obsessed, flesh-denying new religion (though this kind of transformation is frequent, think for instance of the difference between the *Kama Sutra* and Hindu attitudes to sex today). The Jewish Christians might have carried on growing in strength. They might have remained a reforming movement within Judaism. But two-thirds of the Jewish population were killed or fled the country in the subsequent suppression. The aftermath was hostile and bitter, with some Jews like Josephus switching sides to save their skins.

Moving on to the second century most Christians were Gentiles rather than Jews, with Pauline Christianity one strand amongst many. The "Jewishness" of Christianity was being edited out. The idea that Jesus had been a messiah for the Jews and had come for them only (Matthew 10:5-6) had gone. So had other ideas: that he would return in their lifetimes (Matthew 16:27-28; Luke 9:27; 21:32), that the disciples had a role in establishing the new kingdom and judging it (Matthew 19:27-29), and that a new Temple was going to be built (John 2:19). The heartland of Christianity had migrated from Jerusalem and Palestine to the high-rise urban slums of the major towns and seaports of the Eastern Mediterranean. Its appeal was to

Gentiles rather than Jews.

In the first century, Jews account for all the main church leaders and writers (with the possible exception of Luke). After that, for 20 centuries, none are Jews. In the view of the Jews, the Nazarenes/Christians had betrayed both faith and people, selling themselves to the Roman enemy for converts and cash. Christians responded by saying that the Jews had murdered God. This began a state of one-sided war that continued for two millennia until its appalling climax in our grandparents' generation, with the holocaust.

As the movement lost its Jewish identity it increasingly appealed to many known today as "Gnostics" ("those in the know", same meaning as "shaman"). The Gnostics took religion seriously, the "seekers" of their age. They saw themselves as moving beyond the gods of mountaintops and rivers, beyond laws and doctrine, to the worship of God as Spirit. Which means it's hard to know what they thought, their teaching is often vague and contradictory. The central idea is that God is the mind of the cosmos, thinking or dreaming it into existence. And you can know God directly; He is within you. Self-knowledge is knowledge of God. The cosmos is now becoming conscious of itself through conscious beings. In different traditions Gnostics developed a variety of initiation ceremonies and layers of knowledge that enable us to awaken to our shared consciousness with the divine.

There were Gnostics in many religious traditions in the Empire. Most followed various god-men, and it's hard to say how far they changed Christian thinking to their own mold (as conservative Christians claim) or how far the early Christians adopted some of their ideas. Some of their books on similar themes are certainly independent of Christianity, or predate it, like the *Apocrypha of John* (20, 1-8) and the *Apocalypse of Adam* (76, 9-77, 18).

Those who began converting to Christianity saw that the all-too-human books of the Old Testament couldn't have been written by the single almighty good God. Nor could the world, imperfect as it is, have been created by Him. Yahweh, son of El, brother of Baal and Yam, is surely one of thousands of minor tribal deities, with little theology and no sense of individual salvation, or perhaps a rogue god. On their reading of the Jewish scriptures they saw Yahweh as vengeful and arbitrary, favoring the Jews for no good reason, frequently threatening destruction and doing evil; a demonic being who imprisoned man in his material body. Humankind's real father must have been the true God above him, and Sophia its mother. So some worshiped the villains and "anti-heroes" of the Old Testament, like Cain. Others went as far as to say that all gods and demons were figments of our imagination. According to the *Gospel of Philip*, "Human beings made gods, and worship their creation. It would be appropriate for the gods to worship human beings" (71:35-72:4). He had a point.

For Gnostics the idea of Jesus as being literally resurrected from the dead may have seemed a crude simplification, if they had heard of it at all. They did not even believe that Jesus died on the cross. Some thought that Simon of Cyrene changed places with him when he carried Jesus' cross. Others believed that Jesus had a separate spiritual form that descended on him at baptism as a dove, and left him to go back to heaven when he died. But in any case his physical existence was unimportant. What mattered to them was their immediate experience of the still-living Jesus who speaks of enlightenment from illusion rather than salvation from sin, a manifestation of God on earth who showed us how to sweep away all the minor gods and bring us direct to the Highest One.

Up until a few decades ago it was assumed that Gnostic Christians were an unimportant offshoot of the main Christian church. They've been so effectively buried that most of their writings have only been discovered in the last century. Now they're increasingly seen as playing a more important role, though conservatives continue to say that they're not significant, or if they are that they're plain wrong. A few scholars suggest that Christian Gnosticism predates what later became the orthodox tradition and is closer to the teaching of Jesus.

The basic idea of Gnosticism, that the material world is inherently evil and each person is imprisoned within it, to be freed by the spirit of Jesus, comes in the *Gospel of Thomas*, which is probably earlier than any of the New Testament Gospels, and the gospel most likely to have been written by an actual disciple of Jesus, though most Christian scholars dispute this. Some scholars say, on the basis of hints from hostile writers like Polycarp and Tertullian, that Gnostics were in the majority. The literalists were a minority whose vision for a more controlled religion captured the imagination of an authoritarian ruler. We'll probably never know, and it doesn't matter, unless you measure truth in terms of numbers of supporters. In which case we're probably only talking about a townful of people anyway.

Whichever, there was probably never a clear-cut divide between Gnosticism and what was to become orthodox Christianity, any more than there is between conservatives and liberals today. Some of their traditions were assimilated, with the origins gradually forgotten. The sacraments are possibly an example. They early on became the center of Christian worship and identity, as they are today for the huge majority of Christians, but they scarcely figure in the New Testament. The importance of the sacraments in the early church may originate with Christian Gnosticism where membership rituals were important. They probably owe more to works like the early *Gospel of Philip*, which may have been learned and chanted by early Christian believers, than to the New Testament. One of the reasons this gospel didn't make it into the canon was its stress on the earthy, sexual nature of Jesus, particularly in his relationship with Mary Magdalene, which was hard to reconcile with his increasing divinity.

The divine Emperor Diocletian outlawed the Gnostics in AD 295, and their influence waned. By the fourth century AD most believers were taking it all literally, and had started going to the Holy Land as tourists. As in any pagan cult, places and objects were given sacred status, turned into holy sites and relics. In the choice between the Gnostic idea of Jesus as a teacher of wisdom and God within you, or Jesus as the almighty Son of God coming to rule and deliver judgement, the Almighty won.

But it could have gone the other way, in which case Christianity might have ended up much closer to the Eastern religions of today, as indeed did happen outside the Roman Empire in the East. In the *Gospel of Thomas* you can substitute the word "Buddha" for "Jesus" without much altering the sense. Later writings like *The Book of the Blessed* by Justin the Gnostic draw on a range of religious experience including the Hindu Lord Shiva, before pointing to Jesus as fulfilling God's plan. This dialogue between the religions has only really been picked up again in the last few decades.

Gnosticism continued through the centuries in Judaism through the Kabbalists, in Islam through Sufi mystics. In Christianity it remained strong in the Pauline churches of Asia Minor and threads continued through the centuries.

It was also during the second century AD that Christians began to think it would be a good idea to collect their very diverse accounts of the words and life of Jesus (we know of around 70) into a more coherent, single account. By now they were increasingly diverging, becoming more imaginative and magical.

But because the Gospels reflected their different beliefs, the scattered churches found it impossible to agree on one. Some Jews preferred Matthew because of its Jewishness and insistence on adhering to every jot of the Law (Matthew 5:18). Gentiles preferred others that supported non-observance of the Jewish Law. Gnostics liked John, with its rejection of the world, or the *Gospel of Thomas*.

The lead was taken by the Gnostics, those at the cutting edge of the new religion. The first attempt to draw up a definitive list of Christian scripture was made in the middle of the second century by Marcion, a key figure in the early church. He wasn't what we would today call a Trinitarian Christian. The term and the teaching hadn't been thought of yet. And like many Gentiles, he found the morality in the pagan writings to be better than that in what later became known as the "Old Testament."

Marcion thought that there should obviously be only one authoritative Gospel, and he chose that of Luke, but edited it to remove all mention of the Jews and references to the Old Testament. He saw Christianity as a new religion that had no need of Jewish scripture. He also edited the letters of Paul to make him show Jesus teaching a God of love, not fear.

Valentinus was a leading contemporary of Marcion. He hated the idea of a definitive list. Each believer had the truth within himself, so why shouldn't everyone write their own gospel? He showed the way, with his own *Gospel of Truth*.

In the mid-second century Tatian wrote a single harmonized account, based on the four Gospels (the *Diatessaron*). This was accepted by the Syrian but not the Greek and Latin churches. It was probably more widely read by Christians than the canonical Gospels up to the eighth century, when it was banned.

Many Christians in the second century identified with the teaching of Valentinus or Marcion, rather than Paul or James, Peter or Thomas. Despite persecution by other Christians, Marcionite communities were still flourishing in Syria 300 years later. But as the church grew in importance over the next couple of centuries, the pressures to create an established official scripture increased. When Christianity became the state religion the impetus was overwhelming. By now it had responsibility for vast tracts of land, multitudes of slaves, and needed to get its act together to play its role in the management of Empire. The church needed a single "belief" and a "history."

So what was it to be? Was the church going to splinter into a number of different sects or religions, or were Christians going to stick together and exercise power? Numbers or truth? Impact or purity? It's the problem that bedevils all religions down the ages.

The epistles of Paul had widespread support. He was the guy who got it going, who explained the cosmic significance of the Christ figure to the Gentiles. His letters could be read by the now-orthodox as supporting a literal, historical Christ as Savior, and by the Gnostics as supporting a view of Jesus as a spiritual rather than historical figure. He implies further revelation to come in the Gnostic manner. In 2 Corinthians 12:2-4 for instance he refers to a time when he was physically transported to the third heaven (there were usually seven levels, perhaps paralleling the Eastern idea of seven centers of consciousness in the body, described as *chakras*), and also to paradise, where he "heard unspeakable words, which it is not lawful for a man to utter." They were accepted as canonical (authoritative) by around AD 200, and the bulk of the New Testament as we understand it today had general acceptance by AD 300.

Early in the fourth century, a 300-year gap, a similar period from the founding of the USA to now, Eusebius drew up what came to be the list that most agree on today. He leaves out the *Acts of Paul*, the *Shepherd of Hermas*, the *Revelation of Peter*, the *Letter of Barnabas*, which up till then many churches had considered authoritative, and he includes *Revelation* and *Hebrews*, which had previously been excluded. The first "Bibles" now begin to appear, though even then they were referred to in the Greek as "the books" rather than "book."

But it wasn't till the fifth century that Eastern and Western Churches in the Empire finally agreed on the selection, with the former accepting Revelation and the latter accepting Hebrews. Agreement was never universal. The Protestant Reformation brought further changes, dropping 12 of the Old Testament books, the "deuterocanonical"writings or the "Apocrypha." Martin Luther wanted to go further and drop James and Revelation as well.

The definitive "Holy Bible" is an illusion. The Syrian Church still recognizes only 22 of our 27 New Testament books; the Armenian Church includes a *Third Letter of Paul to the Corinthians*; the Ethiopian Church has a different selection again. These may be minor Churches in the twenty-first century but at the time they were important ones. The Syrian Church covered the heartland of Paul's missionary efforts. For the first few centuries more Christians lived there than anywhere else. Ethiopia was one of the first significant Christian areas, and Armenia was the first Christian state. They certainly can't all be right, maybe they all got it wrong.

So where should we draw the line on what to include? Why shouldn't we write a "new" New Testament today? Why stop in the fourth century AD, or the sixteenth? Why not follow the vision and the courage of the early Christians, open Pandora's box, and shape our faith to suit our times, as they did? Perhaps we could then find again the exhilarating sense of liberation they had in the first century, when a bunch of motley peasants believed they could turn the world upside down because they had the vision and the faith for a new one.

14

THE TRUTHS
WE INVENT

"The most scandalous charges were suppressed; the vicar of Christ was only accused of piracy, rape, sodomy and incest."

Edward Gibbon on the condemnation of one of the rival popes in 1425

The Gnostics, following their individual pursuit of truth, were fragmented and disorganized. The diverse range of views in the early church about who Jesus was gradually coalesced in the Empire under the influence of some persuasive philosopher/theologians known today as the early church fathers. Christian history tends to treat them as if they were the only such characters of their time, but they represented only a small range of the intellectual talent around the Mediterranean world, and were perhaps outshone by Buddhist philosophers of the same period farther East, thinkers like Nagarjuna. Even so the majority of scholars, those outside religious institutions at least, do not see them as judicious saints representing the central teaching of Christianity and bringing the church into some already-existing orthodoxy. They were radical, sometimes unstable, certainly heretical (by later standards) teachers who shifted the center of the faith.

Origen for instance believed that the Father, Son, and Holy Spirit were of descending importance, that the sun and moon had souls, and in the pre-existence of the soul (which seems logical, if you believe in its after-existence). Clement believed that Jesus was not wholly human but had a semi-divine body that didn't need to digest food and drink. Justin Martyr, a Samaritan, was perhaps the most important of the early ones. He established Christianity as a credible religion for the intellectuals of the Roman world, and did this by gutting it of its Jewish roots. He describes God as the supreme transcendent Being, operating through His Word, the Logos. This Logos had scattered itself around the world in the hearts of all people, so that everyone had traces of it. For Justin any lover of truth counted as a Christian – Greek philosophers were Christian without knowing it.

With the exception of Justin none of the half-dozen major early apologists for Christianity up till the year AD 180 (after that Irenaeus, Clement of Alexandria, Origen, and Tertullian are rooted in the Gospel tradition) refer to the Gospels in their presentation of Christianity to the Roman world. They appeal to the logic of a single God and a single intermediary, rather than to a historical figure who was born of a virgin and raised from the dead.

The church fathers made Christianity a credible possibility for those particular times, turning Jesus into a kind of avatar of God, much as Krishna is an avatar of Vishnu (there's little suggestion so far that he's co-equal with God). But not a necessary one. Christianity would probably have remained one of many cults in the melting pot of the Empire, to be forgotten or absorbed in the others (if indeed it could be described as one cult rather than several), were it not for the Emperor Constantine.

Constantine clawed his way to the top of the greasy pole in the early fourth century AD. Like a corporate empire builder of today, he wanted a new mission statement. The "Roman Way" of the previous centuries was no longer the driving force that had created the world's most remarkable Empire ever. Its resolution was weakening: too many different peoples and cultures had been assimilated at the bottom; too much wealth and corruption had rotted the top. Energetic tribes on the borders were threatening. The old Roman gods had lost their sway. There were still the mysteries of Eleusis and Orpheus, and the more intellectual faiths of Platonism, Stoicism, and Epicureanism from Greece. But these were remote and abstract for most. As in the West today a gap was left in the popular imagination into which numerous intermediaries flooded. These included the cults of Isis from Egypt, Cybele from Asia Minor, Astarte from Syria, Mithraism from Persia, Judaism and Christianity from Palestine.

Christianity had an edge in that it rooted the esoteric salvation philosophies of the time in a down-to-earth individual, a single god-man, which the majority could readily understand. Now Constantine wanted unity and obedience in matters of state and religion, a common belief that would combine the two. Mithraism had been the main contender in the previous century. The cult of the Sun God, *Sol Invictus*, was also significant – Constantine may have confused this with Christianity, and often switched from one to the other. As indeed did the church, adopting the Sun God's halo for the divine family and saints, changing the Sabbath from Saturday to "Sun"day. The Christian faith may have won out because it was the best organized (we still talk about "dioceses," based on the Roman provinces). It wasn't elitist like Mithraism, it could deliver the mobs. Perhaps the most persuasive argument for Constantine was that as emperor he was able to usurp some of the functions attributed to Jesus (so Eusebius tells us).

So Constantine converted to Christianity, the key moment apparently being at the Milvian Bridge in Rome on 28 October AD 312 when legend has it that he saw a flaming cross in the sky and the words "In this sign conquer" during the decisive battle with his rival for the throne, Maxentius.

There were approximately ten million people in the Empire at the time of Constantine's conversion, about 10% of the world's population, and about 10% of them were Christians – one million is the best guess we have. About three centuries after the death of Jesus 1% of the world's population were Christian. It's around now that historians start talking of Christianity as a religion rather than a cult.

Christianity had taken a big step, but it was a very fragmented one. By the fourth century there were Adoptionists, Antidocommarians, Apollinarianists, Arians, Cerinthians, Collyridians, Docetists, Ebionites, Gnostics, Monophysites, Montanists, Nestorians, Phibionites, and many others, reflecting different fusions of local traditions. And that's just the ones in the Roman Empire. They variously described Jesus as an ordinary man, a teacher of wisdom, the Teacher of Righteousness, a prophet, the True Prophet, the Primal Man, the Messiah, an angel, God's Anointed, the Son of God, the True God, and a score of others.

These beliefs were not mutually exclusive. Much as many today believe that the universal life force can be tapped through a variety of different methods – aromatherapy, astrology, reflexology, etc. – there were many ways in the first couple of centuries of experiencing the liberation that Jesus brought for those looking for a channel to the universal God. Certain beliefs became more precise and dogmatic as they were teased out and separated in Greek, the language of philosophy, and then codified in Latin, the language of law and confession. But for the first ten generations or so you could believe at any one of these points on the spectrum and be a Christian. There was no coherent central belief system to persuade converts. What impressed pagans (in the first century or two) was the love Christians showed, "Christian is as Christian does," not their theology, which hadn't yet been written.

But Constantine wanted clarity and control. He summoned a general assembly of bishops, mostly from the Western provinces of the Empire, none from beyond the borders where his writ did not run, to meet at Nicea, near Nicomedia, to sort out the doctrine. They produced the Nicean creed, still spoken in many churches around the world today as a summary of the essentials of the Christian faith. But the most interesting thing about it is what it leaves out, which is pretty much everything that you would think should go in. It doesn't, for example, quote Jesus at all. It doesn't give any indication of how we should live. It only refers indirectly to the big questions of sin and eternal life. No mention of forgiveness, happiness, justice, love. The core of Jesus' message – "Love the Lord your God . . . love your neighbor as yourself," and the kingdom itself – has disappeared. Most of its ritual chant revolves around Jesus' relationship with the Father, how he was begotten by God and no one else, of the same, and not a similar, substance. The creed is a party platform reflecting the intensity of the spiritual power-politics of the time, every phrase countering what had come to be regarded as heresy by those wanting an authoritarian state religion that glorified the emperor.

So for the last 1,500 years or so the nature of Jesus and his relationship to God has been defined in the doctrine of the Trinity. This is worth exploring further because for many you have to believe in the Trinity to be a proper Christian. Which seems truly bizarre, as it is such a late development. There's no mention of the Trinity as such in the Bible. The clearest reference is in Matthew 28:19, which is probably a later addition. It still doesn't assert that "the three are one," and non-unitarian churches use this formula without drawing the conclusion that it implies belief in the Trinity. There's an oblique reference in 1 John 5:7-8, which doesn't appear in the oldest and most reliable manuscripts and was almost certainly added later, and possibly in a couple of Paul's letters. That's about all, out of 33,173 verses. It doesn't feature in Jesus' teaching. He wouldn't have known what was meant by it. It's one of the Capital Letter Doctrines that the church developed in the first four centuries, and it took a further five centuries or so to become generally accepted in Europe.

But what did the fourth-century Christians think it meant? Short answer, they didn't know, which is why they argued so much. Are there three separate centers of consciousness or not? No one really understands this, and theologians still argue over it, 1,700 years later. Strictly speaking, believing in the Father God and identifying Him with God, which perhaps most Christians do, is a heresy called Monarchianism. The issue goes to the heart of the complication of Christianity, which evolved as a compromise between the Jewish view of a single omniscient God, and the Roman/Greek pantheon of many gods and their different families and relations. It left us a muddle.

Do we now really have one God, or two, or three? It's a new kind of problem, one that didn't exist for those who believed in many gods, or only one God with no family. If Jesus was God's Son, there surely must have been a time when God existed and

Jesus didn't. So wasn't he then of secondary importance? If he was not secondary, and had always been around, and was God, then did he have sex with his own mother? That must logically be the case, and the *Epistula Apostolorum*, a book considered canonical by parts of the early church, thought so: "And I, the Word, went into her and became flesh; and I myself was servant for myself, and in the form of an angel; so I will do after I have gone to my Father."

As well as creating a problem about who exactly God was, the Trinity gave a problem about Jesus. To reconcile those who thought Jesus must be man, and those who thought he must be God, the doctrine of "hypostatic union" (the union of persons) was developed: he was man and God in one. But this only shifted the problem along. If Jesus and God were the same, what was the point of the different entities? An attempt to explain this conundrum was given the name "modalism." This solution, which appeared around AD 200, may have been followed by the majority of Christians. It said that God was one deity with three different phases. God the Father changed into God the Son at the virgin birth, and then became God the Spirit at the resurrection.

Modalism kept both the one God and the deity of Jesus intact. But it caused its own difficulties. If God the Father turned into God the Son, leaving heaven empty, then who was Jesus praying to when he was on earth?

There were other solutions, like Patripassianism, which held that it was really God the Father who suffered on the cross. But the main, obvious alternative, called Arianism, was that Jesus was less than the Father but more than human.

It's hard today, after nearly two millennia of taking the Trinity for granted as the definition for correct belief in God, with Jesus as co-equal with Him, to get an idea of the intensity with which these positions were debated. Today, when the idea of god-men is so incomprehensible, we've just lost the sense of how central it was to the society of the time. At the Council of Nicea the followers of Athanasius combined with those of Marcellus to win the day, fighting it out in the streets, but the controversy continued for 60 and more years afterwards. It was touch and go who would win. Support for one side or the other changed according to fluctuating political and military fortunes, with Athanasius being exiled five times. It was an Arian bishop who baptized Constantine as he lay dying. Success for the Athanasian Trinitarian formula came down to the toss of a political coin, and who could afford the most thugs.

Conservative Christians say that the Spirit of God, who became known as the Holy Spirit, worked through life on earth to insure that the right decisions were made. But church councils were not peaceful affairs where the mind of God was sought in a spirit of love and tolerance. They were often vitriolic and bloody. The stakes were high. Defeated opponents were exiled, not pensioned off. Athanasius was hesitant about attending the Council of Tyre (AD 335) as he feared for his safety. One of his supporters, the presbyter Makarios, had been accused of the kidnapping and murder of Bishop Arsenios. Arius was ultimately struck down by a mysterious illness – caused, some believed, by poison – and according to Athanasius himself ended his life "split in pieces in a public lavatory." Others say he was executed for his beliefs.

Constantine himself was a vicious individual, and being converted did nothing to improve his character. It would be nice to think that the first Christian emperor ushered in a golden period of tolerance, peace, knowledge, artistic achievement, much as did the first Buddhist Emperor, Ashoka. But he murdered his rivals rather than imprisoning or exiling them. He even executed his eldest son, Crispus, and his brother-in-law. He had his second wife Flavia tortured to death by slow immersion in boiling water.

In later years the Empire itself came apart over these linguistic subtleties. The German tribes of central Europe were largely baptized as Arians, and their war cry as they conquered the later Roman capital of Ravenna was, "The Father is greater than the Son." It's reminiscent of Jonathan Swift's Lilliputians in *Gulliver's Travels*, who go to war over whether to cut a boiled egg at the fat or thin end. It was all unnecessary, as Jesus is no more closely related to God than the rest of us. The Trinity just marks the point where Christianity stopped having much to do with the teaching of Jesus and modeled itself on contemporary pagan religion.

There's nothing unique about the Trinity. As soon as gods drop their guard they're likely to be split into threesomes, a magic number of completeness, often representing unity (God), particularity or diversity (Jesus), and a feminine principle (Spirit). There are hundreds of them. The Hebrews would have been familiar with many, some of which feature in the Old Testament. The Egyptians have Osiris, Isis, and Horus; the Babylonians Anu, Ea, Enlil, or the later Apsu, Tiamat, Mummu. Then there's the Sumerian Inanna, Erishkegal, Dumuzi; the

Ugaritic El, Ashtoret and Baal; the Alexandrian Serapis, Isis, and Aubis, etc. Many trinities are more comprehensible than the Christian one. For example, the Hindu trinity of the three forms of God – Brahma the Creator, Vishnu the Preserver, and Shiva the Destroyer – at least reflects more of the rhythm of creation, the reality of life as we know it. Still farther east, Chinese religion has the triad of Heaven, Earth, and Man.

The point of taking the Trinity seriously is not that it's uniquely Christian, but common religious currency. Mystics might say the world is one and we can know it as such. Rationalists that we know it through the particular. Most say you leave out the feminine at your peril. By definition the mystics have difficulty in saying what they're talking about. The rationalists must agree that particulars add up to something else. The feminists mostly agree they need a male to define themselves against.

So some Christians explain the Trinity by saying it represents God outside the world, God acting in the world (Jesus), and through the world (Holy Spirit). Much as Hindus talk of the knower (*Rishi*), the act of knowing (*Devata*), and the object known (*Chhandas*), all aspects of a single reality. The twelfth-century Joachim phrased it progressively: the Hebrew religion centered on God as Father, based on law; Christianity centered on the Son, based on the gospel; today we focus on the Spirit, an age of freedom based on direct spiritual revelation. Or perhaps we can characterize them by different functions. There's the creator Father who gave us life; the Son who came and showed us what matters in life; the Spirit who enables us to do something about it. There's scope here for endless rewriting. It's like having mind, body, and spirit. Ego, superego, and id. But as a precise idea the Trinity is meaningless today to most. Those who believe in it have difficulty saying exactly what it is, or why anyone else should hope to understand it.

The fourth century was the most remarkable ever for Christianity, the turning-point. At the beginning of the century it was a minor cult in the Empire. At the end it was the only permissible religion. This meteoric rise in status drove the writing of the creeds, the establishment of the papacy in Rome (rather than the popes in Antioch and other places) as the supreme power in the church, and the creation of the Bible. The Emperor Julian (AD 361-363) tried to turn the clock back and restore paganism, but failed. Theodosius (379-395) made Christianity the only religion, banning the worship of pagan gods in AD 392. In the *Codex Theodosianus* he declares other religions to be "demented and insane," and states that their followers can be punished and executed. The pragmatic Roman approach of accepting any religion as long as the emperor got his dues was abandoned. Their talent for living comfortably with a number of different perspectives on life began to disappear. Ignorance even came to be seen as a positive spiritual virtue, and intelligent criticism and questioning a vice.

It was Augustine (354-430), a theologian of genius, who unwittingly made this possible. He pulled together various strands of early church teaching into a new definition of the relationships between the individual and God, society and the church. He gave the church a sacred status of its own. Salvation could now only be obtained through it. Sacraments were even valid if administered by unholy priests. The laws of God, as interpreted by the church, were superior to the individual conscience and it was okay to force people into belief. Only God knows and chooses who will be saved. Faith, along the lines started by Paul, was only faith if you could accept what you were told, and by him rather than someone else. His successors drove the nails into the coffin of the kingdom, granting the church a monopoly on permissible belief that lasted for the next millennium.

Christianity accordingly shifted in the fourth century from a religion of the persecuted to the persecutors. The Donatists for instance were a numerous sect who believed in a pure, non-worldly version of the church, for which they were prepared to suffer and die. Augustine made his name by confronting them, and was the first person we know of in history to advocate war and persecution on theological grounds. Donatists became the first Christians to be murdered in significant numbers by other Christians. In the fourth and fifth centuries Christians probably killed more of each other than had been killed by the pagans in the previous three centuries.

In the context of these divisions and developments it's not difficult to understand why, in the seventh and eighth centuries, many turned with relief to Islam, a faith that simply regards Jesus as a very enlightened prophet. Some at first saw Islam as a new Christian movement, maybe even a reformation. Many Christians converted to it as a Roman Catholic might convert to Protestantism, shedding a cartload of doctrines and practices that to Semitic speakers may have seemed like foreign Greek imports, in their place restoring the power, presence, and unity of God. Muslims saw themselves as bringing back the faith of

Abraham, believing in the one true God, shedding the oppressive theology, and the denial of the grace of good works that had developed in the Christian churches.

For Muslims the very idea that God needs to go around begetting bits of Himself to get things done is heresy, reducing His divinity and glory. The Greek language itself is insufficient to convey His majesty. Within a century of Muhammad's death the heartland of Christianity in the Middle East and North Africa was largely Muslim, and has remained that way.

15

THE DAMAGE WE DO

"There lies at the back of every creed something terrible and hard for which the worshipper may one day be required to suffer."

E.M.Forster

The teaching of Jesus built on the best spiritual insights of the time, of all time. It re-interprets God up in the heavens as God living amongst us. In our lives we make Him real. In our actions we create Her kingdom. Later Christians turned this inside out. They interpreted Jesus himself as God coming to earth. They reversed the religion into the pagan ones of the time, putting God back up in the heavens, giving Him a family, turning Him into a fearsome judge and monarch who threatened to destroy humankind for not recognizing Him as such.

What was the result? There's still 1,500 years or so of history between then and now, and I'm running out of space and your patience. So just one chapter to go before we catch up with today.

Christianity had emerged as a significant religion in the world by the fifth century AD, but it didn't turn it upside down in the way that some of the first disciples hoped and Christians today imagine. The record of success was mixed. Centralized control in the West didn't encourage creativity. There are relatively few significant theologians or writers from the second half of the first millennium. Islam in large part replaced Christianity across the Old World from the Atlantic to the Pacific, with the church clinging on in Europe, nearly disappearing under the barbarian invasions from the forests and plains to the east. By the end of the first millennium there were probably fewer Christians in the world than there had been 500 years earlier.

But by the end of the first millennium we can recognize the religion we know today. Churches from that time are still standing. By a few centuries later we're speaking the same languages in Europe that we speak today. We can relate more directly to the writers. We can look back and make some judgements about the religion's impact on the world. Has it been a "good thing?"

We tend to assume it must have been, even if we don't call ourselves Christian. We live within the results, and they've been good for us. We live in relatively peaceful, democratic, stable, and wealthy societies, and up till recently at least they were undeniably "Christian." But all these are new developments and, like anyone who's better off than their neighbors, we also tend to turn a blind eye to the cost of getting there.

We could take any century to explore the implications of this, but let's take a halfway point, 500 years ago. The majority of the world's population followed one of seven major religions: Christianity, Islam, Hinduism, Buddhism, the South American sun religions, and in the Far East Confucianism and Taoism. Each of these cultures had enormously impressive achievements in various fields – science, astronomy, architecture, engineering, literature, art, and so on.

Numerically Christianity was probably the smallest of the seven faiths. The monarchies of Christian Europe were developing a technological edge, but its cities were like villages compared with the metropolises to be found in the Far East and Central America. The idea that white Europeans always conquer colored natives was still centuries away. Christian Europe itself was still at risk from the Muslims, who in the fifteenth century had penetrated as far as central France and besieged Vienna in 1529. From a global historical perspective it's just as likely in those days that the East could have ended up ruling the West rather than vice versa.

Nevertheless the sixteenth century was a good one for Christianity. In contrast to the paucity of Christian leaders and thinkers in the twentieth century, it gave rise in Europe to a number of outstanding ones – Calvin, Colet, Cranmer, Erasmus, Knox, Loyola, Luther, More, Savonarola, Tyndale, Xavier, Zwingli, etc. They all changed the shape of Christianity in different ways, but none had quite the same global impact as Cortez. In 1519 he and 314 fellow-soldiers and adventurers beached their ships at Veracruz (the Rich City of the True Cross) in Central America and set out to conquer the fabled Aztec Empire. The odds against success were incredible: a few hundred against millions. The Spaniards were driven by a powerful combination of extreme greed for gold and glory – for themselves and God. They knew their lives were on the line, it was conquer or die. They took their chance with extraordinary courage and ruthlessness.

They needed these qualities, in abundance. The Aztecs were not peace-loving softies. Their Empire was built on tribute, much of it in the form of human sacrifices. To keep the sun turning in the sky, human beings had to die on their altars, with priests ripping out their still-beating hearts; 20,000 were sacrificed at the dedication of the great pyramid of Tenochtitlan, a city four or five times the size of the largest in Europe. They were a society geared to constant warfare, conquering territory to maintain the supply of sacrificial victims. At the time of the invasion, their emperor, Montezuma, was an aggressive leader and campaigner.

Nor were they primitive. In some ways they were more

advanced than the Europeans. From the Mayan civilization in the Yucatan peninsular they had inherited a calendar more accurate in some respects than the one we use today (based on a solar calendar of 365 days and 6 hours, a ceremonial year of 260 days, and a Venus year of 584 days). The Mayans had made astronomical calculations extending over millions of years. A thousand years ago, they forecast the 1991 eclipse of the sun. We have a more accurate knowledge of the dates of their emperors than of the kings who were their contemporaries in the Dark Ages of Christian Europe.

Yet within a couple of years Cortez was in power and the emperor was in prison, shortly to be killed. How did it happen? There were many factors, notably the defection to Spain of tribute tribes, but the main single reason may have been the confusion of the Aztecs as to who these strange god-like people were, with their horses, ocean-going ships, and guns, which they had never seen before. The Aztecs had a god called Quetzalcoatl or "Feathered Snake" (inherited from the Mayan Kukulcan), who was the re-creator of the world. Born of a virgin, with a cross as a symbol, he was resurrected, and dived to the underworld to regain the bones of the dead, who he re-animated. He had promised to return one day from the east to restore his rule and bring prosperity.

The Aztecs mistook the Spaniards, also coming from the east in their feathered ships, riding extraordinary animals, killing at a distance with flashes of noise and light, for the gods in the story. Montezuma is reported as saying, "This is the same lord for whom we are waiting." The Aztecs thought their gods had actually stepped out of the myth and arrived. The year 1519 was their "Year of the One Reed" when the bearded Quetzalcoatl was to return, when the different calendars synchronized.

The religions we've mentioned so far have been largely in the Old World, but even in the Aztec Empire, 5,000 miles away, with no prior contact, we find the same themes of sacrifice and resurrection, virgin birth and second coming. In the Aztec sacrificial system, the victims represented the gods, the priests consecrated the body and blood, and onlookers shared the flesh to identify themselves with the gods. Spanish priests noted the similarity to the Eucharist and saw the Aztec religion as the devil perverting the truth. And in many ways it was a truly nasty religion, though it has to be said that many victims probably went voluntarily, seeing their death as a passage to paradise.

But the main point of the story is that it shows the dark side of religions that rely on central authority, claiming to be exclusively true for everyone and demanding to be believed, of which Christianity was the first. The arrival of Cortez was the first of the huge land-grabs of modern times, when European Christian nations used superior technology to subdue and largely eliminate the inhabitants of entire continents. It was driven as much by religion as plunder and sanction for it was given to the Spanish and Portuguese by papal bulls of the fifteenth century. The Protestant Dutch and English followed in their wake. By the time Cortez arrived at Veracruz the 3 million-strong native Taino population of Haiti, where Columbus had landed, had already been almost wiped out, with many committing suicide rather than continuing to endure the savage torture and sexual abuse that the Christians routinely inflicted on them. By the middle of the sixteenth century there was not a single Taino left alive.

By the mid-seventeenth century the original population of what is now Mexico had been reduced from 25 million to 1 million. By the mid-eighteenth around 90% of the indigenous population of the whole of South America had been wiped out. In total there are around 1 million pure-blood descendants of the native American population today, north and south, compared with 100 million in the 1600s.

A few, a very few, churchmen questioned whether European nations had the right to conquer, enslave, and kill, and the intention was not genocide, but that was the result. The guns began it all; European flu and smallpox counted for most of the deaths. Churchmen and missionaries did their best to stamp out what was left of the original culture. Native scribes were singled out for persecution, to the extent that within a century of Cortez the art of writing itself had almost disappeared amongst the Mayan people, though they had previously equaled the Europeans in literacy and epic works. Their civilization along with that of the Incas and dozens of other nations was obliterated.

Catholics got to South America first, but much the same happened in North America and Australia with the Protestants, though the numbers involved were fewer, those areas being less densely populated. Africa escaped relatively lightly because the Arabs controlled the north and the mosquitoes the middle. Even so, around 24 million were carried off by Europeans (mostly in English ships) to work as slaves in the newly-emptied lands of the Americas, with another 12 million dying en route. And we're talking here about a period when the population of England itself was around 5 million. Over 70% of the migrants who were shipped into North America between 1580 and 1820 were black. The reason it remained predominantly white is because their treatment was so inhumane. They died young.

Historical population figures involve a lot of guesswork. But best estimates suggest that the worldwide population in the sixteenth century was around 500 million. Christians amounted to about 10%, or 50 million. Over the next century or two, by means of conquest and colonization, Christians killed off another 10%. By the twentieth century Christianity had increased its "market share" to around 30% of the world's population, where it remains today, with most, 60% or so, living in the Americas and Africa, compared with around 1% in the sixteenth century. It's now the number one religion, with the largest following in the world, though on last-century trends Islam is going to overtake it in this new century.

Of the other six religions mentioned at the beginning of this chapter, the sun religions have been wiped out by Christian conquest. Communism, an offspring of Christian Europe, has made large inroads on Buddhism, Confucianism, and Taoism.

So how did Christianity increase its "market share" of the global population from 10% to 30% over the last half millennium? Quite simply, through the greatest episodes of inhumanity and genocide that the earth has ever seen. Genuine Christian missionary effort, motivated by concern for souls rather than conquest, has had little appreciable effect on the other six religions. Today after extraordinary efforts by tens of thousands of dedicated missionaries over centuries there are proportionately fewer Christians in the vast stretch of the globe from Morocco to Indonesia, including all the most populous countries and most of the ancient civilizations, than there were 500 years ago.

So holocaust is not too strong a word to describe aspects of the Christian impact on the world. A comparable genocide today to the sixteenth-century one in Central and South America would involve figures of around 600 million – nuclear war proportions.

Christians see their God as a good God of light and love. But taking a global historical perspective, many more have seen Him as a God of death and destruction, one of the most monstrous and malign of the many demons that have stalked the earth. Satan's wiliest trick of all was to walk the earth disguised as God the Good. Most Christians have danced to his tune rather than that of Jesus, with his priests pulling the strings. The Gnostics weren't so easily fooled. Humankind has paid the price. The Aztecs thought of hell as a period of time rather than a place, a belief they adopted from the Mayans. Their survivors dated it from 1519 when the Christians arrived.

It was the sixteenth century when Christianity really started to motor. The Atlantic trade winds carried Cortez's successors from Spain and other European nations around the world like a new Black Death (a fourteenth-century plague that wiped out one-third of the population of Europe), reshaping most of it as a series of warring Christian empires.

Christians prefer to see it differently. But to look at the broader picture, by the beginning of the twentieth century the Western Christian nations, Catholic, Protestant, and Greek Orthodox, controlled up to 90% of the world's surface and its manufacturing output. With the exception of Japan (still a relatively small and mostly agrarian economy) the industrialized nations were all Christian. Here was an opportunity for the church to create a new order for the world, to bring peace and justice and prosperity. It was the first and hopefully the last time that any one religion has had so much power.

The moment was ripe for a new Augustine to articulate a vision for a new *City of God*, one that would embrace the whole planet, including the knowledge of the new sciences, to see us through the next millennium. But few in the church could see beyond the self-interest of national power-politics. Power attracts conflict, the two are inseparable. The most established Christian nations on earth combusted in civil conflict and war, in particular the first two world wars that left over 70 million dead. The largest Christian nation in Europe, the home of Martin Luther and Protestantism, gave the world the Holocaust itself, humankind's worst crime.

So has Christianity been a "good thing"? Does it make a difference for the better? The most Christian nations on earth today, those with the highest proportion of churchgoers, have had some of the worst records, being amongst the most racist (South Africa and apartheid), the most genocidal (Rwanda), the most tribal and murderous (Northern Ireland), the most nationalistic (Serbia), etc. And the evildoers are often part of their communities, sincere Christians, certain of their salvation. Those who are not, as with Germany in the 1930s, commit acts with the support of the wider Christian community and the church, or they couldn't flourish.

Alternatively you can argue that these are tribal aberrations, nothing to do with the central message. You can argue that Christians have been at the forefront of abolishing slavery, encouraging human rights, developing one of the most tolerant, life-enhancing, and progressive societies the world has seen. You can equally argue that these are the benefits of a secular society with humanist values that the church has done as much to oppose as encourage. The arguments run both ways.

But Christianity should have made a difference that is beyond argument. It makes more explicit claims than any other religion to be both one of love and of equal relevance for everyone. For most of the last 1,000 years Christians have been the overwhelming majority of the indigenous population in the countries where they've lived, with every opportunity to put into practice the teachings of their founder and to be "the light of the world, a city that is set on a hill." Logically history should show a steadily increasing gap between the morality of Christian countries and their pagan neighbors. It hasn't happened.

At the more individual level of course it's different, the record more variable. It's not the point here to sell short the experience of God that Christians have. For hundreds of millions it's the very foundation of their lives. God is as real to them as anything else. Their faith is part of the way they think and act through the day. It's who they are. Many believe life wouldn't be possible without it. Of course, believing in God in the traditional Christian way can work for the individual. Many people have been changed for the better through a commitment to Christ. They're happier, more stable and responsible members of society as a result. There may be few, if any, Christians of the stature and worldwide impact of Gandhi or Nelson Mandela or the

Dalai Lama in the past century. But there are plenty of outstanding individuals who have worked selflessly and sacrificially for the good of others, as there are in all religions, all societies. The fact that Christian sinners outnumber saints is not necessarily a reason to discredit the ideal.

But any honest individual who's worked in a Christian organization (or any other religious one) will tell you that strife, abuse, crime, are no less rife there than anywhere else. Indeed you can argue with reason that being a Christian can make you worse. It's difficult to believe you are "chosen" by the almighty God of the universe and not feel a little special, that you are right and others wrong. Some Christians do not find that their faith makes their lives better. Selfishness can turn to self-righteousness. Problems may be magnified rather than cured. Driven personalities before conversion often remain so afterwards. With membership in overall decline some react by becoming more authoritarian. Many succumb to revivalist or millennial tendencies – they raise the stakes. Double the emotion. Revival or the second coming are around the corner. All the little difficulties and compromises of life get caught up in a dynamic vision of complete renewal or change, in turn creating a further multitude of little problems when the world disobligingly carries on much as before.

Is there any evidence across the overall numbers that being a Christian makes a scrap of difference? At the personal level it's anecdotal. Some Christians seem very impressive. You can want what they have, and be persuaded into faith. Others are not, they can persuade you out of it. It depends on whom you meet. Any individual sample is too small to draw conclusions from.

But the very few surveys that have attempted to analyze changes in behavior after people have become Christians suggest there's no overall improvement. In a 1991 Roper poll in the USA 4% of born-again Christians said they had driven whilst drunk before conversion and 12% had done so after conversion. Across a range of questions behavior had deteriorated rather than improved. There have been several attempts at analyzing comparable divorce rates in the USA, which all tend to suggest that Christians divorce more frequently than non-Christians – 27% for the born-again, 21% for others, 24% for atheists. You can't put much weight on these figures (maybe, for instance, more Christians get divorced because more of them get married?) but there seems no evidence to point the other way.

People aren't stupid where their self-interest is at stake. If there were any clear evidence that being a Christian really made people noticeably better, happier, healthier, or more fulfilled, or that God answered the prayers of Christians rather than those of other faiths or of no faith at all, the churches would be full to the rafters. After 2,000 years everyone in the world would by now be a Christian.

So why aren't Christians better than other people? Partly because the effects of good religion on practice are also true for Buddhists and Muslims, for all believers in all religions. It's the kind of God you believe in that matters rather than the doctrines that churches shape around Her. Sadly, simply believing in God doesn't make you a better or happier person than your neighbor. At most it can make you a better or happier person than you would otherwise have been.

The blunt truth is that no religion or experience of faith in itself necessarily makes you a better person. Individuals can better themselves, develop maturity, improve relationships, come close to God through becoming Christian, or Muslim, or Buddhist, or by leaving formal belief behind. It's down to you. The "God-spot" in your brain is like a spot for music, or sport, or logic. It doesn't improve your character any more than being a concert pianist does.

So how does religion help? Knowledge doesn't bring happiness. Science can't produce it, nor measure it. Nor can wealth. Experience over thousands of generations says that religion can, though which one is immaterial. It adds an extra dimension to the equation, harder to analyze, that happiness is goodness. In transcending the self we can live out of unity with the larger world defined by God, live in its goodness. Religion can sort out your life, bring new friendships, self-worth, and give hope – humor less certain. It can give you strength and courage to spread happiness around. Or it can turn you into an intolerable bigot.

People make different choices as to who they want to be, and what kind of religion they want to follow. But there's no necessary connection between the "church" and "God." Nor is there any necessary connection between Christians and God. If heaven exists, Christians are in a minority there. Judging them by their lives rather than their beliefs, and as a percentage of the population through history, maybe they number 1 in 100.

16

THE CONFUSION WE'RE IN

"The Ninth way is this –
to wander from religion to religion
seeking enlightenment, but ending up in confusion."

The Sutra of Returning to Your Original Nature, 4.26
(Chinese Christian, eighth century AD)

We've covered why we believe, whether it's credible, the differences between good and bad religion, the good teaching of Jesus, the way that got turned into bad religion by the politicians and bureaucrats. This last third of the book takes an overview of where we are, and the way forward. It's easy enough to say that Christianity and religion in general have caused as much harm as good, that Jesus wasn't really God. But what next? What are the good things we can learn and keep from our story?

In some ways we're back to the first century AD. There's one superpower, occasionally directing overwhelming military strength against unruly tribesmen in far-off regions. In politics pragmatism and self-interest rule. There's no one convincing religion, so most make do with bread and circuses, pop stars and celebrities. Religion is once again more of a supermarket than a corner shop, with a mass of competing beliefs pressing their wares in the marketplace. The mysteries of the East are coming back into the frame, gurus gaining their followers in the Western Empire. Maybe we still believe in the Son of God, but perform our sacrificial rituals without much conviction, salve our consciences with the bread and wine, with the occasional nod of a prayer. There's a massive underclass hidden away somewhere in the Third World, equivalent to the slave labor of the Empire. Indeed once again that's where religions of revelation and salvation are flourishing most vigorously. In the more skeptical West choice and tolerance are once again seen by most as virtues rather than decadence. We're all heretics today.

So how should we think of different religions now? Why follow one rather than another? If we're open to truth and honest to God we know that the advances in knowledge, civilized societies, religious achievements from the communal to the individual, have been scattered all over the world in place and time. Qualities like faith, insight, intelligence, and sincerity are universal. We're a global village now. Truth is not tribal. Our aliens are from other planets, no longer from other countries.

Looking superficially at the different religions in the world we might describe Hinduism as being the most successful in terms of being followed by the largest proportion of the world's population for the longest time. Some scholars say that it's the cradle of many of the others, including the monotheistic religions, much as our languages have developed from Sanskrit. Those inclined to mysticism might claim that the central Hindu teaching of *advaita*, of all things being one, is at the root of all religion. Others claim that in its exploration of consciousness it developed sophisticated views of the unity of matter and mind millennia ago that science is only just beginning to appreciate.

But this doesn't necessarily mean Hinduism can work for everyone. It's hard for Westerners to embrace the idea of 350 million gods rather than one (oddly enough very similar to the number of angels that medieval monks believed existed), of duty rather than love at the top of the moral equation, let alone the tolerance of flies and caste. We're conditioned by our past, our present, and they are rare individuals who can determine for themselves quite different futures.

Alternatively many in the West are attracted to Buddhism as the most peaceable and contemplative of the major religions. It seems the most intellectually rigorous, being based on reason rather than revelation, in some respects closer to philosophy. It floats free of dependence on history and miracle much as Christianity freed Roman religion (nearly) from dependence on deities in the sky and statues representing them on earth. But again, it's difficult for most of us to take on board the insignificance of the self, the idea of time as a wheel rather than a line, the endless recycling of life. Though many modern teachers now say all beliefs are secondary, only experience is fundamental.

But there are many options. If you're looking for an intelligently conceived monotheistic religion that makes few demands on credulity and focuses on good practice in this life, then Sikhism is a good bet.

Islam generates a level of sustained prayer and devotion across the whole community that puts Christianity in the shade.

Taoism at times seems closer to the teaching of Jesus than does Christianity itself; a good Taoist has few demands and doesn't exercise power over others. Its vision of the world as determined by principles of balance and order offers an attractive alternative to one ruled by divinities with our kinds of emotions and problems.

Confucianism demonstrates a stronger commitment to the family, the wider social unit, and the principle of good government than most other religions have got their heads around.

Shintoism is the most ancient, beautiful, and simple of all the major religions practiced today.

The still older tribal religions, like that of the Aborigines, have an imaginative power, fusing the soul and the landscape, past, present, and future, that for some dwarfs our own tinkering with the world of spirit.

These religions and many others have enormously rich, varied, and complex traditions, literatures, and rituals. Only the ignorant or foolish say the resources of spiritual and social capital of these religions are less than those of Christianity. No Christian event attracts the number of several million Muslims who visit Mecca every year for the Hajh, let alone the 70 million who at the start of this millennium crowded to the Kumbh Mehla festival on the Ganges.

So what kind of future does Christianity have? At times in the Dark Ages it threatened to disappear. Then just a century ago it promised to dominate. But today it's hard to imagine it having the same legs as say, Hinduism, which has been around nearly three times as long. It's too closely tied to a world-view that's disappeared. It lacks the inclusiveness that characterizes Hinduism on the one hand or the focus and clarity of Islam on the other.

It's still growing in parts of the world, particularly the less developed and the rapidly developing, and will carry on doing so. They're taking on board Western technology, and sometimes its political and economic systems, like parliaments and shopping malls. A culture of individual salvation follows a culture of individual success. They may be throwing out cultural traditions that would suit them better. But in any case, as the influence of the West diminishes in relation to that of Islam and China, in the century or two to come these gains are likely to be reversed.

In Western Europe at least Christianity is in dire straits, and on current trends will virtually disappear in the next couple of generations. Of course religion never "disappears" as such. Some followers always remain. The Zoroastrian religion, which predates it by a millennia or two, still has a few million followers (now called Parsees). Even ancient Egyptian religion is followed by hundreds of thousands. And Christianity may influence new religions like they influenced Judaism.

The problem is that the vision of individual salvation, mediated through the church, achieved through reconciliation with a historical figure who lived 2,000 years ago, doesn't persuade any more. Of course certainties are attractive. The offer of salvation, a place near God's throne, the warmth of a group bound by strong belief, friendship, hardened by small numbers, holds out huge appeal. As cults prove time and time again. Those with the shortest and clearest soundbites get the most votes. Liberals will continue to be edged out of the church by increasingly conservative and small congregations because they aren't radical enough to attract new ones.

But short of a catastrophic decline in educational standards the number of people, in Western Europe at least, who can accept that the Bible is the unique revelation of God to humankind will continue to diminish. And the papacy, particularly the Roman one (there are still others, the Coptic Church for instance has its own), looks increasingly like the ancient Egyptian priesthood, stuck on a riverbank while the world around it moves on and eventually overwhelms it. It's true that you no longer get mad popes; popes you wouldn't trust to mind your daughter in your house; murderous, lecherous, evil popes you wouldn't even want in your house, or in the same street. But in the twenty-first century the idea that popes can pronounce the will of God by virtue of their position is as bizarre a belief as that kings rule by divine right, that slavery is divinely ordained, or blacks are naturally inferior to whites. It's surely just as likely – far more likely – that this series of individuals, hampered as they have been by the trappings of wealth and power that Jesus so strongly condemned, have consistently led the church in the wrong direction, further away from his teaching. They are more likely than anyone to be wrong.

To put it another way, it's not so much that the church's vision doesn't persuade, as that it's hard today to tell the difference between this vision and a thousand others. Substituting literalism in scripture or tradition for moral vision, caught between the rock of age-old creeds and the hard places of modern knowledge, its certainties are crumbling back into the spiritual soup from which they emerged. Many of God's followers, particularly in the growing charismatic and Pentecostal movements, have turned back to the shamanistic practices that have served us well for hundreds of millennia – speaking in tongues, making animal noises, ecstatic dancing, healing, exorcism, and words of knowledge. Here God takes back the characteristics of the ancient weather gods, bringing rain or stopping it, writing the Book of Life for the personal benefit of His followers.

Many more still have turned to New-Age practices. When I started in religious publishing thirty years ago traditional Christian books outsold New-Age, or mind/body/spirit, in the UK by about four or five to one. Now it's the other way around. It's no longer a passing fashion. Practitioners of alternative medicine, who make a living out of it, outnumber general doctors. New-Age followers say with some justification that it's Christianity that's the new upstart, a mere two millennia old, a priestly empire whose time has come and gone.

It's hard today to see the difference between the Christian obsession with the end times, and the New Age with Aquarius; between angels in the Bible Belt, and Beings of Light in Arizona; the routes to easy money and salvation offered by Western evangelists, or by Eastern gurus. Risen Christ, or core crystals; prayer warriors, or light-workers – there's no difference. Eat this wafer, say these words, and you'll touch God. Follow these paths, or rituals, or horoscopes, tap into this force or that, find your inner self, your previous self, or other self, and you'll realize your true potential. Change your way of thinking, your partner, your company, your colors, the position of your furniture, what you eat, how you eat, when you eat, when you pray, who to, and you'll be happier, wealthier, more fulfilled. It can work. Any of it can work. Of course it can. We can believe anything. As with any religion it's a question of distinguishing the worthwhile from the trivial.

Mainstream Christians dismiss New-Age teaching as fantasy, where anything is believed. New-Age followers could justifiably argue that they're closer to the bedrock of Christianity than the church is. The New Testament is chock-a-block with practices many would now think of as New-Age if they were given the names used today: clairvoyance, etheric projection, chanelling, dream visions, numerous forms of healing (by touch, by saliva, and at a distance), summoning spirits, astrological-type signs in the heavens, apparitions, astral planes. The first disciples practiced divination in recruiting to their number. The Old Testament is richer still, full of practices that are now called shamanistic, astrological, etc. Sometimes these practices are condemned, at others not, they're always taken for granted as "real."

And how could it be otherwise? The Hebrews and Jews believed in a world shot through with magic and miracle, in spiritual forces and cosmic struggles, in planetary levels of ascending importance (2 Corinthians 12:2-4), in much the same way as New Agers do today. The practices and beliefs found in the Bible, also developed before the age of science, are common to societies everywhere. It's the Christians who restrict the spectacular workings of God to the pages of the Bible who are out of step with its spirit. The "rationalists" are in the wrong religion. It might be those who think that Jesus thought about God like they do who understand the least about him.

"New Age" is a misnomer. It's a portmanteau term for pre-scientific beliefs from cultures around the world (often the more exotic and ancient or mythical the better). "Old Age" would be more accurate. Much of its teaching draws on traditions that have been known to work for millennia, probably for millions of years, like the healing powers of particular plants, or the therapeutic benefits of grooming and massaging. It's recovering the wisdom of older societies, wisdom that we have lost, insulating ourselves as we do from the world around us with metal and plastic.

In this sense the Bible is the most significant "New-Age" document we have. Christianity the most significant New-Age religion. In trying to hang on to its particular version of Hebrew religion and Greek philosophy the church has simply pushed its congregations out of its doors. With more imagination it could have held on to them. New-Age teaching and practice, having had to make its way in the marketplace, is more prepared to meet people where they are. It focuses on the perennials of "wellbeing" – health and healing, food and diet, sex and love, respect and concern for the planet and other life. It's closer to the Jewish *shalom* of holistic health in mind, body, and spirit than Christianity is.

Some believers go a long way down this line. They travel beyond any particular idea of God to a mystical blend of different strands of Buddhism, Christianity, Hinduism, speculative science, much as many of the first Christians did. We get into the area of egoic time, species mind, transpersonal experience, and the new humankind. For those living in England rather than California it's harder to take these ideas on board. Maybe we're uniquely disadvantaged, living at the tail end of one major religion and before a new one has taken credible shape (and maybe the new one should be led entirely by women to redress the current patriarchal imbalance).

People don't want to be saved today. They don't understand what it means. They want to be happy and healthy. And they'll pay for it, like Christians used to. If the church doesn't change, the wheel will carry on turning, as it always does, and the New-Age teachers will eventually take over and rebuild the churches, like the Christians built over the pagan temples.

If Christians want to turn this around they need to bring our threads of science and religion, experience and tradition, history and conscience into a better kind of balance. This is what different theologians have always tried to do, but as knowledge has expanded, they've largely lost the plot, continuing to work away in the little diminishing bubbles of their own frame of reference. But then as the great Sufi Ghazali taught, theology is ultimately useless anyway. Just think of it as 200,000 lawyers given 2,000 years to describe love and making a mountainous hash of it. What matters is expressing the awareness of God in the simplicity of a loving life. The more we do this, the more we might understand. The more we understand, the more we realize love is all there is.

We need a larger vision, a bigger God. As huge, as extraordinary, as challenging to common practice, as the one Jesus brought to the Jews, or the one expressed in Mahayana Buddhism. One that tells us why we're here and how we should live. Something that lifts us out of who and where we are to where we might get to, what we might become, that ties everything together. That gives enough definition to the uncertainties of life to enable us at least to share the asking of the questions about the journey we're on, even if we can't agree on the answer. We need a vision for that, for what should be at the center of life, for what goodness is and how to be happy. Jesus gave us as good a one as we've got.

The first step is to see where we've gone wrong. For 99% of our history religion has been a collective, tribal matter, a matter of belonging and sharing, of treading lightly on the earth and treating all living things with reverence. With the growth of cities, states, and nations came power, class, and wealth. Within the new religions that grew to accommodate these new structures some continued to find God in solitude, in mysticism, in service, but more used Him as a means of aggrandizement. They defined others as inferior or wrong or even evil rather than just different. The church, in many aspects, came to embody power, class and wealth. This became embodied in everything from its buildings to its theology.

In the case of Christianity we've developed a religion that gives its opponents reason to describe it, especially in its Western capitalist form, as among the worst of religions, the ultimate expression to date of the sanctification of greed rather than giving, growth and profit rather than holiness and happiness. The church today is stuck with the trivia of what used to be a powerful drive to transcendence – with its color and trimmings. Trivial gods concern themselves with what are now trivial issues. They focus on the individual and his/her salvation. They discriminate against those who are different from us, focusing on questions of gender, sexuality, and race, taking primitive tribal laws as universal truth. Serious gods engage with serious issues, and they embrace everyone. Belief today features DNA as well as the devil, looks for inspiration to the stars rather than saints. It returns to the more immediate problem of how we conduct ourselves to enable survival as a species in this world rather than working for salvation in the next. After all, if we screw this world up why should we be trusted with another one?

THE WAY TO GO

"It is the customary fate of new truths to begin as heresies and end as superstitions."

Thomas Henry Huxley

The main theme of this book has been that there are any number of ways of imagining God, good and bad. We progress as individuals and as communities, even as a species, by following the good. For those who call themselves Christians the way forward is to return to what we can recover of the teaching of the founder.

In his vision of the kingdom Jesus challenged his contemporaries to a new understanding of what it meant to be human. He said we could give, love, and receive without limit. We just had to "go further." But Christians today are indistinguishable from everyone else. They have the most, give the least. The historical record is one of the bloodiest. What would Jesus say to us today?

He was born into a people whose self-worth was bound up with their idea of God. The story of how He had succored them as a nation, taken them out of Egypt in the Exodus, out of the Exile in Babylon, enabled them to survive despite the Egyptians, Phoenicians, Assyrians, Babylonians, Persians, Greeks, Romans – this story, whether historical or not, had become the core of their identity. Some of them had backslidden, some had compromised with the oppressors, but some had kept the flame of faith alive. Amongst the most dedicated believers of all were the Pharisees. In the pluralist world of the massive and seemingly impregnable Roman Empire they kept the people to the straight and narrow, honoring the commands of God in the Jewish scriptures, refusing to worship the emperor, making Palestine one of the most troublesome provinces for any governor to handle.

And then here's perhaps the most surprising thing in the New

Testament. Not the virgin birth, or the resurrection, which any old god could do, but the attitude of Jesus to the Pharisees. Despite the support he got from some of them, and the similarity in some respects of their teaching, the people who Jesus consistently cursed were not the pagans or the backsliders, but the believers. Those who had remained steadfast and faithful in the face of great odds, who had devoted every hour of their waking days to serving God. He cursed them not because of what they did, but because of what they did not do. They put law above compassion, God above goodness. He cursed them because they believed they were right, that they were saved in God's eyes. They were proud of what they were doing for God, of the lives they led. They valued their religion, their truth, God's truth, above people, above unconditional love.

The church is no different today. We've just turned into another bunch of Pharisees. If Jesus really did come back today those he would curse, again, are those most sure of their salvation. Indeed today we're doubly cursed. We think we're right, and we also have the wealth and power. We're the Pharisees, priests, and Romans together.

Christianity today is as parochial as any of the competing mystery religions of the first century AD. It doesn't preach the kingdom of God. It blesses the status quo rather than challenges it, produces no prophets. Christian societies are no more kingdom-like than others, Christians no less selfish or prone to evil than non-Christians. There really is no particular good reason to be a Christian today rather than something else, unless it's the place you're starting from. Given a level playing field and a clear head, who would want to believe in the same kind of

God as Ian Paisley, or Pat Robertson, or Cardinal Ratzinger, any more than that of Osama bin Laden? In any religion where being in the right is more important than admitting your own culpability; spreading your beliefs more urgent than preventing starvation; forbidding condoms more important than the spread of AIDS; demonizing your enemy more significant than protecting the rights of the innocent?

Maybe Christianity simply hasn't yet matured into a good religion. It went off the rails too early. It's still at the cultic stage of making impossible truth claims, venerating the leader as God, commanding blind obedience, creating and worshiping idols rather than loving the life we're part of. The orthodox, established church is a river that meandered into the delta for a couple of millennia, turning back on itself, losing itself in creeds and laws, still searching for the wider sea.

It's missing a huge opportunity. Because contrary to the impression given in the public spheres of life religion today grows rather than diminishes in importance. The more complex the world becomes, and the less self-sufficient we are, and the more we are reliant on others, then the stronger our ideas need to be as the glue that binds us. With better technology, everything from medical to military, we confront increasingly complex problems – anything from what a human being is to where life begins and ends, and where the balance lies between freedom and responsibility, force and forgiveness. Defining what our values are and the basis on which we make them have become more important than ever.

To shape our questions and answers Christianity needs to turn itself into something as different from that of today as today's is from the warrior-based, relic-worshiping religion of a thousand years ago. It could happen. Change is as much the lifeblood of religion as of society. Some of the societies in Europe, Christianity's second surviving heartland, have changed in the last couple of generations. They've confronted the demons of racism and nationalism that have been embedded in Christian culture for so long and largely come out the other side. A similar change for the place of Christianity in those societies will mean turning Jesus back from a god into a man, and God back from a personal deity into the Unknown, the ultimate sign of what is beyond our understanding and possession. It will mean taking the kingdom of God seriously on earth, investing our massive economic surplus (relative to the rest of the world) into addressing problems of world poverty rather than consumer goods.

It would be hard. Living the kind of life Jesus describes is. He said it would be. The church should at least try to be there on the line, saying, "This is what it is, what it means. We'll do our best to help you make it." But it's caught up in all this other old stuff. It's turned the teaching of Jesus into another religion of sacrifice. Most religions are based around this idea. God/gods are something "other," fearsome, angry, holy beings who need to be placated. Offerings are made to ensure that the child will be born, our sins forgiven, that the journey will be safe, the crops will grow, the sun will rise again.

Virtually everyone in the Mediterranean area in the first century thought this way. The Greeks, Romans, Jews, all offered sacrifices. Their religions were all temple religions. Sacrifice and law dominated the lives of the Jews. Every hour of the day, in every way, God had to be propitiated. But life itself was still a burden. The Jews were oppressed by the Law, by poverty, by the Romans. They awaited a deliverer, a savior, who would raise their status to what it should be as God's chosen people.

Paul, in a stroke of religious genius, had a new vision of the spiritual world. He turned it upside down. God shows Himself through weakness and shame, not power and strength. He doesn't demand sacrifice, He offers it. In a literal flash of insight Paul saw Jesus as being the sacrifice God Himself had sent as an offering for sin – not just his own, or that of the Jews, but of all humankind. The deliverer had come, and we had crucified him, in line with God's plan. God Himself had freed humankind from the burden of sin and oppression, and all each person had to do in return was realize it.

But Paul was going on hearsay. God is not a remote figure, whether angry or loving, who wants sacrifice, nor does He offer it. He is all consciousness. His image is in all of us, seen most clearly in lepers and children. His love is unconditional, for everyone, not for those who can agree with certain creeds. It's in pouring ourselves out on behalf of others that it is realized, not in building walls of money or power around us.

Today the Trinitarian orthodox God is a glass ceiling on the growth of Christianity, much like the laws of Judaism were for the Nazarenes. True followers of Jesus, as the first of the early church fathers recognized, are those who transcend the self in favor of others, who recognize God everywhere, and are as likely to be found in Kabul as New York. All of life is sacred, it has chosen to be so by coming into being. That's the fundamental religious impulse.

"Jesus said: 'It is I who am the light which is above them all. It is I who am the All. From me did the All come forth, and unto me did the All extend. Split a piece of wood, and I am there. Lift up the stone, and you will find me there.'"

Gospel of Thomas

Smashing this ceiling means being as radical in our approach as Jesus was. And as the previous chapters on the history of belief have suggested the key here is authority, which is the problem in religion much as it is in society, with options ranging from anarchy to tyranny.

Shared systems of belief are helpful in that they encourage individuals to rise above their self-interest. Over the last five millennia we've developed many, much as over the last five centuries we've organized ourselves into many nation states. The trouble is that belief in a system needs commitment. In willingly making the commitment we surrender our power of independent reasoning. Over generations, centuries, a system of collective belief hardens, writes teaching in stone. It even begins to define itself against other systems rather than being open to further sharing. Every now and again it all needs to be pulled down and rebuilt, like Jesus wanted to do with the Temple. Each new religion starts as an act of destruction. If Jesus were here today he'd battle with Catholics and Protestants as back then he did with Sadducees and Pharisees.

We can be better Christians with no God at all than with the Catholic or Protestant God. God is no longer necessary to religion, or to the good life, much as Buddhists have been teaching for longer than Christianity has existed. Perhaps we can just sit lightly to the idea. Now we're "post-Christian" much as the first Christians were "post-Jewish."

This may sound like process theology or Christian atheism of the kind fashionable in the 60s, except that they got rid of Jesus as well as God. But perhaps we could think about religion in the same way we think about science. For instance, Newton's law of gravity is more use to us on a daily basis than Einstein's law of relativity. The first describes the stuff that makes the kettle boil, the tides rise and fall, whereas Einstein's laws operate on a scale beyond our immediate experience, where light bends and time slows. But we can live in the framework of Newton's laws while still accepting those of Einstein as representing a deeper truth. We may know we've moved thousands of miles through space whilst reading this page but it doesn't "matter." We still talk about the sun rising rather than the earth turning even though we know it's not "true."

Similarly Christian atheists are no more "atheistic" than the early Christians, who were themselves called atheists by the Romans. The Romans couldn't understand these people – what were gods if you couldn't represent them in images? Meaningless. How could you worship words?

Churches demonstrate the Roman approach when they insist on Capital Letter Doctrines for truths they've written on paper rather than stone. The doctrines are no more than the old statues. There comes a point where words are just insufficient, where religious language ceases to matter. Maybe we can still just about talk of God as "He," without assuming He has a penis, or a shape, or any existence we can recognize. But there is

258

in the end no real difference between believing in God and not believing, between Christian and Buddhist. When we transcend the self and escape to distant horizons we might think we see God, but God is infinite and has no handles we can hold on to. He's a dance of possibilities, a void, waiting to be called into being. It's how we respond that determines who God is, and what we in turn are.

It might be difficult to think about Christianity this way. It was shaped by Greek philosophy, but its driving force was the Hebrew belief that God intervenes. He made the world, made people, changed His mind, chose a particular tribe, sent a son to earth. We've written this particular story, constructing it around the life of Jesus and overlaying his teaching, and we're good at stories. We've been telling them for hundreds of thousands of years. We shape our response to the real by imagining what our response might be. We turn one into the other. God could be fact or fiction. We change Him at the flick of a switch. And it's not just God. It's ourselves. We can switch ourselves on or off. We can decide to be miserable or happy, to cling to what we have, or let go and travel. You, God, life, it doesn't matter what you call it. One act of friendship to a stranger is worth more than all the God-searching you've done in your life. There's more truth in the patch of grass at your feet than in the theological library.

But if God is not the one the church describes what is there to hang on to in this religion that it has developed? Maybe it's not so much a question of hanging on as of shedding an old skin when it feels too tight. With the same kind of delight the Romans felt when many of them abandoned their worship of household gods for the invisible, almighty, only God. Think of the new picture of God as a similar step on the journey. As larger than the first-century Christian picture of Him as their picture was larger than the statue of Zeus.

For several centuries theology has been moving away from the idea of an objective God. Through twentieth-century theologians like Rudolph Bultmann, Karl Rahner, and Paul Tillich we move to seeing God as a human projection, with Tillich denying that God exists as other than a symbol. The retreat of theology from the classical idea of God mirrors the decline of orthodox Christian faith. And of course Christians might say it's the fault of the theologians. But it's never wise to shoot the messenger. So why do they still talk about God at all? Because most of us feel there is something ultimately real or worthwhile. And we want to know it's "there." We have language, we need a description, it seeks an object.

Religions are the different ways in which we emotionally, intellectually, even physically relate to this feeling of reality. They are a kind of language we have spent a million years developing to help us talk in the broadest sense about the important things in life, the ones we can't explain or measure, the ones that aren't rational, but are still "true" – beauty, happiness, wrong, evil, love, transcendence. These are steps on the ladder of self-awareness, ascending from reptiles, through mammals, through human beings, and maybe to God. No one lives as if these intangible qualities don't exist. Our understanding of them is imperfect, our attempts to describe them and pass them on (religion) worse. But without them we can't love, we can't even think. Each attempt at understanding is worth something, and better than not trying at all. The attempts make a road map of the different journeys we're on. The whole is more than the sum of its parts. It provides a quest to keep us stepping forward. Religion turns this quest into a story, called a myth.

A myth, like the Christian story of God, is our first best guess. It condenses truth down to essentials upon which legends then elaborate. Though it might refer to history it's really outside it, in an eternal "now," using symbols and characters to describe what drives us, which is why it's always relevant. And no religion survives for 2,000 years if it hasn't got a story that helps us along the way. But to say that one story alone is true makes a nonsense of religion, turning it into a lottery.

Claims like that of the infallible *Declaration Dominus Jesus* of a couple of years back, which declares that the Roman Catholic Church is the "only instrument for the salvation of all humankind," are ugly blots, outcrops of insanity in the landscape of theology. They remind us that no organization in history has burnt so many books, persecuted and murdered its opponents so consistently for so many centuries as the Catholic Church, particularly in the second millennium with its office of the Grand Inquisitor and the Congregation of the Index. Apart from being highly offensive to victims of the "religion of love" this kind of dogma presupposes that 99% of belief down the ages has been a great mistake. If Christians then doubt the truth of their own 1%, they can be inclined to disbelieve everything, turning to ideologies of cruelty and despair, or they take refuge in superstition or fundamentalism. The twin bastard offspring of Christianity that made the twentieth century a nightmare for so many – Communism and Fascism – are a product of this reaction.

We underestimate the power of religion to do both good and harm. When we lose sight of the best we let the worst run riot. Popes, evangelists, and ayatollahs turn the world into a battleground of cosmic forces, the demons of their inherited and collective imaginations played out through the psyches of billions, the Darth Vaders of our time. They create division out of unity, evil out of good, building their castles of limited understanding on the plains with each successive generation fortifying the battlements. Good religion works from the bottom up, not the top down. It grinds away in the tiny daily events, the moments of realization, through which matter evolves into love. Decrees from the top, sweeping away huge swathes of searching and suffering, knowledge and experience, set the universe back.

All our certainties are just drops of water in an ocean of probability. What matters is how good our story is, how much it helps us today. Maybe being a Christian today means rejecting the capital C "Church" as it exists now. It has little to do with the teaching of Jesus. Collectively it's responsible for as much human misery as happiness. It acts as a brake on spiritual development as much as a motor. It encourages superstition and ignorance as much as truth, division as much as harmony.

Rejecting it involves working backwards through the last two millennia, undoing the damage the church has caused, the wrong myths it has created. The first hurdle to be jumped is the recent teaching on the infallibility of scripture, then the doctrine of justification by faith, developed in the Reformation. We work back through the establishment of the church by Augustine, the sacraments and priesthood, and the cosmic theology of Paul.

Along the way go the papacy, Capital Letter Doctrines, original sin, guilt, buildings, and wealth. Indeed the whole religious sphere of life goes. Life is a whole, not to be directed for us by priestly specialists. It will only work if we can live it as a whole. In the Christian tradition the Quakers have come as close to this as anyone.

A credible Christianity for today starts with the life of Jesus as a vulnerable human being, from the stable to the cross, who believed in putting the divinity into humanity, and taking religion into the real world of doing good. God is the ideal of the best we can do. He may even exist as the universal mind of which we are fragments. We may be at the beginning of the process that brings Him into conscious being. The closest we get to Him is by embodying love. Jesus saw himself as pointing the way to reconciliation between humankind and God, between one person and another, and within each person, because all are essentially one. In following him, in thought and life, we are Christians. In loving our neighbor we love ourselves. In loving the world we love God. The world is God. It's that simple.

Put simply, in a world we now know to be so much bigger, we need our bigger God back. We need to add what we know to what we feel. We need to recognize the breadth of one, the depth of the other, the power of both, and find a new balance. Believing that the world is flat and was made in seven days, that God will find us a parking place or bring sunshine on Saturday – okay, all religions have these kinds of beliefs, and in themselves they're mostly fairly harmless. Indeed they can be helpful. We know for instance that the mind can cause illness, and can sometimes cure it. If you believe you can be healed you might be.

In that sense all religions work. Actually healing plays only a small part in Christian tradition compared with most others, and has very little emphasis in its theology and teaching, which is part of the reason for the success today of charismatic and New-Age movements. But these beliefs are about as relevant to living a Christian life of the kind Jesus described as an in-grown toenail. Worse, really, because by the time we've filled our heads with this peripheral material there's little space left for the important stuff. We need to join up the dots.

Life is too short and knowledge too vast to do this for yourself. So we'll never know if what we believe is 100% right, or even 50%. If we did it wouldn't be religion, but science. But in every life there comes a point beyond which knowledge doesn't take us, where we set off and say, "I realize that this may not be true, but it works for me. I'm not sure what will happen, but I'll try it." That's what "faith" is. It's believing hopefully. Not a blind trust in formulas, but following our conviction that there's something real here, beyond the surface of appearances, something that can challenge and help us. And this is what being human is about – having faith, risking love, making deeper connections, using both reason and intuition to come to a better understanding of who we are and how we should live.

And we need a vision of the sacred to carry us forward. It will balance God "in here" with God "out there." Many scientists now say what people have instinctively felt since self-awareness developed, what monistic religions describe, and mystics of all traditions experience. What we can all feel in a small way. That mind and matter are in some way related. That how we see the world is as important as the world itself. We not only read the map, we create what it images.

But "we" is not just you and me. What we can add today is the understanding that consciousness is a line that stretches back millions of years and forward for billions. We shade into chimps on the one hand, into angels on the other: maybe one day we'll all play like Beethoven, draw like Michelangelo, and calculate like a computer. We're moving out into this new world as tentatively as the first human beings moved out of Africa, into a world of riches and diversity they knew nothing about. We'll look back and see the "idiot savants" of today, the victims of autism who are occasionally able to unlock the power of the brain in unbelievable ways, as the equivalent of our "Archaic Humans." We'll unravel matter down to the fundamental atomic level where it somehow makes a choice, to be or not to be.

All these trillion trillion choices add up to the incredibly complex universe we live in, defying the laws of probability at every point. We'll find ourselves exercising the choice to create this universe. A choice to be loving. We'll live and move in this loving universe like whales in the ocean, rather than amphibians living half in the world of spirit and half in the body. We know this is going to happen in one form or other, because we're here. If there were no mind of God, there would be no matter, no us. The line is a circle; it exists "now."

Religion has called this process "God," and has called God by a thousand names. Any one of them can do.

18

An Image
For Now

"The ecstasy of religion, the ecstasy of art, and the ecstasy of love are the only things worth thinking about or experiencing."

Don Marquis

The unattainable God, the highest God, the final perfection, the ultimate silence, the absence of everything, the place outside time and space, He is pointed to in virtually all religion. All our traditions are like clumsy rafts we pole out from the shore, believing that at some point we'll find a current that will take us to the Promised Land. But there is no Promised Land, and no map to get us there. The ocean is all there is. How we build the raft is a question of personal psychology; whether we're left-brained or right, whether we're optimists or pessimists, focusing on rules or on freedom, metaphor or fact. Much of the rest is cultural perspective; whether we see God as "in here" or "out there," whether we emphasize His workings in the past, present, or future.

Reaching for the impossible, believing the absurd, this is the practice religion cultivates. Maybe we kid ourselves that it's worthwhile. Maybe it never really happens. It's why most religious founders are relatively indifferent on the description of God; we don't know who He is. Not particularly bothered about the belief system; that just defines who He's not. Uninterested in the organization; that's leading people astray, into thinking they know where they're going. Their priorities are 90% about how we live. It's how you love that counts.

But most of us need more direction than this provides. The hard part of loving is not the inadequate beliefs or the structures they're encoded in. It's coping with suffering and evil that knocks us back. It's knowing how to reach for the good when crunch time comes. When the barbarians are at the gates again. How do we work out what "good" is if it's not the God we've been bought up to believe in? Jesus, however far-sighted he may have been, as a first-century Jew had a conception of God that most of us can't relate to. His God of the Old Testament, of Abraham and Moses, Ezekiel and Daniel, is not ours. His was part of the tradition of the Jewish people, tied into their historical experience and family memories.

One answer to the problems of life is to see them all as illusion. All suffering and illness as self-created. All disasters as a result of collective decisions. If we can raise our awareness high enough we'll no longer suffer. But this seems a long way removed from the daily experience of most. Maybe it's like original sin, with elements of truth but not the whole. Certainly some illness is psychosomatic, self-generated, more than Western medicine gives credit for. But children, healthy people with positive attitudes, all fall ill. Our cousin chimps fall ill. The world was no different when there were no people or chimps around to create karma.

Maybe the Semitic (and Hebrew) view of God as "One" rather than "good" is closer to the truth. We may choose to live a good life. God does not. He is what there is. "Nature" is neutral. Goodness can only be realized through self-awareness and making choices. The Islamic view of "fate" can help us here. A large part of suffering is unavoidable. What will be will be. In the process of creation, of matter becoming mind, it is continuously broken and remade. Over a few years every cell in our bodies is different, 200 billion are replaced every day, but we continue, unaware. We have to see ourselves as part of the ongoing process of creation, not the end product that gets upset if the process doesn't stop at a time that suits us. We're part of the life of the universe. Like cells in our bodies, the larger spirit continues, grows, remaking us in different forms.

Or maybe there's a deeper truth, maybe nature is not "neutral," but a violent communion. Every living thing fights for survival, and has to. It's in doing this that life has created the planet we're on, right down to the air we breathe. Nature is profligate and inexhaustible, but never gentle. Species that don't eat die. All exist at the expense of others. The need to eat is the central fact of life. Maybe all religion, from God's sacrifice of Jesus on the cross to Arjuna of the million mouths, is a way of accepting responsibility for what we are. Our guilt at eating other life is transformed into the higher act of eating God, and being consumed in our turn. All our gods reflect different ways of acknowledging our predatory role and our hopes of transcending it. The East emphasizes acceptance of the Source, the West individual effort, conscious surrender to God. In the balance of the two we find our own truth.

Suffering and self-awareness seem inseparable. There is no appreciation of unity without the experience of separation. Birth and pain, creation and death, they feed on each other. Great artists, musicians, are often suffering individuals, on the edge. They create out of pain. A central religious insight is that perhaps there's no creativity or compassion without suffering. Just as there is no appreciation of "now" without its prior separation into past and future, bitter-sweet memories and hopeful plans. It's through our developing awareness of it that we grow. Indeed most religions, including Christianity, have traditions that encourage suffering. We articulate the pain, the good, and the evil, that other creatures do not yet feel. In embracing it we transcend it. God is to us as we are to them, a further level of awareness in which suffering and love are reconciled.

The power of the Jesus story is in his suffering. In it we see God, represented in him, become the embodiment of suffering, taking it all on Himself. We can see Jesus on the cross as the symbol of a God who is brought into being through suffering, of a universe working through death to create new forms of life, recreating the very idea of God every day. We can see Jesus pushing the very idea of God to its limits, asking questions of us to prompt a new answer.

Indeed the point about being a Christian rather than a Buddhist is that suffering is redemptive rather than illusory. We *can* "choose" to offer ourselves, to triumph over disaster, to be better, to grow in love, we can make a difference here on earth, in our lifetimes, now. This doesn't mean it's the better religion, but it can make more sense in the West. We can forgive ourselves for having damaged our "selves" through our own actions. We can ask forgiveness from those we've hurt. This capacity has been hard won over a million years, but we can exercise it. Zoroaster was grasping at the right idea when he divided the powers of the world into twin brothers of good and evil between whom we have to choose. And the point where Christianity and Buddhism merge is that the nature of the quantum world suggests that at some level this choice has already been made. Whatever the universal mind, or God, is, it is the outcome of trillions of choices that have already happened, and are going to happen. We cannot sin against God, because God is self-determining, at every moment. This is the moment. Don't blame

God or the devil, they are us.

This is the paradox of the best of religion. We find that nothing matters, because all is willed. Our will, God's will, random events, there's no difference. Just pictures from different angles. But it's only out of the acceptance that nothing matters that we can act without ego. Acting out of the awareness that nothing you can do makes a blind bit of difference, because it's happening anyway, but that what you do is supremely important, because otherwise it won't – it's the mystery at the heart of the teaching of the Vedic philosophers, of Buddha, of Jesus, perhaps Muhammad most of all. All good religion boils down to one event. It's the moment of understanding, of seeing the universe and our lives as a whole right now, that enables us to transcend the question, and accept the outcome.

Evil is harder than suffering, but can be seen in the same light. The world is not black and white, people are neither all innocent or guilty, electrons are not waves or particles, all are true. There's no simple "answer." We're all capable of extremes of selfishness and evil given the right conditions. Experiments have shown that average individuals are easily capable of inflicting suffering on patients if told to do so by a figure in authority. A usually selfish individual can do something heroic, jumping into freezing water and rescuing a child. On the other hand generous and well-meaning people can connive in policies of genocide. Supporting the family can edge into nepotism, sex into rape, self-defence into murder, self-awareness into selfishness.

But evil also grows in us collectively; we can become inured to it, as much as any psychopath. It's not the Hitlers that are the problem, but the potential for evil that a Hitler releases in all of us. It's not so much the paedophile priests, but the mentality of church leaders that allows them to continue their ministry. It's not so much that we take food from the mouths of starving children, but that it suits us to be part of a system that allows it to happen. It's defining "us" as more important or worthy than "them." Good religion points us back to the right path. Conscience is the fruit of tens of thousands of generations working out what that is.

An objective real evil force? Demons, possession, Satan? Sometimes it's individual and collective wickedness. Sometimes it's clearly in the mind of the beholder. There are enough reputable accounts to make it credible in some form. But equally it seems to be more common in the past than today, more common in societies that believe in it than those that don't. The obsession with it creates the conditions in which it flourishes. Like Freudians having a disproportionate share of Freudian dreams, we wish it into existence. It's the same with the paranormal. It happens to those who believe in it. If you try to evaluate it objectively, you're not going to see it. Maybe hell exists for those who want to believe in it badly enough. Maybe Christians who are consumed with preaching damnation find out what it's like.

We need the impulse to goodness that the idea of God provides. We need the channels of inspiration that the church has historically delivered through God/Jesus/Spirit. We need a reason to believe we can change, and hope to overcome the evil we meet. And to see that it's first of all in ourselves. We're the barbarians. The people in charge often are. The world and everyone in it is what we've made it. The good and evil we see is

273

how we want to describe it. The plank is in my eye, not that of my enemy. Our problem is we don't realize it, any more than the Pharisees did.

Everything we do, even the best, has its shadow side. So humanists and atheists might say their equivalent of God is represented by the finest of our values and achievements. These might be expressed in terms of individual freedom, human rights, democracy, which add up to the highest form of civilization the world has seen. But individualism can lead to the accumulation of exorbitant wealth at the expense of others. Human rights are important, but so are those of the creatures on whose backs we tread and whose flesh we eat. Democracy is great, but can elect leaders like Hitler. These are Western ideals, but not universal ones. The more collective ideals of the East, organized around the family, have as strong, and a much older, claim to universality.

But we need something more universal than political or social arrangements. Universal values must be something greater than we can understand, more demanding than we can reach, because we don't understand the universe, and probably never will. And if we think we do we create monsters. If we think we've arrived we're just blind to where the shadow falls. We need to learn a better balance between ourselves and our neighbors, ourselves and God, taking God as the totality of everything there is.

How do we keep walking toward the light and away from the darkness we create? The best wisdom traditions say that the only true wisdom is the one you find within yourself, because we're all different. Indeed whatever you believe is only true for you. So make it real for yourself. Look to the different traditions to find the common, best elements that can point you in the right direction. And we need a direction. It's a fearful thing to live in the awareness that everything is down to us. And if we think of "us" as just "me" that's the way to madness. Without a light to aim for and show the way we're struggling in the dark, lost in Plato's cave, squabbling shadows arguing over even more insubstantial words and memories.

Our bigger God is the light we live by. How to describe Her, without slipping into pantheism? Trinities have proved their worth in dozens of religions. So here's a suggestion for a new one. We can think of God as truth: the whole, the One, the ultimate reality. The principle of diversity, or particularity, represented in the Christian tradition by Jesus, becomes that of love. The feminine principle, the Spirit, is represented by beauty.

What Jesus and other religious teachers have is a moment of insight when they see the underlying patterns in the relationships between people and the world. The pattern is not fixed, it's a discovery, a process. It's the same kind of insight that mathematicians have when uncovering a new formula, or musicians finding the right chord. Scientists talk of the "beauty" of a discovery. The more beautiful and simple the answer, the more likely it is to be true.

What they all suggest is that truth is an aspect of beauty, and vice versa. It's the same with love. All the forces in the universe (gravity, electromagnetism, strong and weak nuclear forces) are creating more and more complex and beautiful forms, turning matter into consciousness. In so far as we play a part in bringing things together, creating rather than destroying, loving rather than hating, we are fulfilled. In rising above our "selves" or losing our selves in awareness of the patterns at the heart of the universe and the life we lead together we are practicing religion. If it's not beautiful, if it's not loving, it's not true.

"Beauty," "truth," "love;" the experience of the three together is vivid enough for most people to describe them as "real." Let's be hopeful. The divide in the world is not between religions, or between believers and atheists. If there's a divide anywhere it's between those who have faith that the universe is meaningful and act accordingly, looking to something greater than themselves, and those who don't, and act for their own benefit. Between those who will fight to make the world a better place, and those who can't see the point. Between those who are happy helping others along the way of life, and those who see it as a race to win. Between those who will sacrifice their selves in favor of others, and those who want to impose their cultures or creeds. Between those whose first thoughts are, "How can I bring peace to this conflict? How can I resolve the underlying problems?" and those who turn to aggression or war. Between those who see the potential for unity everywhere and live in its light, and those who see it as reflecting their own interests. Between those who see us as chimps occasionally granted glimpses of the divine mystery, and those who think they're saved and everyone else is going to hell.

Faith says we've turned the corner. If we live in its light the world will follow. There are more people of goodwill in the world than there are of ill. In our hearts we're more inclined to love than hate, to unity than division, peace than war. Materialism says it's only our own interests, our own beliefs that count, and the rest is nonsense.

Faith says that God is not like we are, interested in saving a few friends or followers in one time and place, careless of the rest. Forgiveness was not offered just once, through one man's life and death. He works through every moment and event, creating beauty and love and truth. The universe is not random, it unfolds from God like a tree from a seed, separating out into the 10 to the power of 72 atoms that have formed galaxies, stars, plants, and billions of life forms. There is no other way it could have existed.

This unfolding is expressed in the beautiful patterns of circles, spirals, and helixes that run through everything. It's seen in the Fibonacci ratios first described in the seventeenth century, the golden sequences of numbers that dictate the patterns in nature, from the structure of sub-atomic particles and DNA, to whirlpools and the whorl of galaxies. It's expressed in the most ancient and widespread symbol in religion, that of the spiral. It's what the universe is made of. Mathematicians might say the secret is in the primes, or the never-ending number pi, or a poet might say:

"Beauty is truth, truth beauty, – that is all
Ye know on earth, and all ye need to know."

John Keats

We imitate these patterns in everything we create. Truth is not what we've been told, it's what we make. The practice of all good religion is the "golden rule." We instinctively believe it's right in relationships. We seek harmony and wholeness. The music most of us enjoy listening to is based on chords that can be divided by whole numbers. We instinctively move toward proportion. The main principle in architecture and art is the golden mean proposed by Pythagoras. We can't prove whether this is true, any more than we can analyze what consciousness means, because we're part of the proof. The thing is, it works. It's a good religion, and we need what religion points to. Its defining characteristics are the search for truth, the appreciation of beauty, and the practice of love. They characterize the experience of "oneness." In loving someone, in seeing something as beautiful, in the perception of a truth, we immerse ourselves in the wider reality. We can see what we can become.

Much of what we already appreciate in Christianity is motivated by this. It defines the universe as one of unconditional love. But there's also a lot of "noise" that drowns out the heart of it, a concern to prove things that cannot be proved, to say this landscape is better than that landscape, this definition of God better than that. There is no such "absolute" truth that we can see or realize, any more than there is absolute beauty. We know aspects of it when we see it, but even then struggle to describe it. To be "real," what is one must be the others as well. The universe is the creation of consciousness, the ultimate work of art, and will be seen as a whole when it's complete. Only God knows when that is.

There's nothing scientific in this, nothing that can be proved. And nothing original. It has always played a role in the Christian tradition. In the Middle Ages for instance it was highlighted in a dispute over whether the ultimate vision of God was primarily one of love or of knowledge, with Bonaventura preferring the former and Thomas Aquinas the latter.

In the Renaissance period Marsilio Ficino maintained in his *Theologica Platonica* that the highest Platonic ideals of the Good, the True, and the Beautiful could be found in the human soul. For him these were at the root of all religion. He concentrated on Greek and Persian religions, but another Italian, Giovanni Pico della Mirandola, extended it to embrace Jewish and Muslim wisdom. He suggested that humankind is created to shape itself into whatever form it chooses, and to bear the consequences. Condemned at the time, today he seems right, and we extend his vision to everyone.

Art and music are good ways of communicating all three. Fra Angelico will still speak to us when Aquinas is the province of specialist historians. Compare the people wrestling their way on to the divine stage in Renaissance art with the koan-like stillness of Chinese paintings of the same period and you can understand in an instant a lot there is to know about the difference between the Eastern and Western mind, between Buddhism and Christianity. The Europeans picture God in their image up in the heavens, sending messengers and sons to earth. Simple, glorious, and clear. But impossible to believe today, which is why no one paints like that any more. The Chinese evoke reality (or non-reality) slipping away behind the mist. It wasn't till the late nineteenth century with Impressionism and then Cubism that Western painting began to picture the process of seeing rather than the object seen. The developments in art paralleled the increasing Western interest in Eastern religion, focusing as it does on the workings of the mind rather than its creations.

Storytelling is also a key. It's why there are so many sacred scriptures around the world. The Bible itself is a baseline on which many further stories have been built, like *The Brothers Karamazov* or *Daniel Deronda*. If you're bored with Obadiah and Nehemiah, read Dostoevsky or George Eliot instead. Don't get stuck on the Bible. Think of religious truth like a great universal novel, the story of consciousness. The main characters are the different religious leaders down the ages. Their sidekicks are the great theologians, mystics and philosophers, the artists and writers. Who's the narrative voice? It's you, all of us. We create our story out of these past lives, much as they have created us. In writing new stories we create the future for our children. We're all characters playing roles in the mind of God. Good religion is good art.

Funnily enough the great era of Western fiction coincided with the passing of Christian belief. The first atheists and the first novelists were roughly contemporary. The eighteenth-century novel took the idea that characters could explore their own destinies under the controlling pen of the author far further than previous literary forms. The great flourishing of the novel in the nineteenth and early twentieth centuries seems too remarkable in relation to changing belief patterns to be coincidental. Life came to be seen as a meaningless sequence of ordinary events that we make meaningful, make our own, by giving it shape and form, beginnings and endings. We turn it into our own truth. We make our own novels, our own lives.

The great nineteenth-century novelists knew what they were doing. George Eliot translated liberal German theologians like Ludwig Feuerbach with tears streaming down her face as she saw the basis of Victorian faith disappearing. Charles Dickens created the sentimental Victorian Christmas as a partial substitute for the meaning the Victorians had lost. Thomas Hardy turned the almighty God into a bleak vision of indifference to suffering humankind. In Russia Tolstoy tried to create a new synthesis of rational Christianity and Russian psychology, and Dostoevsky created a Christianity that would survive despite its destruction by reason.

Truth today is a democratic effort, shaped by the consensus of the tribe, as it used to be. A religion that acknowledges its role as fiction and art, a fiction that provides a structure of universal myth and law, will shape our future consciousness. Writers, musicians, and artists are often a generation ahead of their time. Scientists, centuries. Founders of religion, millennia. We need all of them.

19

THE CHURCH WE WANT

"Truth seems to come with the final word; and the final word gives birth to the next."

Rabindranath Tagore

What might a new Christianity look like? A new Christian church would demolish much of the old one. It wouldn't need a "Holy Bible" at all. It would have a collection of writings that are more important than others in expressing faith, but a changing one, and different for each community, as in the first centuries. It could edit out much of the Old Testament, leaving it for the Jewish faith, where it belongs. It would add passages from the scriptures of other religions. It would add new writings. This would not be impossible if the will and imagination were there. The compilers of the Jewish Old Testament had more limited and less promising material to work with. The traditions they merged were as different as many of those in different religious traditions today. It's just a question of being faithful to God and the times together, like they tried to be.

The Bible stories are not there to tell us what to think but to drive us under our emotional surface into realizing what we're capable of, into new understandings. They're riveting in the way they picture the extremities of madness, murder, holiness, freedom, sacrifice, redemption. Moses, David, Solomon, Jeremiah, Amos, Jesus, Paul – along with many others they've become archetypes of certainty, courage, wisdom, frustration, justice, forgiveness, commitment. The whole of life is there. Set against the backdrop of a nation's struggle for identity, for survival and above all for living under the rule of God they can still speak with power if we read them for what they are. They're still relevant to all of us. We still murder Abel, betray like David, scapegoat Jesus. And the greater story of which they're a part can still be our blueprint.

Genesis tells of the creative Spirit breathing life into dust, creating a world that's good in itself. It describes our dawning consciousness, accounting for our sense of separation. God hands over the world to us, and we begin our journey to find our conscious place in it. Noah's ark with the saving of all earth's species is a model for the future of the planet. The prophets warn us against the arrogance of relying on our own resources, the iniquity of oppression, of the disaster to come if we don't keep our faces turned away from ourselves to God and the poor.

The birth of Jesus with the shepherds and stable is a celebration of life and love. It tells us that the most insignificant child on earth is as important as any other, indeed more so than our own selves. Love, helplessness, innocence, these are the things we should treasure, not power and position. Maybe somewhere, in each of us, there's a divine child waiting to be born. And, despite the Herods of this world, it will be, because there are no longer gods "out there." The divine Word has become flesh in the world. It will be realized. We want to believe it.

The crucifixion is perhaps the most powerful story we have. The story of the good man who gave himself unstintingly, refusing wealth and power, who saw that the deeper love is the more it hurts. He accepted betrayal and death to remain true to what he believed. He not only spoke of supporting the victims, of identifying with them, of becoming them, he became one in his life, building on the warnings of the prophets, the cries of the oppressed and murdered going back to Abel. It's as far as the kingdom can go. Our destructiveness is not the last word. To be a Christian is to live without exercising power, to accept without limit. He speaks to us individually because he made it real for himself in his life. If we aren't prepared to follow him as far as he went, it won't happen.

We're close to God today in so far as we are able to relate without dominating, encouraging everyone to be the best they can be. To be the best we can be. It's only through us that He works in the world. He has a hope, a dream, for what we could become. We should not let Him dream alone. In sharing His dream we make it ours, we make our will His will. If we don't, He can't help us off the cross. He won't turn Abraham's knife. We've run out of sacrifices. He's not satisfied with them any more.

It's in our capacity to forgive and love without limit that we bring the divine into existence. Perhaps the deepest meaning that we can draw from the story of Jesus is that love *is* sacrifice. It's a sacred, redeeming force. Everything else is compromise. His teaching on the kingdom and his death on the cross were at one on this. It's in the most intense, sacrificial moments of our lives that the ideal becomes real, that love becomes true. The resurrection is the expression of our hope that this is so, that we are eventually part of a greater spirit that we call God, and are not on our own. Christ on the throne in heaven represents the completion of our journey of understanding, where matter is transformed into spirit. Life does come out of death, hope out of fear, love out of indifference. It's been happening for millions of years. Love and hope deeply enough, and the story will triumph.

It's not difficult to have faith in God with an army behind you. It's when you're at the bottom of the pit, with no light, when you're wrestling with your own failure or despair, that faith is needed and God becomes real. And we then understand there's no difference between them and us, between the self that despairs and the self that hopes, between the person we could become and the one we are, between the God who is imagined and the one who imagines.

Love and power, God and the devil, struggle throughout the Bible, subverting each other. The best of the New Testament expresses the triumph of the first. But then it stops. We need new texts. And out of a new Bible would come a new religious language for Christians, one that doesn't rely on the old categories of "God out there" and Capital Letter Doctrines. We need a language that works for everyone, in the same kind of way that Shamanism worked for everyone before we had Revealed Religion.

Would we still need a church at all? Faith today may be private, but it's also inevitably collective. We're social animals, needing crowds as well as privacy, constructing our stories out of the collective imagination. So churches of some form are needed, though perhaps most of what we have is the packaging that can now be left behind, much like the early Christians left the synagogues.

A community without a church/temple/synagogue at its heart has lost something. The life-changing, life-affirming, life-questioning rites of passage we used to wrestle with and celebrate communally – birth, commitment, marriage, death – are now turned into soulless administrative functions – registry offices, hospitals, crematoria. However hard the good people in these places try, it's not the same. They're not designed to be. For this we need churches. But the point is that they should be forces for change as well as celebration. Beacons of light, practicing repentance, forgiveness, openness, love, tolerance, poverty. They should model in a small way the kingdom we would like to see created on earth. They should "go further," be radical. We bridge the difference between where we are and where we want to be by demanding more change of ourselves than we're willing to give.

But churches, like nations, are too big. Nation states with a population of over 10 million spend disproportionately on armies. They are more prepared to use force than diplomacy. Religions with over 1 million followers are the same. They become authoritarian. Loose networks of smaller numbers with no hierarchy, no property, will represent the good churches of the future. They would draw on different traditions, as the group agreed. Perhaps predominantly Christian in the West, but pagan, humanist, Buddhist, all traditions could play a part. All festivals be honored. Diversity will always be as crucial for religion as it is for species. Let's welcome the coming splits between conservatives and liberals. Let it be clear where they stand, and people be allowed to judge which ideas they want to identify with.

So let's fast with the Muslims, have a Christian confirmation, marry like the Shinto followers, have a Buddhist funeral, dance with the dervishes, if that makes sense to us. And out of the mix new practices will emerge. Let the churches be open to anyone to use, focal points for the community. They should be forces for reconciliation, for the awareness of consciousness as "one," underneath the diversity. That's their job. Spirituality is private, churches represent where we come together. Love transcends differences, it never reinforces them.

Let's draw on the cumulative wisdom and experience of everyone rather than a single tribe or tradition. If it makes sense to be religious it's logical to accept the best practices from the broad range of traditions. Meditation and yoga are as natural a part of a healthy spiritual life as curry and rice are now part of our diet. It's through embracing diversity that we come closer to truth. It's clear that God didn't want us to be too sure of where it lies. Differences are part of the solution rather than the problem. If we added all the religious insights of the world together we'd get a better picture of a tiny part of who He might be.

Would we still have ministers? The standard of ministry is probably higher today than it has ever been. Few go into the church now for power or money. But they're hampered by the system they're a part of. In themselves religious professionals are no closer to God than you are. They're just more practiced at opening the door. If it's the wrong door that's their problem, not yours. Anybody who talks of religion to people they don't know is risking manipulation. But we need to talk, and listen. That's our history. The trouble is, priests, as often as not, are poets who have lost the use of their own words, artists who have forgotten how to paint. Ministers of religion should be trained to be just that, ministers of all kinds of religion, those that have a God and those that don't, rather than preachers of a local version of a particular brand. Offering a range of fizzy drinks rather than diet Pepsi. Or even, perhaps, pointing out that there's always pure water to be had for free.

This already exists in a small way in Eastern religions that are more open to acknowledging truth elsewhere. "The same water is in all the wells," the sage Nisargadatta Maharaj taught in the last century. There is the "Great Church" (*tai chao*), for instance, of the Chinese that blends Taoism, Confucianism, and Buddhism. Cao Dai and Bon Buddhism have the same aim. A nineteenth-century offshoot of Islam, the Bahai faith, preaches world peace and the unity of humankind. Many Hindus also feel comfortable worshiping at shrines devoted to many deities, including Jesus.

In the West, Unitarianism is the strand most open to this, and creates a context for a "do it yourself" religion where individuals can be encouraged to follow their own spiritual journeys. A future "Greater Church," loosely linked, may enable the great religions of the Middle East, India, and the Far East to live peaceably together, at least for those prepared to accept their common humanity and common striving for awareness.

A global "Greater Church" could have an impact on global problems. Already religious institutions worldwide control 8 to 10% of the world's capital markets. Maybe a World Parliament for Religions could match the United Nations and achieve still more. The Parliament would deal with rogue religions like the UN (ideally) deals with rogue states.

The idea of religions working together may seem self-contradictory to many. So at first did the idea of nations doing the same through the League of Nations. But go back a millennium and the idea of nation states would have been incomprehensible. Go back ten millennia and there was probably little basic difference between people's beliefs and the way they organized themselves in different parts of the world, despite the fact that it could take many generations for an idea to travel from one end to the other. Go back 60 millennia to when Cro-Magnon Man first came out of Africa and there was little difference amongst Homo sapiens physically or culturally. Now go forward 60 millennia and the wheel will have come full circle again. The distinctions that developed between races as they settled around the globe will be blurred through intermarriage. It's started to accelerate in the last few centuries. The differences between religions will have diminished in the same way. Why not start preparing for it? Eventually there may even be one universal faith, just as we have one DNA, one planet, one destiny.

The seeds are already there. Representatives of all the world's religions got together for the first time at the World Congress of Faiths in Chicago in 1893. It was influenced by Narenda Nath Datta (Vivekananda, 1863-1902) who emphasized a strain of Hinduism that can accommodate a variety of religious belief. Vivekananda considered that the Divine worked on two levels: the higher level was beyond description, but could be known through meditation. At the lower level God had qualities that were imaged in different ways, through different religions. His teacher, Ramakrishna, had intense spiritual experiences of union with Christ, the Mother Goddess, Kali, Mohammed. All represent different ways to knowledge of the divine. Most of us struggle to realize one. There was another World Parliament in 1993 in Chicago. There are many inter-faith organizations, but the establishment Churches support them as a matter of peripheral goodwill (if at all) rather than seeing them as central to their vision.

Maybe an open-ended religion of this kind isn't distinctive enough to be characterized as "Christian." Maybe this would turn Christianity into a new religion, the first the West has produced, much as Christianity itself developed out of Judaism, Buddhism out of Hinduism. A religion that is shaped by the distinctive contribution the West has given to the human inheritance in the form of individual liberty and rights, democracy and common law, much as early Christianity was shaped by the distinctive Hebrew idea of a single God and a chosen people. And why not? Jesus wasn't a Christian anyway, and it's truer to his teaching than a religion that puts dogma before love.

Maybe we can redefine Christianity to be inclusive of truth from wherever it appears, in the same way that early church fathers like Justin the Martyr did, and the more enlightened sections of Buddhism and Hinduism still do. Judaism was a "tribal" religion of chosen people, and in the couple of millennia since then we've succeeded in reducing salvation from the tribe to the individual. We've gone in the wrong direction. It's the world that God wants to save. It's all creation that is on the path to consciousness. If we could live in the world as it is, seeing it all as reflecting the love of God, rather than trying to change it into our own image, a reflection of our own greed, salvation might come.

We're in a time of transition, much as we were back in the fifth century BC, when across the world new understandings of religion developed. The merger of Greek and Hebrew thought in the first few centuries AD may be paralleled by a merger of

Christian, Hindu, and Buddhist thought over the next few centuries. Improbable as it may seem today, maybe by then everyone will be believing in God again. But this religion will be as diverse as Christianity was in the first couple of centuries.

And that doesn't matter. The religion you choose to operate in is one that suits the culture you are part of and the temperament you've developed. It's not "truer" than another. God has no interest in your theology. By all means have an orthodox Christian faith, have your personal relationship with God, believe in your personal salvation, or however you want to describe it. But recognize it for what it is, a working model, not a final truth. The path to the sacred, not the sacred itself. It's the psychological equivalent of the "household gods" of Abraham. The personal God of Moses, or Jesus, not the Godhead. It's one of the 99 names of Allah, not the hundredth that is unattainable. The Tao that can be spoken, not the Tao that is beyond words.

The almighty, creator God-beyond-God, whoever or whatever it is that holds every atom in His hand, is beyond our reach, for the moment. But He is the end of all our journeys.

"If you know who you are, you can become as I am."
Gospel of Thomas

20

THE CHOICES
WE FACE

"I don't know that atheists should be considered
citizens, nor should they be considered patriots. This
is one nation under God."

George Bush

The first Christians lived in the light of a bigger and better vision. It inspired them to love, to self-sacrifice, and to change themselves and society for the better. It turned sour, conversion changed to conquest, and now it's indifference, or an obsessive focus on personal salvation. But we still need the vision. It's not that life is less dangerous or exciting than in their day. In the last century we've had the first two world wars, Hitler and Stalin, the threat of nuclear destruction, the worst ever famines, the exploration of space, huge advances in knowledge. The best of times, as reflected in the Universal Declaration of Human Rights, and the worst of times, as in the Holocaust. Both generated from Christian societies. In the next century we face over-population, global warming, terrorism, maybe Muslim/Christian conflict, maybe biological war, and the possible waning of Western civilization.

Our power to shape our environment has increased enormously. We can create almost anything we can dream of. But we don't know ourselves any better than the Greeks did. In some ways we're worse off, more divorced from the world around us. And the problems generated by twentieth-century capitalism may overwhelm the successes.

Today we redefine our problems rather than solving them. We no longer leave girl babies out on mountainsides to avoid the cost of extra children, but we redefine the starting point of life instead. In the latter half of the twentieth century the number of abortions was greater than the totalitarian murders of the first half. Instead of lots of little and not-so-little wars we invest in nuclear stockpiles that threaten to destroy all life on earth. We were apparently within minutes of nuclear war at the height of the Cuban missile crisis. If that had taken place it would have given us a quite different perspective on life expectancy and civilization in the twentieth century.

We have this illusion of progress. It's a relatively new one. Every generation since the year dot has tended to think of their grandparents as more upright, less prone to crime and trivia, wiser than they are. Throughout recorded history most societies have looked back on a past golden age rather than forward. Things will get worse before they get better. The successive ages of gold, silver, bronze, iron, and clay (reflected in Nebuchadnezar's dream in Daniel 2) represent steps of universal decline from innocence to corruption. And maybe they're right. History suggests we're just as likely to spend the next couple of centuries going backwards as going forward. It's taken us 2,000 years and more to recover the understanding of the solar system the Greeks had, the flushing toilets of the Cretans, the motorways of the Romans. The average citizen of New York or London today is probably less educated and cultured than the average citizen of Athens 2,500 years ago. In Athens citizens who didn't regularly engage in lengthy public debate were classed as "idiots."

Early in the twentieth century H. G. Wells saw humankind as in a race between education and catastrophe. But education doesn't make us less selfish. It enables us to consume and throw away more, to produce more deadly weapons. There are plenty of educated people in the World Bank, the International Monetary Fund, the World Trade Organization, who are speeding us along on the path to more growth, more pollution, more inequity, more armies. The twentieth century was the most "educated," perhaps the least "religious," the world has known. "Self" triumphed over "soul."

We haven't changed over the last 60,000 years since our ancestors started to settle around the planet. We now have TVs on our walls instead of ochre drawings, we split atoms instead of logs. But we still have the same kinds of conversations about God as they would have had. The only difference is that our options have narrowed, down to one of Bunyan's two paths of destruction or righteousness, the alternate visions of Revelation 19 and 20, or 21 and 22.

"Either the next century will be a spiritual century or there will be no next century at all," as Robert Muller, former deputy secretary general of the United Nations said. And perhaps the best summary of the world of spirit, the alternative path to catastrophe, is faith in the kingdom of God. The idea that you treat other people with the same respect that you would give to God. The challenge that God is only there in so far as we can imagine Him, and there is no one out there to help us. The idea that we can realize heaven on earth if we can die to our selves.

Perhaps this is all over-egging the doom pudding, reading too much of the nightmare of Revelation into our own times. People have been complaining about the decline of moral standards and of civilization itself for thousands of years. It's true that in many parts of the world we don't enslave, torture, mutilate, rape war victims, buy and sell women, like we used to. We now look on that as barbaric, rather than standard practice, approved by society and God. Murder rates in regions like Europe are one hundredth of what they were in the Middle Ages. Much of the world has expanded its moral circle. But the world population is twice what it was 40 years ago, three times what it was 100 years ago. Virtually all commentators agree that our 300 million-year-old stock of fuel is going to run out in the next half century. Some say it's all going to come right, once capitalism has been properly taken on board by everyone, but they've been saying that for centuries now, and the imbalance between rich and poor, between consumption and resources, keeps growing. Put these trends together and crunch time is getting closer.

And in this century religion threatens to be the mega-disaster that helps push us into a darker age than we've seen before. Through the twentieth century as belief in the traditional God/Yahweh/Allah has become more difficult believers have retreated into fundamentalism. It's the reverse of good religion, breeding evil like poverty breeds crime.

In large sections of the church today Christians are as regressive and dangerous as their compatriots in other religions. They don't have the power to torture and murder like they used to, but dark undercurrents keep resurfacing. There's a disturbing new "final solution" emerging today for instance in fundamentalist thinking on Armageddon (the imminent apocalyptic return of Jesus, which involves the destruction of most of humankind). In the USA the best seller of all books in the 1970s was *The Late Great Planet Earth*, which through a crude identification of the biblical land of Gog with Russia placed nuclear Armageddon in the immediate future. Ronald Reagan believed it. Most Americans did. The equivalent in the 90s was a series of books called *Left Behind*, with over 60 million copies sold. In these books a proportion of the population suddenly disappear, carried off to heaven. Their clothes are left behind, their meals are uneaten on the table, cars run off the road, planes fall out of the sky.

Admittedly fundamentalism is only one strand in the tapestry of Christian thinking, but the doctrines that have allowed it to flourish in different forms over the centuries are central to the faith. Fundamentalists simply follow their particular religious logic to its inhuman conclusion.

Of all the world religions it's only Christianity, and its successor, Islam, which condemn people to eternal damnation. Through its history Christianity has seen the majority as heading for hell. It's one of the reasons the Chinese rejected the Jesuit missions in the seventeenth century. Xu Dashou said of their teaching: "The books of the Barbarians say: if you have done good throughout your life but have not made yourself agreeable to the Master of Heaven, all your goodness will have been in vain. If you have done evil all your life but for one single instant did make yourself agreeable to the Master of Heaven, all the evil you have done will immediately be absolved."

Xu hits it on the nail. If Hitler had repented in the last moments of his life, and then been shot by the approaching Russians, good Christians should believe that he went to heaven, and that the millions of Jews he gassed went to hell. It's as irrational and immoral a doctrine as you can find anywhere in the history of world religion.

The ideas that the world is about to end, that Christians are a persecuted minority, that you can take the Bible literally, that what is not "Christian" is in some way evil, breed the extremist "survivalist" groups. "Christian Identity" and "Aryan Nations" in the USA prepare for holocaust and anarchy. No Muslim terrorist movement on earth comes close to matching the atrocities of the evangelical Lord's Resistance Army in Northern Uganda. Today their more mainstream counterparts are closer than ever to having the power that could make their wishes come true. In this respect only are prophecies realized, when they are self-fulfilling.

It's the Garden of Eden scenario – given enough time, if there's a wrong decision to be made and the capacity to make it, someone, somewhere, is going to pick the apple, press the button. And if the world is about to end anyway, and if precipitating it will bring God to earth, why negotiate? Why compromise? Why bother to look after what we have? Why waste time on love? For fundamentalists of all religions "peace" is a delusion. It would prove them wrong. God's agenda is for conflict, for holocaust, for the extermination of all except the few saved. This is the religion of the emperors, the Aztecs, the Nazis, a religion that consumes its own base in the form of real people. It's the triumph of the ancient Sun God, bent on destroying the moderating gods of moon and rain, turning the kingdom of God into an inferno, self-destructive, and evil.

Will Homo sapiens survive? The probability of bringing about our own extinction must be high. The current British Astronomer Royal, Martin Rees, gives humankind only a 50/50 chance of surviving this century. So what are the chances of surviving another 5,000 years? Or 5 million? Will fingers stay off the trigger (nuclear, biological, or whatever comes next) for that long?

Even at the more prosaic daily level of warfare and politics it's not difficult for instance to imagine a situation quite soon where increasing fundamentalism in the Islamic world collides with increasing geo-political dominance by the Christian West, maybe itself led by fundamentalists in the White House. It will be fuelled by pressures of population growth and ever-increasing consumption of diminishing resources like water, all highlighted and concentrated in the flash point of Jerusalem, still sacred to the three monotheistic religions.

Despite the interdependence of Christianity and Islam in so many ways, with the same scriptures and the same God at their heart, the two civilizations have spent much of the last two millennia in conflict. Our appreciation of this has been dimmed by the economic and military superiority of the West in the last couple of centuries. A long-running global war between the two, fed by the passions that monotheistic religions in particular can ignite, with their competing claims to superiority, could dwarf the 200 million or so casualties of the last century.

What Jesus said was that the kingdom of God is here. We're actually in the Garden of Eden if only we could see it. The world is wonderful if only we could realize it. There's enough food for everyone if only we could share it. But it only takes one bad guy, or one computer error, and we're all history. Our collective fates may, in real life this time, rest on the decision of an individual. And it's hard to have confidence in our leaders today. Great societies are built on vision, moral rigor, and literacy. As they age their wealth and military power increase but the foundations decay. Compare the speeches of USA presidents of the first century of the USA with those of the twentieth century. The difference is striking. Or the letters home from soldiers in the Civil War with those of the Vietnam War. Self-interest and superstition take over. When these societies are apparently at their peak they're a generation or two away from failure. Every such generation thinks they're immune from the cycles of history, under the special protection of their God, but none are. Their accumulated wealth is plundered by the "uncivilized." It happens every time.

If the apocalypse that we risk creating by our own efforts doesn't arrive then we have the chance of surviving, but on a planet that by definition has limited resources that are rapidly being used up. And this is the paradox of the global capitalism we hold up as the model for the world, the final stage of history. The more we have the more we want. Today 5% of the world's population consumes 60% of the world's resources, producing the same proportion of its pollution. This is not just. In a global economy on a small planet it's hard to describe countries like the USA and those in Western Europe in any real sense as "Christian" when they maintain their standard of living while 60% of the world's population lives on under $2 a day, and millions of children starve to death every year. It can't last.

It also doesn't take a rocket scientist to work out that even if the problem of justice could be ironed out by bringing everyone up to the same level we would then face the bigger problem of unsustainability. How long would the earth's resources last if 6 billion (coming up to 10) people were consuming at the same rate as the 1 billion in the developed countries? Maybe the capitalist model is the best we have, maybe it's "moral" (doubtful), but it's not "Christian."

We have the example of past civilizations to show us what happens when the soil, or fuel, has run out, only this time there's no virgin territory to move into. The Easter Island scenario then beckons. It's the only case in history of a society that through circumstance and geography developed in complete isolation. As the trees and soil disappeared the fishhooks got smaller because there were no canoes to get to the fishing grounds, the crops ran out, warfare between the villages increased, till an extraordinary society collapsed and disappeared. In 1992 110 out of the world's 138 living Nobel Prize winners signed the *World Scientists' Warning to Humanity* that we're at the same point. The planet is just a larger Easter Island. Our future as a species is in more doubt than at any other time over the last million years, and the best many in the church can do is bicker over whether women and gays should really have the same status as heterosexual males. And are then surprised that many feel the church is irrelevant.

The wheel of history always turns again. What we sow we reap. In times to come we're going to be on the receiving end of the generosity or brutality of people we currently dismiss as having created their own problems. Global capitalism will go the same way as every other social model, and may be one of the shorter-lived ones. It's sheer hubris to think otherwise. The pursuit of pleasure and wealth at the expense of moral sense and sanity, the lifestyle and economics of Hollywood, will come to be seen as extreme and useless as the Egyptian pursuit of life after death.

And the ascendancy of a particular culture or nation gets shorter as technology develops faster. In the period we call BC, it shortens from tens of millennia to millennia; in AD, it narrows to centuries; in recent times, to decades. Christianity is becoming so closely identified with capitalism that it may go down with it. Future generations of Homo sapiens or some other species may look at our vast cathedrals, towers pointing to the sky, and wonder what on earth the people who built them were trying to reach for, who they were trying to worship. Much as we puzzle over stone circles and pyramids, or the huge stone faces on Easter Island itself, looking for ever out to the horizon, perhaps for the salvation that never arrived.

Maybe human consciousness, civilization, is just a momentary spark, one that will be extinguished just as it was getting started, unnoticed and unlamented in the history of our galaxy, let alone the universe. Maybe with the wisdom of hindsight future galactic historians of another species will simply say our brains grew too fast. A couple of million years ago the brain spurted to its present size, pushing out the skull to allow room for the skills of communicating and organizing that went with the development of language. But like the insects too heavy to turn themselves the right way up if they fall over, and the arthropods whose brains grew around the food channel and stifled it, we're an evolutionary dead-end. After years of trying we won the lottery, and then killed ourselves on the proceeds, competing to accumulate more than others, without a thought for the effects farther down the line, on the generations to come.

To put it in biological terms the human brain got too big for the body, leading to the pains and dangers of childbirth and midwives. Our jaws retracted, leaving us with too many teeth, giving us dentists. But more significantly the newer and older parts of the brain haven't integrated well. We've lost many of our natural instincts – like regulating our breeding rates according to food supply – without developing an intelligence large enough to compensate. And indeed, there you have the Catholic Church in the forefront waving us, lemming-like, over the cliff edge.

Having lost the biological imperative of sharing food along certain genetic lines, we haven't developed enough compassion to avoid absurd inequalities in the distribution of wealth. The result is crime and lawyers, social unrest and police, revolution and armies, over-population and starvation, legacies of suffering and bitterness. We've developed the power of individual choice, but not sufficiently the moral capacity to act out of selflessness rather than greed. We've created monster cities and monster ideologies to match them. We can't even find sufficient self-control to avoid over-fouling our own nest, sawing away the branch on which we're sitting.

Maybe the third millennium will be a time of disaster, human-made, on a scale we haven't seen before. Our imaginary galactic historians will shake their heads and write their epitaph over a desolate planet: "Here are the lords of creation. They weren't doing too badly, till they lost respect for the God who is bigger than they could imagine."

But then it's not the fact that we're perfectly adapted to our environment that makes us human, but that we're such misfits. Otherwise we'd still be up in the trees. It's our sense of separation and inadequacy that drives us forward, creating visions of perfection and salvation in our heads, enabling us to dream of a better, more self-aware, and happier future. We need a big idea to aim for, something to carry us through the next million years, or we won't make it. We need to grow to the next level of consciousness.

So hold the idea of God in your head as a possibility. Live it as if it's true. It's in living by faith that we grow. By imagining that we can get to the next step, overriding our genetic programing. It's in growing that we meet God. Maybe He exists out there, maybe He's all in our heads. Maybe it comes to the same thing. It's worth believing, but it's not worth a moment's argument, a single wrong action.

21

THE FUTURE
WE FOLLOW

"Space travel is bilge."

Britain's Astronomer Royal, in 1956, the year before Sputnik

Let's believe in God, rather than in the ways we describe Him. Original sin, life after death, sacrificial love, these and a dozen other major ideas are there to be tested, adapted, absorbed into a tradition that makes sense to us, that enables us to move forward. Out of these we shape our own definition of God. God is the hook by which we can step into a state of grace. Grace is what happens when truth and love snap together in our heads and we can act unselfconsciously out of that awareness. Grace gives us the best kind of happiness, unreserved, undeserved, 15 billion light years' worth of time and space on our side.

Religion describes grace. At its best Christianity is a religion of grace. Grace provides assurance that the universe makes sense, our lives have a purpose, that we are evolving toward a glory greater than we can imagine. But we'll never know. That's why it's faith, religion rather than science.

And it always will be. There are no clear answers. If this universe is all there is there are always further questions: Why is it made this way? Why is there something rather than nothing? What role should we be playing in it?

If we could account for every molecule and event in this universe since time began we would still be left with the idea that there may be vastly more universes than there are molecules in this one. If the universe is infinite God will always be a bigger question than we can find an answer to. Mystery, not certainty, is at the heart of existence, and the acceptance of it at the heart of good religion.

There will always be a "beyond," and there's no reason why it should be within the grasp of our particular animal minds. The sages in the East say even the right questions take the form of unanswerable riddles, and if we can understand them we've probably got it wrong. Most of the great teachers talk in puzzles, paradoxes, parables, asking questions rather than giving answers. But for the unenlightened the questions are worth asking. If we keep questioning we progress. We may get to the point where we don't need the answers, when we simply understand.

Jnana, the path of knowledge, involves exhausting the mind's possibilities, transcending it. Salvation involves the complete surrender to the will of God. The results are the same. It doesn't matter what you believe. It's like your language or your skin color. It's who you become that's important. Better to be a happy and loving Hindu or atheist than a mean and intolerant Christian, and vice versa. Perhaps more significantly it's what you believe that you can become. It's by the collective exercise of faith that we might become what we hope to be.

Imagine a soap bubble. It materializes out of space-time foam and floats free, like a feather on the breath of God. For a fleeting second, threads of biology, history, culture are knitted together by personality. We have this moment to enjoy and through a few simple actions hope to leave the world a fraction better than we found it. The actions are hopefully defined by love, which represents the fullest form of self-awareness that we know of. Developing this is cultivating a state of mind we call prayer. Prayer is perhaps the most basic way of thinking, an internal dialogue between the two halves of the brain to find the best course of action, to question who we are, and where we're going, which defines us as human. Worship is a state of gratitude.

At times this feeling is so overwhelming that it might take on the form of a Higher Power, of God. The flip side of awareness is accountability. We're responsible for what we become and do, for this second of time. The kingdom of God is a measure that we don't live up to. Faith is the belief that the bubble dissolves again back into the mixture we call God, that the awareness we have developed somehow survives in the bubbling ferment of creation. Nothing ever disappears, everything is remembered in the quantum world. Everything is forgiven, or it could not exist. There is no rubbish bin, no "off" button in the universe. No hell or heaven. All we do and think and dream is added like yeast to the mixture.

We can believe this because we're here, because we're having this conversation. Because through 15 billion years the universe has been evolving toward consciousness, and will continue to do so. We're part of this. You, here, now, is all that matters.

But what of our children, and God in the future?

Think of conscious life on earth as a giant game of snakes and ladders. We've crept past a couple of dozen snakes to get this far. Religious fundamentalism is one of the next big perils. Just a few thousand years ago it didn't exist. Now it's one of the threats to the planet. If we go down, it's back to cockroaches and rats, if we're lucky. The path to self-awareness that began with the mammals, when the extinction of the dinosaurs gave them their opportunity, would then start anew. The age of reptiles, followed by the age of mammals, will be followed by something different again.

If we get past that snake of global warfare, that evolutionary test, maybe fuelled by different interpretations of God, managing to work together, and keep going, the balance between ourselves and the world might change far more radically than anything we've seen to date. For one thing, we're going to end up looking a lot different. Even in the short span of recorded history the average height of human beings has decreased and risen through changes in lifestyle and diet. As we create our own environment and have the power to genetically manipulate our own bodies the rate of change will increase. It's likely to prove impossible to resist the drive to improve human beings genetically, much as we have already been improving grapes and crops, dogs and cows, for thousands of years. Ironically African genes may be the most highly valued, as they have a greater diversity in the gene pool.

Evolution hasn't had time yet to explore more than a tiny fraction of the potential combinations that exist in DNA, or the possible power of the brain. Artificial evolution can speed this process up by many factors of 10. The replacement of human organs and tissue by that of other species or with man-made materials is already advanced. The ability to clone people may be just a few years away. There's every reason to suppose that the science of genomics will be able to fashion human beings and intelligence in every conceivable form.

But will this be a democratic process, undertaken for the good of everybody, or will it lead to different classes of people more extreme and rigid than anything Hinduism or the Hebrews could have dreamt of? If you successively replace different parts of the human body with organs from other people, or animals, or mechanical devices, how far can you go? Where does a "person" begin and end? How will a thousand-year life expectancy change our view of pleasure, families, salvation? Traditionally wisdom comes with age, but increased life expectancy over the last couple of centuries doesn't seem to have taken us forward much. Would the sense of adventure, of curiosity, of religion as a series of conversions leading us on to a greater understanding be stronger than the pull of self-righteousness and greed?

Maybe this is where our problems will really begin. We struggle at the moment with the "simple" issues of abortion and euthanasia, addiction and mental illness. But our very ideas of what a human being is and how to order society accordingly will be up for grabs again. If we can't get our act together now, defining what it means to be human, how we relate to each other fairly, how will we cope with a world of a few million-dollar-super-humans who are genetically and physically superior to the rest of us?

We're as yet just a blink of an eyelid in the planet's history. If we can overcome tribal desires to rule, accumulate, and convert, the future will open out, and we'll shape our environment to enable consciousness to continue and develop, rather than be driven to a dead end. The world of science fiction will then increasingly become fact.

We could start to tap the resources of the planet's core, rather than scratching at the surface. Then we'll tap the energy of the sun, which produces more energy each second than humankind has so far consumed in its history, and be able to work with and create planets. Later the galaxy, working with stars. Perhaps the dialogue between the two halves of our brains will be extended to quarters, tentiles, to all brains. Or perhaps the part that some scientists describe as the fourth level, the pre-frontal lobe in the cortex, will grow larger. It's where our empathy and moral sense seem to reside, and doesn't reach its full proportionate size till we're around the age of seven. Or perhaps our place at the table will be taken by a different species, who will look back at our fourth level as we look back at our third, and wonder how we ever got to where we are.

Perhaps we'll go further. Maybe the "mind" will be cased in forms other than the organic – maybe electrical energy, who knows what. The brain by then would be free to grow to an indefinite size, not restricted by the uncomfortably small birth canal, taking it to 10 to the power of 11 neurons, or 12. Maybe we'll develop a more collective kind of consciousness of the kind already possessed by some other species, like the termites. Maybe we'll go back to our first home, the sea, and talk over family matters with our far-distant cousins, the whales. We could ask forgiveness for the last few centuries of one-sided slaughter.

Maybe we'll escape our biology altogether. After all it's not true that death is the natural end of everything, that all life is programed to die. Bacteria and amoeba for instance do not. Over a couple of billion years we've traded off immortality for complexity, self-awareness, and knowledge. As many of the greatest myths indicate, there's a price to be paid for life, and a still greater one for love.

And science today suggests that time is not the straight line we thought. The past and future are no less "real" than the present. If we could have surfed a light wave from the beginning of the universe we would see all the past and future simultaneously, and could pick out our lives like an email from the ether. In the quantum world there's no distance, no time, only "here and now."

With self-consciousness we've come to an awareness of time passing. Is there a further level of consciousness that is aware of time past, present, and future? Of the "one" that includes them all? Where we live with the awareness of dimensions that we can currently only trace in maths? This is an idea that all religions grasp the edges of. Is that more unlikely than that the descendants of your hamster, who shares our ancestry, could be reading and writing books? Having eaten of the Tree of Knowledge, would we then be grasping the fruit of the second of the trees in the Garden of Eden, the Tree of Life? And if we could, are we then equal to God, as He feared (Genesis 3:22, 23)?

Maybe by then we'll be free of the guilt of flourishing at the expense of other species. Maybe the future for religions of sacrifice is progressively to deny ourselves the "first fruits" of our relatives. We'll encourage life rather than destroy it. Maybe the stardust of which we're made will be converted to starlight. Perhaps the angels we see are the beings we could become.

If this took a million years that's a quarter of the time we've been around for, a fifteenth of the average life of a species, an infinitesimal amount of the time the universe still has to run. If we stay in the game we may be part of the consciousness that in 10 billion or so years' time, when the universe comes to an end, finds itself at the beginning, ready to play again.

Or perhaps we're not going to raise our game, and we'll go the way of Home erectus, Homo neanderthalensis, and our many other cousins. Perhaps the God we've created in our image is more of a destroyer than a savior, a figure of wrath rather than love. Perhaps the future is elsewhere, and this planet really is as utterly insignificant as it appears to be. Think of the many trillions of planets there probably are in the universe, and how rapidly consciousness has evolved on earth in the last billion years or so. There may be millions of life forms elsewhere who would see us as barely out of the slime stage. If life is not unique to earth, then, if we survive, we should be preparing ourselves to confront another image of God that is unlike any of our own.

We probably won't know in our lifetimes. We've only just got to the point of being able to tell that there are indeed planets around nearby stars, and that most of the 100 billion stars in our galaxy probably have them. It will be another generation or two before we're able to view them through telescopes. But if out of all the planets in the universe only the earth supports life then life itself is "religious" in the highest possible sense. Every form of life on the planet relates to every other. Every one is "sacred." Any religion that doesn't see this isn't worth the name, doesn't even match up to a comprehensive dictionary definition of what "religion" is.

At the moment we're exterminating species at a fantastic rate, some say tens of thousands a year, others hundreds of thousands. We've no idea even how many there are, some say 5 to 10 million, some 50 to 100. Shake a tree in the Amazonian rainforest and new species fall out. Humankind has upped the average extinction rate by a hundred- to a thousand-fold, leading to the kind of mass destruction of life that the planet hasn't seen since the dinosaurs disappeared 65 million years ago.

The history of life over the last few billion years suggests that any one of them could hold the key to the future.

Our story has come full circle. We've found the keys to the Garden of Eden. We can clone species, we're on the edge of creating them, of fashioning ourselves in new forms. We've unpicked the metabolism of life and death, pulling its fruit down from the tree. But we don't have a new story for this. We seem to have lost the facility for writing new chapters. We're still stuck in chapter 1. This story is an interpretation of Genesis that says that to be self-aware, to gain knowledge, is to transgress against God. Thinking is bad, obedience is good. The church still promotes this. It has lost the alternative vision of Job, one of the greatest of books in that muddled miscellany we call Holy Scripture, that God is there to be questioned and argued with. That's His role in life, life calling to life, words shaping life. But in the words the writer puts into the mouth of God, the answer will always be beyond us. The church has forgotten the new story that Jesus offered, where personal growth and sharing take priority over law and nature. He called it the kingdom of God.

And the Christian nations who claim to take their morality from Jesus and dominate the world economy have in the last century invented concentration camps and nuclear bombs, colonizing the ocean with submarines, and space with missiles. Roughly half the scientists in the world, mostly Christians, work at least part-time for the military establishment. In the ultimate ironic twist it is as likely to be well-meaning, God-believing Christians, as much as anyone, who will destroy the planet, and the life on it that He's spent 3.5 billion years shepherding through to consciousness. That really would give the devil the last laugh. If the "Rapture" really happened tomorrow the world might be a safer place.

This book began out of a question one of my kids asked me. "Do you believe in God?" I can't answer yes or no. I don't believe in those kind of certainties. But I can tell a story. This one's about the grand project of the third millennium AD, which is to produce a quantum computer. It would be made of electrons existing in the "in-between" state, in which they haven't yet decided where to appear. In such a system the electrons would calculate probabilities in all the possible universes simultaneously. It would be so powerful that if you enlarged the biggest computer we have to the size of the planet it would still take tens of millions of years to calculate what the quantum computer could do in an instant. A microscopic quantum computer with just 300 electrons would have more components in its parallel states than there are atoms in the universe, and the power of larger ones would increase exponentially. In theory it could simulate the universe. It's a difficult thing to build, because organizing electrons that don't exist yet is a hard act. It sounds like science fiction, but scientists around the world are working on it, and some say that 2002 saw the decisive breakthrough. Anyway, imagine it made. The greatest human achievement ever.

The world leaders gather around it for the opening ceremony. The Pope is allowed to ask the first question: "There's only one question worthy of this historic moment," he says. "Does God exist?" The machine whirrs, and after a moment comes back with the answer, "He does now."

"Believe nothing because a wise man said it.
Believe nothing because it is generally held.
Believe nothing because it is written.
Believe nothing because it is said to be divine.
Believe nothing because someone else believes it.
But believe only what you yourself judge to be true."
The Buddha